LIFE IN CHRIST

Reverends
JAMES KILLGALLON
and
GERARD WEBER

LIFE

IN

*Instructions in the
Catholic faith*

CHRIST

Life in Christ : *720 N. Rush Street, Chicago 11, Illinois*

Introduction

GOD, OUR FATHER, has spoken to us, revealing to us the meaning and purpose of our life. He sent his Son, Jesus Christ, to redeem us and to teach us the truths by which we are to live as children of God.

The study of a catechism is a study of the teachings of our Saviour, Jesus Christ. The more diligence and thoroughness we bring to such a study the better we shall know the life-giving truths which Christ came to teach us.

But mere study will enable us to know only the *teachings* of Jesus Christ. It is not enough to know his teachings. We must know Jesus Christ himself. We must know him and love him and, by living according to his teachings and his example, strive to become more and more like him. It is only by being united to Christ, his Son, and by loving him and all men in him that we can be pleasing to our heavenly Father.

While studying the teachings of Jesus Christ, therefore, we must pray to him. We must pray for help to understand those teachings, and we must make an effort to apply to our daily life the truths we are coming to know. We must also enter into the prayer-life of the Church, in which we re-live every year the life of Christ and pray to the Father through Christ.

One of the chief aims of this catechism is to help those who study it to become familiar with the inspired word of God, the Holy Scriptures. The many scriptural references and texts which are contained herein are meant to be studied in connection with the lessons in which they appear. Such a study, the authors believe, is really necessary for a truly effective use of *Life in Christ.*

For this reason those who use this catechism should have their own copy of the New Testament, in order that they might read and study it in connection with the lessons. The quotations used herein are taken from the Confraternity of Christian Doctrine edition.

An attempt has been made, too, to introduce prospective converts gradually to the liturgical life of the Church and to the private devotional practices which are part of the life of the Church. The seasons and feasts of the liturgical year have been woven into the lessons, and some of the more important devotions are explained after a treatment of the doctrinal matter on which they are based.

At the end of most of the lessons there is a suggested practice. In the first half of the catechism these practices are mostly concerned with learning and saying certain prayers and with the reading of Scripture, particularly the New Testament. It is the hope of the authors that the priest instructor will call attention to these practices and add others which he thinks appropriate. In this manner the will as well as the intellect will be brought into use right at the outset.

Contents

7

part IV: Growth in the Divine Life

part V: The Commandments of God

PART I

THE GIFT OF LIFE

part **I** : *THE GIFT OF LIFE*

section **1** | **Happiness**

God, who at sundry times and in divers manners spoke in times past to the fathers by the prophets, last of all in these days has spoken to us by his Son, whom he appointed heir of all things, by whom also he made the world; who, being the brightness of his glory and the image of his substance, and upholding all things by the word of his power, has effected man's purgation from sin and taken his seat at the right hand of the Majesty on high—HEB. 1:1-3.

SOME two thousand years ago there lived one whose influence on the world is unique in history. He did not live in one of the great centers of civilization, but in a remote corner of the world. He was not born with the material advantages that wealth and social position can give; he was born in a stable. He did not have a long career, nor one which carried him into many countries; his life span was only thirty-three years; his activity was confined to an area of a few hundred miles. His life did not end on a note of triumph; he suffered the shameful death of crucifixion.

Yet today, twenty centuries later, this man is worshipped by hundreds of millions in every country of the world as the Saviour of mankind. Through the centuries since his death millions have gladly renounced all that the human heart holds dear, home, family, riches and friends, to carry his name to other corners of the earth. He is loved throughout the world as no other man has been loved. His cross, once a symbol of a criminal death, is now displayed triumphantly atop churches throughout the world, a

11

symbol of hope and love. His teachings have humanized and ennobled men and nations.

What is it that makes Jesus Christ unique among all the men in history? What is it that accounts for the influence he has had and still has on the world? The answer is, of course, that Jesus Christ was not merely a great teacher and religious leader; he is the Son of God. He is the Redeemer promised by God, who brought salvation to the human race, who ransomed man by his death on the cross.

Jesus Christ is a true man. He is the mediator between man and God. No man can come to the Father except through him. Jesus Christ is also God. His teachings, therefore, are the word of God revealed to man.

Jesus Christ is "the way, and the truth, and the life"—JOHN 14:6. It is by union with *him* that men receive the life of grace. It is through the acceptance of *his* teachings that men find salvation. It is by submission to *his* rule that men find the freedom of the sons of God.

Jesus said to his disciples, "Behold, I am with you all days, even unto the consummation of the world"—MATT. 28:20. Although he ascended into heaven, and we can no longer see and hear him as did his mother and his contemporaries, Jesus in his great love for us remains with us in his Church. He continues to give life and truth and guidance to those who are joined to him.

1. Does Jesus Christ promise happiness to those who love him?

Yes. Jesus Christ promises eternal happiness to those who love him.

2. Does Jesus Christ promise us happiness in this life?

Yes. Christ promises us happiness in this life, but not the kind of happiness the world seeks.

> Peace I leave with you, my peace I give to you; not as the world gives do I give to you. Do not let your heart be troubled, or be afraid—JOHN 14:27.

3. How does the happiness which Christ promises differ from that which the world seeks?

The kind of happiness which Christ promises in this life comes from loving God and being loved by God, and from the expectation of eternal happiness in heaven. Christ does not promise us pleasure or wealth. Rather, he tells us that it is only through suffering and self-denial that we can attain joy and peace of soul in this life.

> *Do not lay up for yourselves treasures on earth, where rust and moth consume, and where thieves break in and steal; but lay up for yourselves treasures in heaven, where neither rust nor moth consumes, nor thieves break in and steal. For where thy treasure is, there thy heart also will be*—MATT. 6:19-21.

4. In what words did Christ tell us how to attain happiness in this life?

In the Sermon on the Mount Christ said:

> *Blessed are the poor in spirit,*
> *for theirs is the kingdom of heaven.*
> *Blessed are the meek,*
> *for they shall possess the earth.*
> *Blessed are they who mourn,*
> *for they shall be comforted.*
> *Blessed are they who hunger and thirst for justice,*
> *for they shall be satisfied.*
> *Blessed are the merciful,*
> *for they shall obtain mercy.*
> *Blessed are the pure of heart,*
> *for they shall see God.*
> *Blessed are the peacemakers,*
> *for they shall be called children of God.*
> *Blessed are they who suffer persecution for justice' sake,*
> *for theirs is the kingdom of heaven*—MATT. 5:3-10.

a. Christ here is promising happiness. The word blessed means happy.

b. The reward promised in each of these Beatitudes is primarily heaven. But if we live according to the plan of Christ we shall have a foretaste of the happiness of heaven in this life.

c. Christ tells us that we will be happy by doing for his sake the very things which we think will make us unhappy.

d. Christ tells us that we must not set our hearts on money, whereas most men want even more money than they have.

e. Christ tells us that we must forgive our enemies and love them, whereas most men want to "get even with" or at least avoid those who hurt them.

f. Christ tells us that we must avoid all sin, that we must be willing to take a lower place, that we must suffer for him, etc. These are things which are distasteful to us and which we think would make us unhappy. But the Lord says just the opposite.

5. How is it possible for us to live according to these high standards set by Christ?

Christ has not only *told* us how to live; he has *shown* us by his example. What is more, he gives us all the help we need to follow his example. If we love Christ and try to follow his example we shall receive the strength he promised when he said,

> *I am the vine, you are the branches. He who abides in me, and I in him, he bears much fruit; for without me you can do nothing*—John 15:5.

Practice

▶ The greatest thing that Catholics do and the greatest expression of our unity is the worship we give to God in the Mass.

One who is taking instructions in order to be received into the Church should begin at once the practice of assisting at Mass on Sundays and Holydays of obligation.

God, Our Father

*Let not your heart be troubled. You believe in God, believe
also in me. In my Father's house there are many mansions.
Were it not so, I should have told you, because I go to prepare a place for you. And if I go and prepare a place for you,
I am coming again, and I will take you to myself; that where
I am, there you also may be. And where I go you know, and
the way you know.*

*Thomas said to him, "Lord, we do not know where thou
art going, and how can we know the way?" Jesus said to
him, "I am the way, and the truth, and the life. No one comes
to the Father but through me. If you had known me, you
would also have known my Father. And henceforth you do
know him, and you have seen him."*

*Philip said to him, "Lord, show us the Father and it is
enough for us." Jesus said to him, "Have I been so long a
time with you, and you have not known me? Philip, he who
sees me sees also the Father. How canst thou say, 'Show us
the Father'? Dost thou not believe that I am in the Father
and the Father in me? The words that I speak to you I speak
not on my own authority. But the Father dwelling in me,
it is he who does the works. Do you believe that I am in the
Father and the Father in me? Otherwise believe because
of the works themselves. Amen, amen, I say to you, he who
believes in me, the works that I do he also shall do, and
greater than these he shall do, because I am going to the
Father. And whatever you ask in my name, that I will do, in
order that the Father may be glorified in the Son. If you ask
me anything in my name, I will do it"*—JOHN 14:1-14.

JESUS tells us that God is his Father. He
tells us that God is also our Father. This is Christ's great message.
God is not a remote power, who rules the universe from afar. He
is our loving Father, who sent his Son into the world in order

that he might share his life with us.

God wants to unite us to himself. Therefore we must know him. We must know him not merely by observing the world about us, the work of his hands, but by hearing what he has told us of himself.

1. Who is God?

God is the Father of all men. He calls all men, regardless of their race, color or social condition, to unite themselves with him.

2. Why is God called the Father of all men?

God is the Father of all men because:

a. He has created all men.

*God created man in his image.
In the image of God he created him.
Male and female he created them—*GEN. 1:27.

b. He provides for the needs of his children.

But he said to his disciples, "Therefore I say to you, do not be anxious for your life, what you shall eat; nor yet for your body, what you shall put on. The life is a greater thing than the food, and the body than the clothing. Consider the ravens: they neither sow nor reap, they have neither storeroom nor barn; yet God feeds them. Of how much more value are you than they! But which of you by being anxious about it can add to his stature a single cubit? Therefore if you are not able to do even a very little thing, why are you anxious concerning the rest?

"See how the lilies grow; they neither toil nor spin, yet I say to you that not even Solomon in all his glory was arrayed like one of these. But if God so clothes the grass which today is alive in the field and tomorrow is thrown into the oven, how much more you, O you of little faith!

*"And as for you, do not seek what you shall eat, or what you shall drink; and do not exalt yourselves (for after all these things the nations of the world seek); but your Father knows that you need these things. But seek the kingdom of God, and all these things shall be given you besides"—*LUKE 12:22-31.

c. He loves men so much that he sent his Son to save them.

*For God so loved the world that he gave his only-begotten Son, that those who believe in him may not perish, but may have life everlasting. For God did not send his Son into the world in order to judge the world, but that the world might be saved through him—*JOHN 3:16-17.

d. He has shared his life with men.

*Behold what manner of love the Father has bestowed upon us, that we should be called children of God; and such we are. This is why the world does not know us, because it did not know him. Beloved, now we are the children of God, and it has not yet appeared what we shall be. We know that, when he appears, we shall be like to him, for we shall see him just as he is. And everyone who has this hope in him makes himself holy, just as he also is holy—*I JOHN 3:1-3.

3. How do we know that God exists?

We know that God exists because the world in which we live proclaims his existence.

For the wrath of God is revealed from heaven against all ungodliness and wickedness of those men who in wickedness hold back the truth of God, seeing that what may be known about God is manifest to them. For God has manifested it to them. For since the creation of the world his invisible attributes are clearly seen—his everlasting power also and divinity—being understood through things that are made
—ROM. 1:18-20.

a. The world about us gives witness to the existence of a supreme being. Everywhere in nature we find order and design. To try to explain order and design as the result of chance is foolish. Order and design are clearly the result of an intelligence at work. No one would ever seriously maintain that a watch simply came into being, that the metal out of which it is made happened to form itself into the shape of a watch, that the numerals on the face of the watch *just happened* to form themselves in the sequence of one to twelve and locate themselves in mathematical precision just so far from one another as to allow the hands of the watch to move (again by chance) precisely this fraction of an inch every minute. Even if one allowed millions

17

of years for all this to have happened one could not reasonably claim that anything as orderly and complex as a watch was produced by blind chance.

If this is true of a watch, what is to be said about the earth, the planets, the solar system, the universe itself? Everywhere in nature there is order and design. Everywhere we find the "laws of nature." Only a living, intelligent being could have designed the universe. This being we call God.

b. We also know that God exists because he has told us so.

God, who at sundry times and in divers manners spoke in times past to the fathers by the prophets, last of all in these days has spoken to us by his Son, whom he appointed heir of all things, by whom also he made the world—HEB. 1:1-2.

When God spoke to Moses, commanding him to lead his people out of Egypt and into the promised land he told Moses his name: *"I Am."*

"But," said Moses to God, "when I go to the Israelites and say to them, 'the God of your fathers has sent me to you,' if they ask me, 'What is his name?' what am I to tell them?" God replied, "I am who am." Then he added, "This is what you shall tell the Israelites: 'I AM sent me to you' "
—Ex. 3:13-15.

4. What has God told us about himself?

Speaking through men whom he inspired, God has told us:

a. **God is love.**

And we have come to know, and have believed, the love that God has in our behalf. God is love, and he who abides in love abides in God, and God in him—1 JOHN 4:16.

God is all good. He created the world in order to show forth his glory and to share his happiness with the beings he created.

Holy, holy, holy the Lord God of hosts, all the earth is full of his glory—Is. 6:3.

He shares his life with men.

. . . he has granted us the very great and precious promises, so that through them you may become partakers of the divine nature . . .—2 PET. 1:4.

18

He loves all men and wills that all men be saved.

I have loved thee with an everlasting love: therefore have I drawn thee, taking pity on thee—JER. 31:3.

For God so loved the world that he gave his only-begotten Son, that those who believe in him may not perish, but may have life everlasting—JOHN 3:16-17.

. . . God our Saviour, who wishes all men to be saved and to come to the knowledge of the truth—I TIM. 2:4.

He is all-merciful, ready to forgive any sinner who repents.

Merciful and gracious is the LORD, slow to anger and abounding in kindness. For as the heavens are high above the earth, so surpassing is his kindness toward those who fear him. But the kindness of the LORD is from eternity to eternity to those who fear him—Ps. 102:8, 11, 17.

I say to you that, even so, there will be joy in heaven over one sinner who repents, more than over ninety-nine just who have no need of repentance—LUKE 15:7.

b. **God is all knowing.**

> *And there is no creature hidden from his sight; but all things are naked and open to the eyes of him to whom we have to give account*—HEB. 4:13.

> *He plumbs the depths and penetrates the heart;*
>   *their innermost being he understands.*
> *The LORD possesses all knowledge,*
>   *and sees from of old the things that are to come:*
> *He makes known the past and the future,*
>   *and reveals the deepest secrets.*
> *No understanding does he lack;*
>   *no single thing escapes him*—SIR. 42:18-20.

c. **God is just.**

> *The Lord will reward everyone according to his justice, and his faithfulness*—I KINGS 26:23.

> *A faithful God, without deceit, how just and upright he is!*—DEUT. 32:4.

> *Life eternal indeed he will give to those who by patience in good works seek glory and honor and immortality; but wrath and indignation to those who are contentious and who do not submit to truth but assent to iniquity*
> —ROM. 2:7-8.

19

d. God is infinite.

There is no limit to his life.

Great is the LORD *and highly to be praised*—Ps. 144:3.

From everlasting you are, O LORD—Ps. 92:2.

e. God is unchangeable.

Every good gift and every perfect gift is from above, coming down from the Father of Lights, with whom there is no change, nor shadow of alteration.—JAS. 1:17.

f. God is eternal.

He had no beginning and will have no end.

Before the mountains were begotten and the earth and world were brought forth, from everlasting to everlasting you are God . . . For a thousand years in your sight are as yesterday—Ps. 89:2-4.

. . . before Abraham came to be, I am—JOHN 8:58.

The Lord shall reign forever and ever—Ex. 15:18.

g. God is all-powerful.

Adonai, Lord, greatest art thou, and glorious in thy power, and no one can overcome thee. Let all thy creatures serve thee, because thou hast spoken, and they were made. Thou didst send forth thy spirit, and they were created, and there is no one that can resist thy voice
—JUD. 16:16-17.

h. God is everywhere.

Where can I go from your spirit?
  from your presence where can I flee?

If I go up to the heavens, you are there;
  if I sink to the nether world, you are present there.

If I take the wings of the dawn,
  if I settle at the farthest limits of the sea,

Even there your hand shall guide me,
  and your right hand hold me fast.

If I say, "Surely the darkness shall hide me,
  and night shall be my light"—

For you darkness itself is not dark,
  and night shines as the day.
    [Darkness and light are the same.]

—Ps. 138:7-12.

i. **God is a spirit.**

He is the one limitless, almighty, all-knowing spirit. He does not need anything or anyone outside of himself. He depends on nothing and on no one, but all things depend on him. Yet God cares for and sustains all the things which he has created. And he calls all men to become his adopted children.

Practice

▶ There are many people who know very little about God and his goodness towards men. As we study and learn more about God we should share this knowledge with our friends and neighbors.

We should strive, too, to realize more and more how much we depend on God and to acquire a sense of his continual presence. God himself will give us this realization if we pray for it. One type of prayer which is well suited to give us a sense of the continual presence of God and to unite us with him throughout the day is an offering of ourselves made to God in the morning and renewed frequently during the day.

We may make this offering in our own words. The best time to make it is immediately upon rising. A good time to renew it is just before meals. A simple form of the morning offering is as follows:

My God, I offer thee this day all I shall think or do or say, uniting it with what was done on earth by Jesus Christ, thy Son.

Begin the practice of making the morning offering now.

section 3 | The Gift of Life

Now there was a certain man among the Pharisees, Nicodemus by name, a ruler of the Jews. This man came to Jesus at night, and said to him, "Rabbi, we know that thou hast come a teacher from God, for no one can work these signs that thou workest unless God be with him." Jesus answered and said to him, "Amen, amen, I say to thee, unless a man be born again, he cannot see the kingdom of God." Nicodemus said to him, "How can a man be born when he is old? Can he enter a second time into his mother's womb and be born again?" Jesus answered, "Amen, amen, I say to thee, unless a man be born again of water and the Spirit, he cannot enter into the kingdom of God. . . . For God so loved the world that he gave his only-begotten Son, that those who believe in him may not perish, but may have life everlasting"
—JOHN 3:1-17.

WE can appreciate the astonishment of Nicodemus, hearing these words for the first time. "Unless a man be born again of water and the Spirit, he cannot enter into the kingdom of God." This rebirth demands the giving of a new kind of life, the life to which Christ referred when he said, "I came that they may have life, and have it more abundantly." It is the divine life, that gift of God which makes men share in the very life of God.

No wonder, then, that Jesus Christ sums up his whole work of redemption by speaking of re-birth and a new kind of life. No wonder, too, that without an understanding of this new life we should never be able to see in proper focus the great realities which God has revealed to us, or to appreciate the wonderful destiny that is ours.

1. What does Jesus mean when he says that we must be "born again"?

Jesus means that in order to achieve the supernatural destiny

22

for which God has created us we must receive a new kind of life, a supernatural life, which is a created share in the life of God.

This is the life to which Jesus referred when he said:

I came that they may have life and have it more abundantly
—JOHN 10:10.

I am the vine, you are the branches. He who abides in me, and I in him, he bears much fruit; for without me you can do nothing. If anyone does not abide in me, he shall be cast outside as the branch and wither; and they shall gather them up and cast them into the fire, and they shall burn
—JOHN 15:5-6.

. . . I am the way, and the truth, and the life—JOHN 14:6.

I am the bread of life. Your fathers ate the manna in the desert, and have died. This is the bread that comes down from heaven, so that if anyone eat of it he will not die. I am the living bread that has come down from heaven. If anyone eat of this bread he shall live forever; and the bread that I will give is my flesh for the life of the world—JOHN 6:48-52.

. . . If thou didst know the gift of God, and who it is who says to thee, "Give me to drink," thou, perhaps, wouldst have asked of him, and he would have given thee living water. . . . Everyone who drinks of this water will thirst again. He, however, who drinks of the water that I will give him shall never thirst; but the water that I will give him shall become in him a fountain of water, springing up into life everlasting
—JOHN 4:10-15.

2. What is this supernatural destiny for which God has intended us?

God intends that after death we share his own happiness in a heaven which is not natural to human beings or to any other creatures, but to God alone.

3. How can we live in a heaven which is natural to God alone?

We could not live in heaven just as we are, with merely our human life. To live in heaven it is necessary to have a share in the life of God. We have no right whatever to such a gift. But since God wants to share his happiness with us he has willed to share his life with us.

4. What is this share in the life of God called?

This share in the life of God is called the *divine life* or *sanctifying grace.*

"Grace" means a free gift, something to which we have no right. We have a right to our human life because we were created as human beings. Human life is *natural* to us. But to share God's life is something which is totally *above* man. For this reason sanctifying grace is also called *super-*natural life. It is called "*sanctifying*" because it makes us like God, our Father, who is holiness itself.

5. In what way does the divine life make us like God?

The divine life makes us "partakers of the Divine Nature" (2 PET. 1:4) because it empowers us to live as God lives, that is, to know God as he knows himself and to love him as he loves himself.

6. Do we have any idea of the life of God?

The life of God is the deepest of all mysteries. God is ". . . the King of Kings and the Lord of Lords; who alone has immortality and dwells in light inaccessible, whom no man has seen or can see . . ."—I TIM. 6:16. However, we have a hint as to the life of God in our own life. We know and love in our own limited way. God knows and loves without limit. His life consists in knowing and loving himself, the highest truth and the greatest good.

7. How shall we know and love God when we share his life in heaven?

In heaven, because we shall be united to God, we shall know and love him as he knows and loves himself. God will fill our minds with himself, dazzling, immeasurable truth, and our wills with himself, goodness so inexhaustible that all created love is but his shadow, in a fulfillment of love which is beyond all power of imagination.

8. Does the divine life make us divine?

The divine life makes us divine in the sense that we share

24

God's life. It does not make us divine in the sense that we become God or "part of God." Such an idea would be absurd. Even in heaven, seeing and loving God face to face, we shall never lose our identity, our individuality, or our complete dependence on God.

9. How does the divine life make us adopted children of God?

St. John tells us,

Behold what manner of love the Father has bestowed upon us, that we should be called children of God; and such we are. This is why the world does not know us, because it did not know him. Beloved, now we are the children of God, and it has not yet appeared what we shall be. We know that, when he appears, we shall be like to him, for we shall see him just as he is. And everyone who has this hope in him makes himself holy, just as he also is holy—1 JOHN 3:1-3.

By nature we are creatures of God, the work of his hands. When we receive the divine life we live with the life of God and take on an inner resemblance to him. Our relationship with God becomes then not merely that of creature and creator but that of child and Father.*

10. What is the greatest gift which comes with the gift of the divine life?

The greatest gift which comes with the divine life is *God himself.*

. . . if anyone love me, he will keep my word, and my Father will love him, and we will come to him and make our abode with him—JOHN 14:23.

11. Why does God come and dwell within us?

God comes and dwells within us to begin, in an incomplete way, the possession of him which we will have in heaven.

---

* This divine adoption is much more thorough and real than human adoption. When a married couple adopt a child they merely go through a legal process. No internal change takes place in the child they adopt; they must choose a being who is already like them, who has the same kind of nature. But when God adopts us as his children he actually transforms us internally. We take on an inner likeness to him because we share his life.

12. What is actual grace?

Actual grace is help from God. It is light for our minds and strength for our wills. It is the kind of grace for which we should constantly pray because we constantly need it.

Often the thought comes to us, "I ought to pray more," "I should try to correct this fault in my character," "I should help this man." Often, too, we suddenly see a truth about God, ourselves, and our relation to God a little more clearly. These promptings and enlightenments are not accidental, trivial occurrences. They are sent by God. They are actual graces. God sends us these actual graces in order that we might perform actions which will merit for us an increase of the divine life. One who has lost the divine life through mortal sin cannot repent unless God gives him actual graces which will enable him to do so.

Practice

▶ 1. God is always offering us actual graces. We should strive to realize how completely we depend on them and to cooperate with them at all times. To this end prayer is a necessity, prayer for ourselves and for others. We should pray for more and more actual grace. Without it we are helpless.

2. The Communion service in the Mass begins with the prayer of the children of God, the one taught us by Christ himself, the Lord's Prayer:

Our Father, who art in heaven, hallowed be thy name. Thy kingdom come, thy will be done on earth, as it is in heaven. Give us this day our daily bread, and forgive us our trespasses as we forgive those who trespass against us; and lead us not into temptation, but deliver us from evil. Amen.

As you say this prayer at Mass try to realize the unity we have with one another as children of God, our Father. That unity is demonstrated best when we offer Mass together.

God, OUR FATHER, shows forth his beauty, his power and his majesty in the world he created. He gave his children a wonderful world in which to live. God's original plan was beautifully simple. He gave man the gift of divine life at the instant he created him, and placed him in the world in order that he might prepare for heaven. We were to be born in possession of the divine life and were to keep it always. There was to be no disorder, no sickness, no death, provided man remained faithful to God and did not rebel against him by sinning. But Adam, the head of our race, failed God and us, his descendants. He sinned and thereby lost his and our most precious possession, the divine life, which makes us children of God.

The story of God's creation of the world and of our first parents, of their elevation to the divine life and of their rebellion against God is told in the first book of the Bible, the book of Genesis.

In the beginning God created the heavens and the earth; the earth was waste and void; darkness covered the abyss, and the spirit of God was stirring above the waters.

God said, "Let there be light," and there was light. God saw that the light was good. God separated the light from the darkness, calling the light day and the darkness night. And there was evening and morning, the first day.

Then God said, "Let there be a firmament in the midst of the waters to divide the waters." And so it was. God made the firmament, dividing the waters that were below the firmament from those that were above it. God called the firmament heaven. And there was evening and morning, the second day.

Then God said, "Let the waters below the heavens be gathered into one place and let the dry land appear." And so it was. God called the dry land earth and the assembled waters seas. And God saw that it was good. Then God said, "Let the earth bring forth vegetation: seed-bearing plants and all kinds of fruit trees that bear fruit containing their seed." And so it was. The earth brought forth vegetation, every kind of seed-bearing plant and all kinds of trees that bear fruit containing their seed. God saw that it was good. And there was evening and morning, the third day.

And God said, "Let there be lights in the firmament of the heavens to separate day from night; let them serve as signs and for the fixing of seasons, days and years; let them serve as lights in the firmament of the heavens to shed light upon the earth." So it was. God made the two great lights, the greater light to rule the day and the smaller one to rule the night, and he made the stars. God set them in the firmament of the heavens to shed light upon the earth, to rule the day and the night and to separate the light from the darkness. God saw that it was good. And there was evening and morning, the fourth day.

Then God said, "Let the waters abound with life, and above the earth let winged creatures fly below the firmament of the heavens." And so it was. God created the great sea monsters, all kinds of living, swimming creatures with which the waters abound and all kinds of winged birds. God saw that it was good, and God blessed them, saying, "Be fruitful, multiply, and fill the waters of the seas; and let the birds multiply on the earth." And there was evening and morning, the fifth day.

God said, "Let the earth bring forth all kinds of living creatures: cattle, crawling creatures and wild animals." And so it was. God made all kinds of wild beasts, every kind of cattle, and every kind of creature crawling on the ground. And God saw that it was good.

God said, "Let us make mankind in our image and likeness; and let them have dominion over the fish of the sea, the birds of the air, the cattle, over all the wild animals and every creature that crawls on the earth."

God created man in his image. In the image of God he created him. Male and female he created them.

Then God blessed them and said to them, "Be fruitful and multiply; fill the earth and subdue it. Have dominion over the fish of the sea, the birds of the air, the cattle and all the animals that crawl on the earth." God also said, "See, I give you every seed-bearing plant on the earth and every tree which has seed-bearing fruit to be your food. To every wild

28

animal of the earth, to every bird of the air, and to every creature that crawls on the earth and has the breath of life, I give the green plants for food." And so it was. God saw that all he had made was very good. And there was evening and morning, the sixth day.

Thus the heavens and the earth were finished and all their array. On the sixth day God finished the work he had been doing. And he rested on the seventh day from all the work he had done.

God blessed the seventh day and made it holy because on it he rested from all his work of creation"

—GEN. 1:1-31, 2:1-3.

THE STORY of creation as it is given in the Bible was written by Moses, who drew on the oral traditions of his people. It was written with these people in mind. It is, of course, inspired by God. It is not, however, a scientific account. We must not expect in it answers to scientific questions. It is up to human learning and research, guided by the teachings of the Church, to determine, for example, the age of the earth and the question of evolution. The Bible was not intended to answer such questions.

1. What does this Biblical account of creation teach?

This account teaches certain important religious truths:

a. There is only *one* God.

b. God is the creator of everything, even of the sun, moon and the stars (which some of the neighboring peoples worshipped as gods).

c. God created everything effortlessly, merely by his word.

d. All things created by God are good.

e. God has given man dominion over the things on this earth.

2. Does this account teach us that the world was made in six days?

No. The six days are a purely literary device, i.e., a manner

29

of speaking which made it easier for the audience to understand and remember.

Thus God is described as creating "places" on the first three days and the inhabitants of these "places" on the second three days. The "work" of the first and the fourth day is described as the separation of light and darkness on the one hand, and on the other the creation of the heavenly bodies which regulate light and darkness. The "work" of the second and fifth days is described as the separation of the waters on the one hand (the Jews thought that there were waters above the sky and under the earth) and on the other the creation of the fish which live in the waters and the birds which live in the air separating the waters.

The "work" of the third and sixth days is described as the creation of the earth and plant life and of animals and man.

3. Why did Moses use this literary device?

a. If Moses had known what science now knows about the origin of the world and had stated this information in scientific terms, the people would have been bewildered and would not have understood his religious message.

b. Moses wished to stress the holiness of the Sabbath day, which the Jews were already bound to observe. So he represented God as working six days and resting on the seventh (the Sabbath).

4. Does this account rule out evolution?

This account of creation reveals that God is the creator of all things. The manner in which creation took place is not revealed in the Bible. Modern science teaches us the evolution of plant and animal life. As long as this teaching does not exclude God as the creator and director of the process of evolution, it does not contradict revelation.

5. What is the meaning of the word create?

To create means to make something out of nothing. Human beings can make things, using materials which already exist, but the power to create belongs only to God.

Creation means more than making something out of nothing.

30

When God creates something he also keeps it in existence. If he did not, it would return to nothing.

6. Was it necessary that God create?

No. God is absolutely free. He need not have created anything. God has no need of anything outside of himself.

7. Why, then, did God create?

God created in order to manifest himself and to share his goodness with the beings he created. He has shared his existence with the whole of creation, which mirrors him in various degrees of clarity.

The heavens declare the glory of God, and the firmament proclaims his handiwork—Ps. 18:2.

He has created images of himself in the spiritual world, angels and men; and in his infinite goodness he has willed to give to angels and men as an utterly free and undeserved gift a share in his nature, the divine life.

8. What are angels?

Angels are spiritual beings created by God. They, like human beings, are created in the image of God, more clearly in God's image than man because they are completely spiritual, having no need of bodies or of anything material.

9. How do angels differ from God?

Angels are creatures, i.e., they were created by God; they depend absolutely upon God's sustaining hand for their existence and activity. Although of a higher nature than man, they, too, are limited beings.

10. What is the story of the elevation and fall of the angels?

At the moment he created them God gave the divine life to the angels. Since they are beings with free will they, too, had to prove their fidelity to God before being admitted to heaven. A vast multitude of the angels rebelled against God and fixed their powerful wills forever on evil. These evil spirits live now in hell and are called "devils."

The angels who remained faithful to God enjoy the vision of God in heaven.

11. Do angels play any part in our lives?

Yes. Our guardian angels protect and help us. The devils tempt us and try to lead us into sin. Satan, the leader of the devils, tempted Eve to sin and to lead Adam into sin.

Practice

▶ In the Mass, at the conclusion of the Canon, a beautiful scene is presented to us; all God's creation is gathered around the cross of Christ, who by his death has redeemed the world and drawn all things to himself:

Through him and with him and in him all honor and glory is given to you, God, almighty Father, in the unity of the Holy Spirit. World without end. Amen.

Everything in the world was created to give glory to God. We, the greatest of all his earthly creatures, must praise him with our minds, our hearts, our whole being. The worship of God is our first, our most important and our most exalted function.

The Church worships God, above all, in the Mass. Strive to realize when you assist at Mass that you are worshipping God in the highest possible way.

Make your own the short prayer of praise which the Church uses so often:

Glory be to the Father and to the Son and to the Holy Spirit, as it was in the beginning, is now, and ever shall be, world without end. Amen.

section 5 | # The Creation of Man

*O God, who in a wonderful manner created and ennobled human nature and still more wonderfully renewed it; grant that, by the mystery of this water and wine, we may be made partakers of his divinity who was pleased to become partaker of our humanity, Jesus Christ, your Son, our Lord, who being God, lives and reigns with you in the unity of the Holy Spirit, forever and ever. Amen—*MISSAL.

THIS PRAYER, recited by the priest at Mass as he puts water into the chalice of wine, emphasizes the point that Jesus Christ, when he came to bring men the divine life, was *restoring* something which had been lost. God, in creating man, exalted human nature very wonderfully by giving man the divine life. Then, by a great tragedy which occurred at the very beginning of the human race, man lost the divine life and the means of attaining heaven. Jesus Christ, therefore, "vouchsafed to share our manhood" in order that we might have part in his Godhead, i.e., might receive from him the divine life, which had been lost in Adam. Through Christ God has "yet more wonderfully established it (human nature) anew." Our restoration to the divine life is yet more wonderful than the original gift.

I came that they may have life, and have it more abundantly
                                                        —JOHN 10:10.

I. The Creation of Man

The creation of man is described twice in the Book of Genesis, in the first chapter and again in the second.

God said, "Let us make mankind in our image and likeness; and let them have dominion over the fish of the sea, the birds of the air, the cattle, over all the wild animals and every creature that crawls on the earth."

God created man in his image.
In the image of God He created him.
Male and female He created them—GEN. 1:26-28.

Then the Lord God formed man out of the dust of the ground and breathed into his nostrils the breath of life, and man became a living being—GEN. 2:7.

Then the Lord God said, "It is not good that the man is alone; I will make him a helper like himself." . . . The Lord God cast the man into a deep sleep and, while he slept, took one of his ribs and closed up its place with flesh. And the rib which the Lord God took from the man, he made into a woman, and brought her to him. Then the man said,

> *"She now is bone of my bone,*
> *and flesh of my flesh;*
> *She shall be called Woman,*
> *for from man she has been taken."*

For this reason a man leaves his father and mother, and clings to his wife, and the two become one flesh
—GEN. 2:18, 21-24.

1. What are the main points which God teaches us in this account of the creation of man?

The main points which God teaches us here are these:

a. the body of man was made in a special manner by God;

b. all human beings are descendents of Adam and Eve.

c. woman is of the same nature as man and is dependent on man;

d. the soul of man was created directly by God;

2. Could the origin of man's body be explained by the theory of evolution?

The Bible does not give us the answer to this question. The theory of the evolution of man's body could fit into the story as we have it in the Bible, provided of course, that we understand by evolution a process directed by God, not by chance.

Revelation makes it very clear, however, that the *souls* of Adam and Eve were created directly by God, as is the soul of every human being.

3. *What is man?*

Man is a creature with a material body and a spiritual soul, made by God in his likeness.

All creatures reflect God in the sense that each mirrors in its own limited way the boundless reality and beauty of God. Man, because he has a spiritual soul, has dominion over the other earthly creatures and is a more perfect image of God than anything else on this earth.

When I behold your heavens, the work of your fingers,
*   the moon and the stars which you set in place—*
What is man that you should be mindful of him,
*   or the son of man that you should care for him?*
You have made him little less than the angels,
*   and crowned him with glory and honor.*
You have given him rule over the works of your hands,
*   putting all things under his feet:*
All sheep and oxen,
*   yes, and the beasts of the field,*
The birds of the air, the fishes of the sea,
*   and whatever swims the paths of the seas*

—Ps. 8:4-9.

4. *Has the soul a life of its own?*

Yes. The soul is a living thing. Without the soul the body would not have life. But the soul, even after it leaves the body, will live forever. Since it has not any parts it cannot "fall apart" or die. It would cease to live only if God were to destroy it.

After death human souls are separated from their bodies, but they are not angels. God has created us as men and has revealed that at the end of the world our souls and bodies will be reunited. We shall always be men.

II. The Gift of the Divine Life and Its Loss by Our First Parents

Now the serpent was more cunning than any beast of the field which the Lord God had made. He said to the woman, "Did God say, 'You shall not eat of any tree of the garden'?" The woman answered the serpent, "Of the fruit of all the trees in the garden we may eat; but 'Of the fruit of the tree in the middle of the garden,' God said, 'you shall not eat, neither shall you touch it, lest you die.'"

But the serpent said to the woman, "No, you shall not die; for God knows that when you eat of it, your eyes will be opened and you will be like God, knowing good and evil." Now the woman saw that the tree was good for food, pleasing to the eyes, and desirable for the knowledge it would give. She took of its fruit and ate it, and also gave some to her husband and he ate. Then the eyes of both were opened, and they realized that they were naked; so they sewed fig-leaves together and made themselves coverings. When they heard the sound of the Lord God walking in the garden in the cool of the day, the man and his wife hid themselves from the Lord God among the trees of the garden. And the Lord God called the man and said to him, "Where are you?" And he said, "I heard you in the garden, and I was afraid because I was naked; and I hid." Then he said, "Who told you that you were naked? You have eaten then of the tree of which I commanded you not to eat." The man said, "The woman you placed at my side gave me fruit from the tree and I ate." Then the Lord said to the woman, "Why have you done this?" The woman said, "The serpent deceived me and I ate." Then the Lord God said to the serpent:

> *"Because you have done this, cursed are you among all animals, and among all beasts of the field; on your belly shall you crawl, dust shall you eat, all the days of your life. I will put enmity between you and the woman, between your seed and her seed; he shall crush your head, and you shall lie in wait for his heel."*

To the woman he said:

> *"I will make great your distress in childbearing; in pain shall you bring forth children; for your husband shall be your longing, though he have dominion over you."*

And to Adam he said, "Because you have listened to your wife, and have eaten of the tree of which I commanded you not to eat:

> *Cursed be the ground because of you; in toil shall you eat of it all the days of your life; thorns and thistles shall it bring forth to you, and you shall eat the plants of the field. In the sweat of your brow you shall eat bread, till you return to the ground, since out of it you were taken; for dust you are and unto dust you shall return."*

(And the man called his wife Eve because she was the mother of all the living.)
—GEN. 3:1-20.

Here, in terms of the earthly paradise, the tree of life, the serpent and the tree of knowledge of good and evil God reveals to us the story of his gift of the divine life and its loss through Adam. Our first parents were to pass on the divine life to their descendants. But first they had to prove their fidelity to God. Instead of remaining faithful, they listened to the suggestion of the evil spirit, deliberately turned their wills against God and lost the divine life, with tragic results for themselves and their descendants.

1. What gifts did God give to our first parents?

By far the greatest gift was the gift of the divine life. But in addition God gave Adam and Eve other gifts:

> They were immune to sickness and death.
> Their emotions and even their desires were under the control of their higher nature.
> They had knowledge and skills without having had to acquire them.

2. What was the sin which our first parents committed?

The exact nature of the sin has not been clearly revealed to us. From the figures of the tree of the knowledge of good and evil and the words of the tempter, "Your eyes will be opened and you will be like God, knowing good and evil" (GEN. 3:5), it appears to have been a sin of pride, a refusal to acknowledge their complete dependence on God. This sin of our first parents is called original sin.

3. How were Adam and Eve affected by their sin?

By far the most tragic consequence was their loss of the divine life. But they also lost other gifts. Although the union of spirit and matter is in itself one in which there would naturally be some conflict, there was no such conflict in the case of our first parents. Adam and Eve had received a special gift, a harmony between body and soul which is not natural to man. All the inclinations of the body were under the perfect control of the soul; all the powers of the soul were oriented to God. By their sin our first parents lost this special gift. They suffered disharmony with-

37

in themselves. Their bodies were no longer completely subject to their souls; their souls no longer oriented to God. They became subject, too, to sickness, suffering and death.

4. How are we affected by the sin of Adam?

Because of the sin of Adam we come into the world deprived of the divine life and subject to death, sickness and the inclination to sin.

> For we know that the Law is spiritual but I am carnal, sold into the power of sin. For I do not understand what I do, for it is not what I wish that I do, but what I hate, that I do. . . . For I do not do the good that I wish, but the evil that I do not wish, that I perform—ROM. 7:14-19.

Original sin—the fact that we come into the world without the divine life—must not be confused with actual or personal sin, which we ourselves commit. Actual sin may be either *mortal* or *venial*. Mortal sin is an offense against God which is so serious that it destroys our divine life and breaks our friendship with God. Venial sin is an offense against God which does not destroy the divine life, but which weakens our will and paves the way for mortal sin.

5. What was God's response to the sin of Adam and Eve?

God did not restore the lesser gifts, such as freedom from death. But what is much more important, he promised that his own Son would become man in order to redeem us and restore the divine life.

When the Son of God became man he took the name Jesus, which means saviour.

6. What did Jesus mean when he said that he came that we might have "life more abundantly"?

Since God has become man we have been honored and exalted more than the angels. We have Jesus Christ as our head, teaching us and sanctifying us through the Church. We have the sacraments, through which the divine life flows into our souls. We eat and drink the body and blood of Christ in the Eucharist. We have the Mass, the re-offering of Christ's death, in which we now have a part.

We have as our mother and model the greatest of all God's creatures, the only human person who was conceived without original sin, Mary, the Mother of God.

Despite the tragic sin of Adam and the struggle for salvation in which we must now engage; despite the suffering and evil which is in the world as a consequence of that sin, the Church still exults in a most striking and beautiful song, which is sung in the Easter Vigil service.

> *O wondrous condescension of your mercy towards us! How far beyond our understanding is your loving affection, that you should ransom a slave at the price of your own Son! O necessary sin of Adam, which was blotted out by the death of Christ! O happy fault, that merited such a redeemer!*

Practice

▶ Because of the sin of Adam we have inclinations which will lead us into sin unless we keep them in check. We all have tendencies towards pride and selfishness. Even our natural desires, good in themselves, can easily get out of hand and cause us to go to excess. We must, therefore, from time to time deny ourselves even legitimate pleasures in order to strengthen ourselves. The Church helps us to do this by requiring us to forego meat on Fridays and to fast at certain times. She encourages us to do more on our own initiative.

Even if we are not yet bound by law to do so we should adopt the practice of giving up meat on Fridays and other days of abstinence in order to strengthen ourselves against these inclinations which might lead us into sin.

Glories of Divine Grace, SCHEEBEN. St. Meinrad, Ind., Grail, five booklets, Vol. 1—30c; Vol. 2—35c; Vol. 3—30c; Vol. 4—25c; Vol. 5—35c.
> Five excellent, reasonably priced, easy to read booklets on the supernatural life, written by a great theologian; a section of Scheeben's masterpiece, Mysteries of Christianity.

The Church Today, SUHARD. Chicago, Fides, $4.75.
> The collected pastoral letters of the late Emmanuel Cardinal Suhard. There are two excellent pastorals on God: God's Providence and The Meaning of God. The latter is not easy reading, but is well worth the effort.

The Divine Pity, VANN. New York, Sheed & Ward, 220 pp., $2.75.
> An explanation of the Beatitudes and their meaning in the life of a Christian. Inspiring reading. Poetic in tone.

Theology and Sanity, SHEED. New York, Sheed & Ward, 407 pp., $3.50.
> Nothing better, for anyone who is not afraid to read a book which *makes* one reason. The chapters on the attributes of God are demanding on the reader, but will give him a really mature idea of the Supreme Being.

The Holy Ghost, LEEN. New York, Sheed & Ward, $3.50.
> One of the best books available on the divine life and God's work in the soul. Not easy reading, but worth a great deal of effort.

PART II CHRIST THE LIFE

section 6 | The Preparation for the Redeemer

Then Paul arose, and motioning with his hand for silence, said, "Israelites and you who fear God, hearken. The God of the people of Israel chose our fathers and exalted the people when they were sojourners in the land of Egypt, and with uplifted arm led them forth out of it. And for a period of forty years he bore with their ways in the desert, and after destroying seven nations in the land of Canaan, he divided their land among them by lot after about four hundred and fifty years. After that he gave them judges, until the time of Samuel the prophet. Then they demanded a king, and God gave them Saul, the son of Cis, a man of the tribe of Benjamin, for forty years. And removing him, he raised up David to be their king, and to him he bore witness and said, 'I have found David, the son of Jesse, a man after my heart, who will do all that I desire.'

"From his offspring, God according to promise brought to Israel a saviour, Jesus . . ."—ACTS 13:16-23.

THOUSANDS of years elapsed between the sin of Adam and Eve and the coming of Christ. During that time men fell deeper and deeper into sin and drifted farther and farther from the idea of the one true God. A great part of the world worshipped idols and had so debased religion that vice was sometimes considered virtue. Yet God had not abandoned men. Immediately after the fall of Adam he promised a redeemer. Throughout all the centuries which elapsed as man floundered in sin and unbelief, God's providence was still at work. Then, in his own time, God began the immediate preparation for the coming of his Son into the world.

1. How did God begin the immediate preparation for the coming of Christ?

About 2,000 B.C. God began the immediate preparation for the coming of Christ when he said to Abraham:

*Leave your country, your kinsfolk and your father's house, for the land which I will show you; I will make a great nation of you. I will bless you, and make your name great, so that you shall be a blessing. I will bless them that bless you, and curse them that curse you. In you shall all the nations of the earth be blessed—*GEN. 12:1-3.

2. Who was Abraham?

Abraham was the founder of the Jews,* the people whom God chose as his own, the people to whom God spoke through the prophets in the Old Testament.

3. What was the importance of the Jews in the plan of God?

The Jews were the people through whom God kept alive belief in the one true God during the centuries before Christ. God's ancient revelation was given to the Jews. It was they who preserved it and handed it down. When the Son of God became man he chose to be born a Jew.

The Jews, therefore, are our spiritual ancestors. Christianity is the Jewish religion brought to its fulfillment in Christ and opened up to the whole world.

4. Who was Moses?

Moses was the great leader and law-giver whom God chose to lead the Jews out of captivity in Egypt into the land he had promised them. It was to Moses that God gave the Ten Commandments on Mount Sinai when he entered into his covenant with the Jews. To Moses, also, is attributed the authorship of the first five books of the Bible.

5. What is the Old Testament?

The Old Testament is the collection of the sacred books of

---

* The chosen people were not called "Jews" until later in their history. For the purpose of simplification, however, the word "Jews" will be used throughout these lessons.

44

the Jews which tell the story of their relationship with God. It is usually classified as forty-five books, which vary in length and literary form: twenty-one books of history, eighteen books of prophecy and seven books of wisdom literature.

These books are to be understood in the light of the literary style and of the mentality of the times in which they were written. Recent archeological studies have in many cases indicated the geographical and historical reliability of the Old Testament, where it has been attacked. The books were written by many authors over a long period of time. The traditions of the Jews recounted in the first five books certainly go back to the time of Moses (1,400-1,200 B.C.), while the story of the Machabees, told in the last two books, was written about 100 B.C.

6. Why is this collection of books called the Old Testament?

These books are called a TESTAMENT because they are an account of the covenant (agreement) entered into by God with his chosen people through Moses on Mount Sinai. This testament, or covenant, is called OLD to distinguish it from the NEW one which God entered into with all men through Christ on Mount Calvary.

The prophet Jeremias foretold the transition from the old to the new testament five hundred years before the birth of Christ.

> *Behold the days shall come, saith the Lord, and I will make a new covenant with the house of Israel and with the house of Juda; not according to the covenant which I made with their fathers, in the day that I took them by the hand to bring them out of the land of Egypt: the covenant which they made void, and I had dominion over them, saith the Lord. But this shall be the covenant that I will make with the house of Israel after those days, saith the Lord: I will give my law in their bowels, and I will write it in their heart, and I will be their God, and they shall be my people*
> —JER. 31:31-34.

7. What kind of history is recorded in the Old Testament?

The Old Testament is the history of God's dealing with his chosen people.

45

a. The Old Testament is the history of God's kingdom on earth. The Jews were God's people. He was their king, who exercised his authority through the prophets, judges and kings. God separated the Jews from all other people and promised them large families, good harvests, peace and his continual presence and protection if they were faithful to him. He theratened them with war, famine, plague and exile if they were unfaithful. The Jews frequently turned from God. In each case God chastised, forgave them and accepted them again as his chosen people.

b. The Old Testament tells the story of only one people, the Jews. Other people are mentioned only incidentally. It does not give a complete history of even that people, but treats of only those events which have direct bearing on the plan of God. There are gaps of hundreds of years in the narrative, and only men who have a direct relationship to Christ figure prominently in it.

c. The Old Testament is centered on the coming of the Messiah. It tells of the historical events leading up to his coming. It records the prophecies which he was to fulfill.

8. *What is a prophet?*

A prophet is a man sent by God to tell the people the will of God and to bring them his message. The prophets of the Old Testament strove continually to keep the Jews faithful to God; they reminded them of his promises to them, of his past benefits and of their future glory if they remained faithful to him. Some of the prophets also foretold future events such as the destruction of the kingdom of Israel. Many of the prophets spoke of the coming of the Messiah and of his kingdom.

> *And the word of the Lord came to me, saying: "Before I formed thee in the bowels of thy mother, I knew thee: and before thou camest forth out of the womb, I sanctified thee and made thee a prophet unto the nations." And I said: "Ah, ah, ah, Lord God, behold, I cannot speak, for I am a child." And the Lord said to me: "Say not: I am a child: for thou shalt go to all that I shall send thee, and whatsoever I shall command thee, thou shalt speak"*—JER. 1:4-7.

9. What things were foretold by prophets concerning Christ and his kingdom?

Many individual traits of the person, character, kingdom and rule of the Messiah were foretold by the prophets. These facts were revealed over a long period of time and were never gathered into one picture in any book of the Old Testament. Many of the prophecies were obscure. Most likely the prophets themselves did not understand exactly how their prophecies would be fulfilled. In fact, various prophecies seemed to contradict one another. One group showed a victorious king ruling in justice over a peaceful people, while another group foretold the humiliation, the rejection, the suffering and the violent death of the Messiah. Many of the prophecies were not clearly understood until after Christ came and by his life and actions fulfilled them, even those which had seemed to be contradictory.

Now when Jesus was born in Bethlehem of Judea, in the days of King Herod, behold there came Magi from the East to Jerusalem, saying, "Where is the newly born king of the Jews? For we have seen his star in the East and have come to worship him." But when King Herod heard this, he was troubled, and so was all Jerusalem with him. And gathering together all the chief priests and Scribes of the people, he inquired of them where the Christ was to be born. And they said to him, "In Bethlehem of Judea; for thus it is written through the prophet,

" *'And thou, Bethlehem, of the land of Juda,
     art by no means least among the princes of Juda;*

*For from thee shall come forth a leader
     who shall rule my people Israel'* "

—MATT. 2:1-6 cf. MICH. 5:2.

*And after they had crucified him, they divided his garments, casting lots, [to fulfill that which was spoken through the prophets, saying,
     "They divided my garments among them, and upon my vesture they cast lots"]*—MATT. 27:35 cf. Ps. 21:19.

Liturgy

Every year the Church re-lives the period of preparation for the coming of Christ during the season of Advent. Throughout this liturgical season, which extends for about a month, beginning four Sundays before Christmas, the mood is one of longing and expectation. The Gloria is omitted, and violet vestments are used at Mass; the Masses and offices of the season express the need for redemption, our longing for the Saviour:

> O Lord, stir up your might and come! Rescue us from the dangers that threaten us because of our sins, and be our salvation. . . . (Collect of the Mass of the First Sunday of Advent).

> Drop down dew, you heavens, from above, and let the clouds rain the just one. Let the earth be opened and bud forth a Saviour (Is. 45:8—Introit of the Mass of the Fourth Sunday of Advent).

The liturgy of Advent admonishes us to do penance for our sins and to purify our hearts for the coming of Christ at Christmas. But underneath is the note of joy and hope; our deliverance is almost at hand; he is coming!

Practice

▶ We should become acquainted with the Old Testament. It is important, first of all, because it is the word of God. It is a great source from which we can gain a deeper appreciation of the greatness and the goodness of God, his providence, and his love for us. It contains a wealth of inspiring thoughts and stories.

The Old Testament is important, too, for a fuller understanding of the New Testament. Christianity has its roots in the Old Testament. In order to understand Christianity more fully one must know and understand its background, which is the Jewish religion. Both are based on belief in the same God and his *one* plan for mankind.

It would not be wise, however, to approach the Old Testament without any preparation and to try to read it from cover to cover. It would be less difficult to read certain selections first.

Read some part of the Old Testament. Suggestions:

> **Some of the Psalms**
>
> **The Book of Job**
>
> **Parts of the Books of Proverbs, Wisdom and Ecclesiasticus (Sirach).**

✠ ✠

section 7 | **Jesus Christ, the God-Man**

All that the Father gives to me shall come to me, and him who comes to me I will not cast out. For I have come down from heaven, not to do my own will, but the will of him who sent me. Now this is the will of him who sent me, the Father, that I should lose nothing of what he has given me, but that I should raise it up on the last day. For this is the will of my Father who sent me, that whoever beholds the Son, and believes in him, shall have everlasting life, and I will raise him up on the last day—JOHN 6:37-40.

W HEN, "in the fullness of time," God sent the long promised Redeemer, he sent not merely a man empowered to teach and act in his name, but his only-begotten Son. Jesus Christ is no mere man; he is God become man that he might be the mediator between God and man.

Jesus Christ expressed the threefold office he holds as the God-Man in his words, "I am the way and the truth and the life."

Jesus is the life—our priest, who redeemed us by his death on the cross, who shares with us his divine life.

Jesus is the truth—our teacher, who reveals to us by word and example the eternal truths of the kingdom of heaven.

Jesus is the way—our king, who came to draw all men to himself in a spiritual kingdom, begun here on earth in his Church and to be completed in his everlasting kingdom in heaven.

It is as man that the Son of God fulfills these three offices. It was as man that he first revealed himself to men. Later he openly proclaimed and proved his divinity. But first he won the love and trust of men by showing them his humanity.

In studying the life of Christ, therefore, we shall approach the God-Man as he revealed himself, through his human nature.

1. *Who is the mother of Jesus?*

The Blessed Virgin Mary is the mother of Jesus.

2. *How did the Blessed Virgin become the mother of Jesus?*

We read in St. Luke's Gospel:

Now in the sixth month the angel Gabriel was sent from God to a town of Galilee called Nazareth, to a virgin betrothed to a man named Joseph, of the house of David, and the virgin's name was Mary. And when the angel had come to her, he said, "Hail, full of grace, the Lord is with thee. Blessed art thou among women." When she had seen him she was troubled at his word, and kept pondering what manner of greeting this might be. And the angel said to her, "Do not be afraid, Mary, for thou hast found grace with God. And behold, thou shalt conceive in thy womb and shalt bring forth a son: and thou shalt call his name Jesus. He shall be great, and shall be called the Son of the Most High; and the Lord God will give him the throne of David his father, and he shall be king over the house of Jacob forever; and of his kingdom there shall be no end." But Mary said to the angel, "How shall this happen, since I do not know man?" And the angel answered and said to her, "The Holy Spirit shall come upon thee and the power of the Most High shall overshadow thee; and therefore the Holy One to be born shall be called the Son of God. And behold, Elizabeth thy kinswoman also has conceived a son in her old age, and she who was called barren is now in her sixth month; for nothing shall be impossible with God." But Mary said, "Behold the handmaid of the Lord; be it done to me according to thy word." And the angel departed from her

—LUKE 1:26-38.

3. Why did the angel greet Mary, "Hail, full of grace"?

The angel greeted Mary thus because, destined to be the mother of God, she was the most highly privileged of all God's creatures. She is the only human person who was preserved immaculate from all stain of original sin at the first moment of her conception. Moreover, so perfectly did she cooperate with God that she is the holiest of all his creatures. Throughout all her life she was never guilty of the slightest sin.

4. What is meant by the words, "The Holy Spirit will come upon thee, the power of the Most High will overshadow thee"?

These words mean that Jesus was conceived in the womb of Mary miraculously, without the aid of a human father.

5. Why was Jesus born of a virgin?

Jesus was born of a virgin because his Father willed it. It would have been possible for Christ to have had a human father; but it was eminently fitting that his mother be a virgin and his conception miraculous. Throughout the centuries of preparation for the coming of Christ, God had worked wonders in the conception of his servants who prepared the way for the coming of his Son. Abraham received a son from Sarah only when she was old and past the child-bearing period. Elizabeth, who had been sterile, miraculously, in her old age, conceived John the Baptist, the precursor of Christ. An even greater miracle should mark the conception and birth of the Redeemer himself. He should have no earthly father. He is God's own Son. It was fitting too, that the womb which bore the Son of God should not thereafter bear a mere human child. Mary, the Mother of God and the

Spouse of the Holy Spirit, remained a virgin after the birth of Christ.

6. Who was St. Joseph?

St. Joseph was the husband of Mary and the foster father of Jesus.

7. Who are the "brothers of Jesus" mentioned in the Bible?

They are not brothers, but relatives. The word brother was commonly used at that time to express blood relationship. The word first-born, too, does not imply that there were any other children. It is a technical term referring to the first-born male, who had to be offered to God under Jewish law—cf. Ex. 13:2.

8. What is the story of the birth of Christ?

We read in St. Luke's Gospel:

*Now it came to pass in those days, that there went forth a decree from Caesar Augustus that a census of the whole world should be taken. This first census took place while Cyrinus was governor of Syria. And all were going, each to his own town, to register. And Joseph also went from Galilee out of the town of Nazareth into Judea to the town of David, which is called Bethlehem—because he was of the house and family of David—to register, together with Mary his espoused wife, who was with child. And it came to pass while they were there, that the days for her to be delivered were fulfilled. And she brought forth her firstborn son, and wrapped him in swaddling clothes, and laid him in a manger, because there was no room for them in the inn—*LUKE 2:1-7.

9. Where did Jesus live most of his life?

After his birth in Bethlehem and an exile in Egypt (to escape King Herod, who sought to kill him) Jesus lived in the little town of Nazareth until he was about thirty years of age.

10. Why did Jesus spend thirty years in a hidden life?

He did so in order to give us an example of the perfect human life. Most men cannot imitate Christ in his life of preaching and teaching. But all men can imitate him in the quiet family life of Nazareth.

11. Did Jesus feel and act as other men do?

Yes. In becoming man he took to himself all that belongs to human nature, sin and ignorance alone excepted.

12. What are some of the incidents in the Gospels which show us the humanity of Jesus?

Throughout his boyhood the behavior of Jesus was that of a normal boy, so much so that when as a man he proclaimed himself to be the Messiah the people of his own town refused to believe him—cf. LUKE 4:16-30.

There was only one unusual episode in the boyhood of Jesus, his teaching in the temple at the age of twelve—cf. LUKE 2:42-51.

He felt hunger, thirst, fatigue—cf. LUKE 4:2; JOHN 19:28; JOHN 4:6.

He was fond of children—cf. MARK 10:13-16.

He felt sorrow and wept—cf. JOHN 11:32-36; LUKE 19:41-44.

He knew loneliness—cf. MATT. 26:37-46.

He enjoyed human companionship—cf. JOHN 2:1-12.

He visited the homes of his friends—cf. LUKE 19:1-10.

He felt keenly the betrayal of Judas and the denial of Peter—cf. LUKE 22:39-62.

He experienced the agony of his passion and death. The very anticipation of it caused him such mental suffering that he sweat blood—cf. LUKE 22:41-44.

The tender love of Jesus for all men is evident continually throughout the Gospels. In no place is it so beautifully shown as in his discourse to the apostles which St. John relates in his narration of the Last Supper. This discourse and prayer of Christ for his apostles runs through four chapters of St. John's Gospel
—cf. JOHN 14-17.

13. When did Jesus begin his public life?

Jesus began his public life when he was about thirty years of age. At that time he left Nazareth and went about preaching, teaching and working miracles.

Liturgy

Christmas in the liturgy begins with Mass at midnight. There are three different Masses for Christmas, the midnight Mass, the Mass at dawn and the Mass later in the morning. At the midnight Mass the emphasis is on the eternal generation of the Word of God before all time:

Amid the brightness of the saints, before the day-star was made, I have begotten you
—Ps. 109:3; Communion Antiphon, Midnight Mass of Christmas.

But the Gospel, even at this first Mass on Christmas, gives us St. Luke's wondrous account of the birth of our Saviour in Bethlehem.

In the dawn Mass the emphasis is on Christ as the light of the world.

In the third Mass once again the emphasis is on the divinity of our Lord. God has sent his Son into the world to save all men. All who hear him and follow him will be made sons of God.

During the octave of Christmas we celebrate the feasts of St. Stephen, the first Christian martyr, St. John the Evangelist, the Holy Innocents, St. Thomas of Canterbury and St. Sylvester. The octave day of Christmas is the feast of the Circumcision of our Lord, New Year's Day.

On the great feast of the Epiphany, twelve days after Christmas, we celebrate the manifestation of Christ to the gentiles. This manifestation is epitomized in the persons of the three Wise Men, who came from the East to pay homage to the Christ Child.

Devotion

We worship Jesus Christ even in his human nature, because that human nature belongs to the Second Divine Person, the eternal Word of God. One of the ways in which we worship Christ in his human nature is through devotion to the Sacred Heart of Jesus. The heart of Jesus is here taken as a symbol of his manhood and of the infinite love of Christ and the mercy he has for sinners.

The first Friday of every month is set aside for special devotion to the Sacred Heart of Jesus. The Church encourages all to receive Holy Communion on these first Fridays. Our Lord has promised that whoever does so for nine consecutive first Fridays will not die without receiving whatever help is necessary for his salvation.

Devotion to the Sacred Heart of Jesus is one of the best means of acquiring a deeper love of our Lord.

The feast of the Sacred Heart is celebrated on the Friday following the Second Sunday after Pentecost.

Practice

▶ The prayer which recalls the scene of the Annunciation, the moment when God became man, is the Angelic Salutation. This prayer, one of the most beloved prayers of the Church, contains the words of Scripture itself, the greeting of the angel to Mary and the greeting of her cousin Elizabeth to the Mother of God.

Hail Mary, full of grace, the Lord is with thee; blessed art thou among women, and blessed is the fruit of thy womb, Jesus. Holy Mary, Mother of God, pray for us sinners, now and at the hour of our death. Amen.

We should learn this prayer by heart and make it a part of our daily prayer.

And he spoke to them many things in parables, saying, "Behold, the sower went out to sow. And as he sowed, some seeds fell by the wayside, and the birds came and ate them up. And other seeds fell upon rocky ground, where they had not much earth; and they sprang up at once, because they had no depth of earth; but when the sun rose they were scorched, and because they had no root they withered away. And other seeds fell among thorns; and the thorns grew up and choked them. And other seeds fell upon good ground, and yielded fruit, some a hundredfold, some sixtyfold, and some thirtyfold. . . .

"Hear, therefore, the parable of the sower. When anyone hears the word of the kingdom, but does not understand it, the wicked one comes and snatches away what has been sown in his heart. This is he who was sown by the wayside. And the one sown on rocky ground, that is he who hears the word and receives it immediately with joy; yet he has no root in himself, but continues only for a time, and when trouble and persecution come because of the word, he at once falls away. And the one sown among the thorns, that is the man who listens to the word; but the care of this world and the deceitfulness of riches choke the word, and it is made fruitless. And the one sown upon good ground, that is he who hears the word and understands it; he bears fruit and yields in one case a hundredfold, in another sixtyfold, and in another thirtyfold"—MATT. 13:3-8; 18-23.

CHRIST WAS SENT into the world by his Father to tell fallen men of God's saving love for them and of the coming of the kingdom. It was to the Jews that he preached because it was to the Jews that God had promised the Redeemer. Our Lord spent the three years of his public life seeking out the people to tell them of his kingdom.

He preached in the towns and in the country, in the streets

56

and on the hillsides, in the temple and in the homes of the people. When his life had but a day to run our Lord summed up his teaching of the word of his Father thus:

I have manifested thy name to the men whom thou hast given me out of the world. They were thine and thou hast given them to me, and they have kept thy word. Now they have learnt that whatever thou hast given me is from thee; because the words that thou hast given me I have given to them. And they have received them, and have known of a truth that I came forth from thee, and they have believed that thou didst send me—JOHN 17:6-8.

Our Lord was a courageous teacher. He did not modify his doctrine to please the leaders of the people or the people themselves. He knew that many of his words would fall upon deaf ears, but he also knew that those who received his words with joy "would yield fruit a hundredfold" and would carry his message to the ends of the earth.

1. What did our Lord teach the people?

Our Lord taught the people that salvation and redemption were at hand and that the kingdom of God was come. St. Mark says that he was heralding the joyful tidings of God's kingdom— cf. MARK 1:14. St. Matthew says that he went about preaching "the gospel (the good news) of the kingdom"—MATT. 4:23.

Jesus *reaffirmed* the teachings of the Old Law, which the Jews had received from God, purging it from the legalistic elements which the Scribes and Pharisees had introduced.

Jesus *fulfilled* the Old Law. He took each part of the old revelation, doctrine, moral law and worship, and brought it to completion in a new, more perfect revelation of doctrine, law and worship.

Do not think that I have come to destroy the Law or the Prophets. I have not come to destroy but to fulfill
—MATT. 5:17.

In preaching his Gospel Jesus told men of the infinite love of God for them, of the mystery of the Trinity, of his own divinity, of his Church and of the sacraments. All the teachings of the Catholic Church can be traced back to the teachings of Jesus Christ.

57

2. How did Jesus teach?

Jesus taught in various ways. Some of his teachings, for example, the law of love, he stated simply and directly. Some of his teachings he gave by means of parables, stories such as that of the sower. Although Jesus taught in words which carried great authority and worked miracles which amazed the people, he taught most effectively by his example. St. Augustine, referring to the example of Christ says, "He did not say, 'Learn from Me how to build a world and raise the dead' but 'Learn from me; I am meek and humble of heart.'"

3. What is a parable?

A parable is an illustration of a truth by means of an example or a story. By using parables Jesus was able to present great religious truths in a form which allowed them to be grasped and remembered by all, the unlearned as well as the learned.

For example, Jesus taught

—the necessity for good works, in the parable of the barren fig tree—cf. LUKE 13:6-9;

—the virtues of humility and contrition, in the parable of the Pharisee and the publican—cf. LUKE 18:9-14;

—the necessity of being prepared for death at any moment, the need of being in possession of the divine life at all times, by the parables of the wise and foolish virgins—cf. MATT. 25:1-13 and the marriage of the king's son—cf. MATT. 22:1-14;

—the necessity of forgiving one's enemies by the parable of the unmerciful servant—cf. MATT. 18:23-35;

—the necessity of loving one's neighbor, by the parable of the good Samaritan—cf. LUKE 10:30-37;

—the love and mercy of God, by the parable of the prodigal son—cf. LUKE 15:11-32.

4. What are some of the doctrines which our Lord taught by his example as well as by his words?

Our Lord exemplified all his teachings in his life, particularly those on the love of God and one's neighbor, prayer, submission to the will of God and poverty.

5. How did Jesus teach love?

Jesus taught:

*You have heard that it was said, "Thou shalt love thy neighbor, and shalt hate thy enemy." But I say to you, love your enemies, do good to those who hate you, and pray for those who persecute and calumniate you, so that you may be children of your Father in heaven, who makes his sun to rise on the good and the evil, and sends rain on the just and the unjust. For if you love those who love you, what reward shall you have? Do not even the publicans do that? And if you salute your brethren only, what are you doing more than others? Do not even the Gentiles do that? You therefore are to be perfect, even as your heavenly Father is perfect—*MATT. 5:43-48.

He exemplified this teaching by freely laying down his own life for all men.

*Greater love than this no one has, that one lay down his life for his friends—*JOHN 15:13.

On the cross he prayed for those who crucified him, ". . . Father, forgive them, for they do not know what they are doing"
—LUKE 23:34.

Most of his miracles were worked out of compassion for the sick and the suffering.

The cure of the centurion's servant—cf. MATT. 8:5-13.

The raising from the dead of Jairus' daughter—cf. MATT. 9:18-26, the widow's son—cf. LUKE 7:11-16, and of Lazarus—cf. JOHN 11:1-44.

The cure of the paralytic at the pool of Bethsaida
—cf. JOHN 5:1-9.

The cure of the man who had been born blind
—cf. JOHN 9:1-38.

6. How did Jesus teach prayer?

Jesus taught the true spirit of prayer, insisting on sincerity and simplicity, and denouncing hypocrisy and wordiness in prayer—cf. MATT. 6:5-9.

59

The whole life of Jesus was lived in constant union with his Father. All his actions were in perfect accord with the will of the Father. His whole life, therefore, was one continual prayer.

But Jesus also spent long periods absorbed in prayer. The Gospels frequently state that he spent the whole night in prayer.

He prefaced his public life by retiring to the desert, where he spent forty days and nights in prayer and fasting—cf. Luke 4:1-2.

When he was about to choose his disciples, Jesus spent the whole night in prayer—cf. Luke 6:12.

A great many of his miracles were preceded by prayer, e.g., the healing of the deaf mute—cf. Mark 7:34; the raising of Lazarus from the dead—cf. John 11:41; the multiplication of the loaves—Matt. 14:19.

He began his passion with prayer at the Last Supper—cf. John 17, entire chapter.

He prayed during his agony in the garden—cf. Matt. 26:36-44.

He prayed as he hung on the cross—cf. Luke 23:34, 46.

7. How did Jesus teach perfect submission to the will of God?

Jesus said:

> . . . of myself I do nothing: but even as the Father has taught me, I speak these things. And he who sent me is with me; he has not left me alone, because I do always the things that are pleasing to him—John 8:28-29.

The outstanding characteristic of Jesus is his total, unreserved surrender to the will of God, his mighty burning love for his Father. No other man has ever so completely fulfilled the first commandment of the law, "Thou shalt love the Lord thy God with thy whole heart and with thy whole soul, and with thy whole strength."

The first recorded words of Jesus, then a boy of twelve, were, "Did you not know that I must be about my Father's business?"—Luke 2:49. These words he spoke to Mary and Joseph to explain why he had remained in Jerusalem. Yet, having uttered these words, he went down to Nazareth and "was subject to them"—LUKE 2:51, because such was the will of his Father.

Every action of Jesus' was dictated by his love for his Father. In the anguish he endured in contemplating the sufferings and death he was about to undergo he prayed, "Father, if it is possible, let this cup pass away from me; yet not as I will, but as thou willest"—MATT. 26:39.

8. How did Jesus teach poverty and detachment?

Jesus taught:

Therefore I say to you, do not be anxious for your life, what you shall eat; nor yet for your body, what you shall put on. Is not the life a greater thing than the food, and the body than the clothing? Look at the birds of the air: they do not sow, or reap, or gather into barns; yet your heavenly Father feeds them. Are not you of much more value than they? But which of you by being anxious about it can add to his stature a single cubit?

And as for clothing, why are you anxious? See how the lilies of the field grow; they neither toil nor spin, yet I say to you that not even Solomon in all his glory was arrayed like one of these. But if God so clothes the grass of the field, which today is alive and tomorrow is thrown into the oven, how much more you, O you of little faith!

Therefore do not be anxious, saying, "What shall we eat?" or, "What shall we drink?" or, "What are we to put on?" (for after all these things the Gentiles seek); for your Father knows that you need all these things. But seek first the kingdom of God and his justice, and all these things shall be given you besides. Therefore do not be anxious about tomorrow; for tomorrow will have anxieties of its own. Sufficient for the day is its own trouble—MATT. 6:25-34.

Do not lay up for yourselves treasures on earth, where rust and moth consume, and where thieves break in and steal; but lay up for yourselves treasures in heaven, where neither rust nor moth consumes, nor thieves break in and steal. For where thy treasure is, there thy heart also will be—MATT. 6:19-21.

He exemplified this teaching by his own complete detachment:

He was born in a stable.

He worked as a carpenter in the tiny town of Nazareth.

61

During the three years of his public life, he had no home and no possessions. He said of himself:

The foxes have dens, and the birds of the air have nests; but the Son of Man has nowhere to lay his head

—MATT. 8:20.

He had special love and concern for the poor.

He chose as his apostles, for the most part, men of little means, and required that they give up all things in following him.

Practice

▶ Christ still teaches his doctrines to the world. Now he does so through his Church. One of the most effective ways in which our Lord teaches us today is through the liturgy of the Church.

Remind yourself that it is Christ who is teaching you as you listen to the reading of the Epistle and Gospel and to the sermon at Mass.

Read with care the parables of our Lord which are mentioned in question 3 of this lesson. Try to understand the lesson Christ is teaching in these parables, and make an application to yourself.

Christ's Great Teaching, the Blessed Trinity

And now I am going to him who sent me, and no one of you asks me, "Where art thou going?" But because I have spoken to you these things, sadness has filled your heart. But I speak the truth to you; it is expedient for you that I depart. For if I do not go, the Advocate will not come to you; but if I go, I will send him to you. And when he has come he will convict the world of sin, and of justice, and of judgment: of sin, because they do not believe in me; of justice, because I go to the Father, and you will see me no more; and of judgment, because the prince of this world has already been judged.

*Many things yet I have to say to you, but you cannot bear them now. But when he, the Spirit of truth, has come, he will teach you all the truth. For he will not speak on his own authority, but whatever he will hear he will speak, and the things that are to come he will declare to you. He will glorify me, because he will receive of what is mine and declare it to you. All things that the Father has are mine. That is why I have said that he will receive of what is mine, and will declare it to you. A little while and you shall see me no longer; and again a little while and you shall see me, because I go to the Father—*JOHN 16:5-16.

JESUS CHRIST has revealed to us the secrets of the kingdom of heaven. In the greatest of his teachings he has revealed to us the secret of God himself. He has told us of the inmost life of God, the deepest of all mysteries, the mystery of the Blessed Trinity. God, he has told us, is not one Person alone, as we would think, but rather three Persons, Father, Son and Holy Spirit.

All the truths of our faith are mysteries which we cannot fully understand. The Blessed Trinity is the deepest of all mysteries.

Nevertheless God has revealed it to us. He has done so because he wants us to know him as he is, to know as much about him as we can in order that we might in some measure return the boundless love he has for us.

1. How did Jesus teach us of the inmost life of God?

Jesus taught, as indeed the Jews of his time already knew, that there is only one God, one supreme Creator and Law-giver.

But in revealing the inmost life of God, Jesus taught that in the one God there are three distinct Persons, each absolutely equal to each other. He told us the names of these three Divine Persons: Father, Son and Holy Spirit.

2. How did Jesus tell us that there are three Divine Persons?

a. Jesus spoke continually of his Father, calling him always by that name. When he drove the money changers from the temple, he said, "Take these things away, and do not make the house of my Father a house of business"—JOHN 2:17.

He said to his apostles, "In this is my Father glorified, that you may bear very much fruit, and become my disciples. As the Father has loved me, I also have loved you. Abide in my love. If you keep my commandments you will abide in my love, as I also have kept my Father's commandments, and abide in his love"—JOHN 15:8-10.

b. Jesus said that he is the Son, the only-begotten Son of that Father, equal to the Father.

Speaking of himself he said, "For God so loved the world that he gave his only-begotten Son, that those who believe in him may not perish, but may have life everlasting"—JOHN 3:16.

At the Last Supper he prayed to the Father, ". . . Father, the hour has come! Glorify thy Son, that thy Son may glorify thee, even as thou hast given him power over all flesh, in order that to all thou hast given him he may give everlasting life . . . and now do thou, Father, glorify me with thyself, with the glory that I had with thee before the world existed"—JOHN 17:1-5.

He said to his apostles, "All things that the Father has are mine"—JOHN 16:15.

In response to Philip's words, "Lord, show us the Father," Jesus answered, "Have I been so long a time with you, and you have not known me? Philip, he who sees me sees also the Father. How canst thou say, 'Show us the Father?' Dost thou not believe that I am in the Father and the Father in me?"—JOHN 14:8-10.

c. Jesus promised to send a third Divine Person, the equal of himself and the Father.

At the Last Supper he told the apostles, "And I will ask the Father and he will give you another Advocate to dwell with you forever, the Spirit of truth whom the world cannot receive, because it neither sees him nor knows him"—JOHN 14:16-17.

"But the Advocate, the Holy Spirit, whom the Father will send in my name, he will teach you all things, and bring to your mind whatever I have said to you"—JOHN 14:26.

"But when the Advocate has come, whom I will send you from the Father, the Spirit of truth who proceeds from the Father, he will bear witness concerning me"—JOHN 15:26.

d. When he sent the apostles to preach the Gospel to the whole world Jesus told them to baptize "in the name of the Father, and of the Son and of the Holy Spirit." Here Christ expresses in one short formula the idea of one God (in the name) in three distinct and equal Divine Persons (*of* the Father, and *of* the Son, and *of* the Holy Spirit—cf. MATT. 28:19.

3. *Why is the First Divine Person called the Father?*

The First Divine Person is called the Father because it is he who begets the Second Divine Person, the eternal Word, who is "the brightness of his glory and the image of his substance"— HEB. 1:3.

4. *Why is the Second Divine Person called the Son?*

The Second Divine Person is called the Son because he is the perfect image of the Father, "God of God, light of light, true God of true God, begotten not made, of one being with the Father" (Nicene Creed).

5. Why is the Third Divine Person called the Holy Spirit?

The Third Divine Person is called the Holy Spirit because he is the Person of divine love, breathed forth by the Father and the Son. He is the "Lord and lifegiver, who proceeds from the Father and the Son, who together with the Father and the Son is likewise adored and equally glorified, who spoke through the prophets . . ." (Nicene Creed).

6. How did Jesus teach us to distinguish between the three Persons in God?

a. Jesus spoke of the Father as creator and ruler, because we naturally think of a father in this role. All the time we know it is the three Divine Persons who create and rule.

b. Jesus told us that he, the Second Divine Person, became man and lived and died among men. As God, Jesus is called the Word, the eternal Knowledge of the Father. That is why St. John, speaking of the Second Divine Person, says: "In the beginning was the Word, and the Word was with God; and the Word was God. . . . All things were made through him, and without him was made nothing that has been made. . . . And the Word was made flesh, and dwelt among us"—JOHN 1:1-3, 14.

c. Jesus spoke of the Holy Spirit as the one whom he and the Father would send to enlighten and inspire us. We naturally associate works of love and inspiration with the Holy Spirit, since he is Divine Love. All the time we know, however, that it was the three Divine Persons who descended upon the infant Church on Pentecost and who dwell in all who possess the divine life.

7. Do we find any manifestations of the Blessed Trinity in the New Testament?

Yes. When Jesus was baptized by John in the river Jordan:
Now it came to pass when all the people had been baptized, Jesus also having been baptized and being in prayer, that heaven was opened, and the Holy Spirit descended upon him in bodily form as a dove, and a voice came from heaven, "Thou art my beloved Son, in thee I am well pleased"
—LUKE 3:21-22.

When Jesus was transfigured before Peter, James and John, the Father spoke from heaven, "This is my beloved Son; hear him"—MARK 9:6.

On Pentecost the Holy Spirit manifested his coming by the sound of a mighty wind and parted tongues of fire.

*And when the days of Pentecost were drawing to a close, they were all together in one place. And suddenly there came a sound from heaven, as of a violent wind coming, and it filled the whole house where they were sitting. And there appeared to them parted tongues as of fire, which settled upon each of them. And they were all filled with the Holy Spirit and began to speak in foreign tongues, even as the Holy Spirit prompted them to speak—*ACTS 2:1-4.

8. How do we honor the Blessed Trinity in the liturgy?

The Church usually addresses her prayers to God the Father, through the Son, in union with the Holy Spirit.

On the great feast of Pentecost, fifty days after Easter, we celebrate the coming of the Holy Spirit upon the Church.

We celebrate Trinity Sunday every year on the first Sunday after Pentecost.

9. How may we pray to the Blessed Trinity.

We may pray simply to God, i.e., to the Blessed Trinity.

We may pray to any one of the three Divine Persons.

We may pray as the Church does most often—to the Father, through the Son, in union with the Holy Spirit. Our Lord promised: "Amen, amen, I say to you, if you ask the Father anything in my name he will give it to you"—JOHN 16:23.

The equality of the Persons of the Blessed Trinity, their oneness in nature and their distinctness in person is expressed in the Athanasian Creed.

Now this is the Catholic faith: that we worship one God in Trinity, and Trinity in unity; neither confusing the persons nor distinguishing the nature.

The person of the Father is distinct; the person of the Son is distinct; the person of the Holy Spirit is distinct.

Yet the Father and the Son and the Holy Spirit possess one God-head, equal glory and co-eternal majesty.

As the Father is, so is the Son, so also is the Holy Spirit.

The Father is uncreated, the Son is uncreated, The Holy Spirit is uncreated.

The Father is infinite, the Son is infinite, the Holy Spirit is infinite.

The Father is eternal, the Son is eternal, the Holy Spirit is eternal.

Nevertheless there are not three eternals, but one eternal; even as there are not three uncreateds but one uncreated, and one infinite.

So likewise the Father is almighty, the Son is almighty, the Holy Spirit is almighty. And yet they are not three almighties, but one almighty.

So also the Father is God, the Son is God, the Holy Spirit is God. And yet they are not three Gods, but only one God.

So, too, the Father is Lord, the Son is Lord, the Holy Spirit is Lord. And still there are not three Lords, but only one Lord.

For just as we are compelled by Christian truth to profess that each Person is individually Lord and God, so also are we forbidden by the Catholic religion to hold that there are three Gods or Lords.

The Father was made by no one, being neither made nor created nor begotten.

The Son is from the Father only, being neither made nor created, but begotten.

The Holy Spirit is from the Father and the Son, being neither made nor created nor begotten, but proceeding.

Consequently, there is one Father, not three Fathers; there is one Son, not three Sons; there is one Holy Spirit, not three Holy Spirits.

Furthermore, in this Trinity there is no "before" or "after," no "greater" or "less"; for all three Persons are co-eternal and co-equal.

In every respect, therefore, as has already been stated, unity must be worshipped in trinity, and trinity in unity. . . .

Practice

▶ The Blessed Trinity dwells within us because we possess the divine life. We should try to realize this presence of God within us.

St. Paul tells us:

Or do you not know that your members are the temple of the Holy Spirit, who is in you, whom you have from God, and that you are not your own? For you have been bought at a great price. Glorify God and bear him in your body—I Cor. 6:19-20.

We should remember these words wherever we are, at work, at home, at places of amusement. God is within us. We should act accordingly. We should also be anxious to share the presence which is ours with others who do not yet know and love God as we are privileged to.

The sign of the cross is a profession of faith in and an act of adoration of the Blessed Trinity.

Take particular care to realize that you are praying even as you begin your prayers by signing yourself:

In the name of the Father, and of the Son, and of the Holy Spirit. Amen.

section **10** | ## Jesus Christ, High Priest and Redeemer

For every high priest taken from among men is appointed for men in the things pertaining to God, that he may offer gifts and sacrifices for sins. He is able to have compassion on the ignorant and erring, because he himself also is beset with weakness, and by reason thereof is obliged to offer for sins, as on behalf of the people, so also for himself. And no man takes the honor to himself; he takes it who is called by God, as Aaron was. So also Christ did not glorify himself with the high priesthood, but he who spoke to him,

> *"Thou art my son,*
> *I this day have begotten thee."*

As he says also in another place,

> *"Thou art a priest forever,*
> *according to the order of Melchisedech."*

*For Jesus, in the days of his earthly life, with a loud cry and tears, offered up prayers and supplications to him who was able to save him from death, and was heard because of his reverent submission. And he, Son though he was, learned obedience from the things that he suffered; and when perfected, he became to all who obey him the cause of eternal salvation, called by God a high priest according to the order of Melchisedech—*Heb. 5:1-10.

IN THESE WORDS St. Paul explains the idea of priesthood (a priest is a mediator between God and man) and emphasizes the fact that Jesus Christ, the God-Man, is the priest of priests. The essential function of a priest is to offer gifts to God in the name of the people and to be the bearer of sacred gifts from God to man. Jesus Christ, the anointed of God, came to offer himself on the cross for the salvation of men. Christ is the mediator between God and man. His sacrifice on the cross is the supreme gift offered to God. Christ, by his death, has made reparation for the sins of men and has made the divine life once more available.

1. What do we mean when we say that Jesus Christ is our high priest?

When we say that Jesus Christ is our high priest we mean that he offered his life as the supreme gift to his Father by dying on the cross for us, and that he brings to us from God all the things which make men holy.

2. What do we mean when we say that Jesus Christ is our Redeemer?

We mean that Christ by the sacrifice of his life on the cross has paid the price for our sins and has made the divine life once more available to us.

3. Does Christ still exercise his office of priest?

Yes. Christ as head of the Church continues to exercise his priesthood. Through the Church Christ offers Mass and administers the sacraments. Therefore we can say that it is Christ who baptizes, Christ who forgives sin, etc.

4. What is the history of the passion and death of Jesus?

Jesus began his passion by eating the Last Supper with his twelve apostles.

At this meal he instituted the Holy Eucharist and ordained the apostles priests:

> And having taken bread, he gave thanks and broke, and gave it to them saying, "This is my body, which is being given for you; do this in remembrance of me." In like manner he took also the cup after the supper saying, "This cup is the new covenant in my blood, which shall be shed for you"—LUKE 22:19:20.

He underwent a night of agony in the garden of Gethsemani:

> Then Jesus came with them to a country place called Gethsemani, and he said to his disciples, "Sit down here, while I go over yonder and pray" . . . and he began to be sad-

71

dened and exceedingly troubled. Then he said to them, "My soul is sad, even unto death. Wait here and watch with me"
—MATT. 26:36-39.

He was betrayed by Judas and taken prisoner:

And while he was yet speaking, behold Judas, one of the Twelve, came and with him a great crowd with swords and clubs, from the chief priests and elders of the people. Now his betrayer had given them a sign, saying, "Whomever I kiss, that is he; lay hold of him." And he went straight up to Jesus and said, "Hail, Rabbi!" and kissed him
—MATT. 26:47-49.

He was taken before the high priests, where he professed that he was God:

And the high priest said to him, "I adjure thee by the living God that thou tell us whether thou art the Christ, the Son of God." Jesus said to him, "Thou hast said it. Nevertheless, I say to you, hereafter you shall see the Son of Man sitting at the right hand of the Power and coming upon the clouds of heaven."

Then the high priest tore his garments, saying, "He has blasphemed; what further need have we of witnesses? Behold, now you have heard the blasphemy. What do you think?" And they answered and said, "He is liable to death"
—MATT. 26:63-67.

He was denied by Peter:

But Simon Peter was standing and warming himself. They therefore said to him, "Art thou also one of his disciples?" He denied it, and said, "I am not." One of the servants of the high priest, a relative of him whose ear Peter had cut off, said, "Did I not see thee in the garden with him?" Again, therefore, Peter denied it; and at that moment a cock crowed
—JOHN 18:25-27.

He was taken before Pilate, the Roman governor:

He was scourged, mocked, crowned with thorns and condemned to death:

Pilate, then, took Jesus and had him scourged. And the soldiers, plaiting a crown of thorns, put it upon his head, and arrayed him in a purple cloak. . . . When, therefore, the chief priests and the attendants saw him, they cried out, saying, "Crucify him! Crucify him!" Pilate said to them, "Take him yourselves and crucify him, for I find no guilt in him." The Jews answered him, "We have a Law, and according to that

Law he must die, because he has made himself Son of God."

Pilate therefore, when he heard these words, brought Jesus outside, and sat down on the judgment-seat, . . . And he said to the Jews, "Behold your king!" But they cried out, "Away with him! Away with him! Crucify him!" Pilate said to them, "Shall I crucify your king?" The chief priest answered, "We have no king but Caesar." Then he handed him over to them to be crucified. And so they took Jesus and led him away—JOHN 19:1-16.

He was crucified between two thieves:

And when they came to the place called the Skull, they crucified him there, and the robbers, one on his right hand and the other on his left—LUKE 23:33.

After three hours' agony on the cross he died:

It was now about the sixth hour, and there was darkness over the whole land until the ninth hour. And the sun was darkened, and the curtain of the temple was torn in the middle. And Jesus cried out with a loud voice and said, "Father, into thy hands I commend my spirit." And having said this, he expired—LUKE 23:44-46.

5. Was it necessary for Christ to suffer and die in order to redeem us?

No. It was not absolutely necessary for Christ to suffer and die in order to redeem us. Any action or prayer of Christ would have been of such great value that it could have redeemed any number of worlds. But God decreed that it be by the sufferings and death on the cross that his Son redeem the world.

6. Why did God require the death of his Son?

God required the death of his Son in order to teach us the seriousness of sin and to prove his love for us.

Greater love than this no one has, that one lay down his life for his friends—JOHN 15:13.

a. The passion and death of Christ teaches us, above all, the immense love and mercy of God. If one is ever tempted to doubt the mercy of God, one need only look at a crucifix to be reminded that God's love knows no bounds. The outstretched arms of Jesus on the cross, moreover, illustrate the fact that no one, however great a sinner he be, is excluded from the love and mercy of God.

    b. The passion and death of our Lord teaches us the enormity of sin. It was sin which caused Christ to suffer such agony and to die. All the efforts of the world to minimize or to glamorize sin fail before the image of the crucified Saviour.

Liturgy

The Church re-lives the Passion and death of Jesus in the liturgy of Holy Week. On Second Passion Sunday, the Sunday before Easter, palms are blessed and distributed. Carrying these palms, we walk in procession singing, "Hosanna to the Son of David," as did the children of Jerusalem at Christ's triumphal entry into the Holy City as he came to begin his Passion. At the Mass which follows the whole story of the Passion and death of Christ is recounted as the Passion of our Lord according to St. Matthew is sung. On Tuesday and Wednesday of Holy Week the story of the Passion as told by St. Mark and St. Luke is read in the Mass. On Holy Thursday evening we celebrate the anniversary of the Last Supper by a Mass which expresses both our joy and gratitude for the great gifts of the Eucharist and the priesthood, and our deep mourning at the Passion of Christ, which began on that night. The service on Good Friday is not a Mass, not the unbloody sacrifice of Christ; it is a service which concentrates, rather, on the bloody death of Christ on the first Good Friday. The service consists of readings, prayers, the singing of the Passion according to St. John, veneration of the cross and Holy Communion. After the services of Good Friday night the Church is empty and silent; the altar is bare. Until the Easter Vigil service on Holy Saturday night we re-live the time when the dead body of Christ lay in the tomb.

Devotion

All Catholic churches have a series of fourteen pictures depicting various scenes in the Passion and death of Jesus. These pictures are in sequence, beginning at the front of the church and continuing down one side wall and up the other. They are called "The Way of the Cross" or "The Stations of the Cross." To make the way of the cross or to make the stations, as the practice sometimes is called, all one has to do is to walk from picture to picture meditating on the Passion of Christ. One may "make the stations" privately at any time; the devotion is held publicly in most churches on the Fridays of Lent.

This devotion is one of the most highly blessed devotions in the Church, and one which will give us a deeper realization of the love and mercy of God as well as a greater sorrow for our sins.

Prayers and meditations which can be used in making the way of the cross are to be found in most prayer books or in booklets which can be obtained from pamphlet racks or Catholic book stores.

Practice

Read St. Matthew's account of the Passion of Jesus. It is to be found in chapters 26 and 27 of St. Matthew's Gospel.

. . . and if Christ has not risen, vain is your faith, for you are still in your sins. Hence they also who have fallen asleep in Christ, have perished. If with this life only in view we have had hope in Christ, we are of all men the most to be pitied. But as it is, Christ has risen from the dead, the first-fruits of those who have fallen asleep. For since by a man came death, by a man also comes resurrection of the dead
—1 Cor. 15:17-22.

IF JESUS CHRIST had not risen from the dead his life would have been essentially no different from that of any great teacher. He would have been remembered only as a good and wise man who had taught a beautiful doctrine and who had been put to death unjustly. His life would have ended not in apparent failure but in real failure. He would have been conquered by sin; evil would have triumphed over him and destroyed him. He would have shown himself to be a mere man, subject to death as are all men.

But Jesus Christ has risen from the dead. By his resurrection he shows that he is not merely a great teacher but the eternal Son of God. By his resurrection he shows that his life was not a failure but a glorious success. By his resurrection he shows that, far from having been overcome by evil, he is the conqueror of both sin and death. By his resurrection he shows that he has the power to give eternal life, as he promised, to all who follow him.

1. Did Jesus Christ claim to be God?

Yes. At his trial the Jews recognized that Jesus was claiming to be the Son of God, the equal of God the Father, and they condemned him to death precisely for making that claim.

76

We read in St. Matthew's Gospel:

Then the high priest, standing up, said to him, "Dost thou make no answer to the things that these men prefer against thee?" But Jesus kept silence. And the high priest said to him, "I adjure thee by the living God that thou tell us whether thou art the Christ, the Son of God." Jesus said to him, "Thou hast said it. Nevertheless, I say to you, hereafter you shall see the Son of Man sitting at the right hand of the Power and coming upon the clouds of heaven."

Then the high priest tore his garments, saying, "He has blasphemed; what further need have we of witnesses? Behold, now you have heard the blasphemy. What do you think?" And they answered and said, "He is liable to death"
—MATT. 26:62-67.

On various other occasions, too, Jesus claimed to be God. For example, he had announced to a paralyzed man that his sins were forgiven. The Pharisees, who had heard him, thought in their hearts, "Who is this man who speaks blasphemies? Who can forgive sins, but God only?"—LUKE 5:21. Jesus, giving expression to their thoughts, worked a miracle that all could see showing that he could, indeed, forgive sins, i.e., that he was God.

Jesus even applied to himself the very title for the Almighty, "I am."

The Jews therefore said to him, "Thou art not yet fifty years old, and hast thou seen Abraham?" Jesus said to them, "Amen, amen, I say to you, before Abraham came to be, I am"—JOHN 8:57-58.

2. Is it not possible that Jesus when he said he was the Son of God was merely claiming to be a prophet sent by God?

No. In the first place such a claim would not have been taken as blasphemy. Moreover Jesus called God "my Father" in a way in which no mere man could speak of God. On one occasion he said openly, "My Father and I are one." The Jews thereupon took up stones to cast at him, saying, "Thou, being a man, makest thyself God"—JOHN 10:33.

In speaking to Philip, Christ said, "Dost thou not believe that I am in the Father and the Father in me?"—JOHN 14:10.

And again at the Last Supper he prayed to the Father: "And now do thou, Father, glorify me with thyself, with the glory that I had with thee before the world existed"—JOHN 17:5.

3. Does not Jesus at times speak as if he were inferior to the Father and at other times as if he were equal?

Yes. For example, he said, "The Father is greater than I"— JOHN 14:28, and also, "All things that the Father has are mine"—JOHN 16:15.

Jesus Christ is one person. But that one person is both God and man. At the time of the Incarnation he took a human body and soul. As God, the Second Divine Person, he always existed. The Second Divine Person, therefore, now possesses two natures, a human and a divine. In the Gospels he acts and speaks sometimes in his human nature, i.e., as man, sometimes in his divine nature, i.e., as God. He spoke in his human nature when he said, "The Father is greater than I," in his divine nature when he said, "All things that the Father has are mine."

4. Did Jesus says that we would rise from the dead?

Yes. On many occasions Jesus said that he would rise from the dead.

The Jews therefore answered and said to him, "What sign dost thou show us, seeing that thou dost these things?" In answer Jesus said to them, "Destroy this temple, and in three days I will raise it up." The Jews therefore said, "Forty-six years has this temple been in building, and wilt thou raise it up in three days?" But he was speaking of the temple of his body. When, accordingly, he had risen from the dead, his disciples remembered that he had said this, and they believed the Scripture and the word that Jesus had spoken—JOHN 2:18-22.

Then certain of the scribes and pharisees answered him saying, "Master, we would see a sign from thee." But he answered and said to them, "An evil and adulterous generation demands a sign, and no sign shall be given it but the sign of Jonas the prophet. For even as Jonas was in the belly of

*the fish three days and three nights, so will the Son of Man
be three days and three nights in the heart of the earth"*
—MATT. 12:38-40.

5. How was Jesus put to death?

In addition to being scourged mercilessly Christ was forced
to carry his heavy cross through the city to the place of crucifixion. His condition during this journey was such that his enemies feared that he would die before reaching Calvary. Hence
they forced Simon of Cyrene to help carry the cross—cf. MATT.
27:32.

Jesus was nailed to the cross and hung there for three hours.
At the moment of his death there was a sign from heaven:

> *But Jesus again cried out with a loud voice, and gave up his
> spirit. And behold, the curtain of the temple was torn in
> two from top to bottom, and the earth quaked, and the rocks
> were rent, and the tombs were opened, and many bodies of
> the saints who had fallen asleep arose; and coming forth
> out of the tombs after his resurrection, they came into the
> holy city, and appeared to many—MATT. 27:50-53.*

The Roman soldiers broke the legs of the two thieves who
were crucified with Christ in order to hasten their death. But
when they came to Jesus they saw that he was already dead;
there was no need to break his legs. One of the soldiers, however,
took a lance and opened up the side of Christ, piercing his
heart—cf. JOHN 19:31-37.

6. What were the circumstances of Christ's burial?

The body of Jesus was placed in a tomb by his friends, and
a heavy stone was rolled against the opening to seal the tomb.
But the enemies of Christ, taking every precaution, and mindful
of our Lord's prediction that he would rise on the third day,
placed a guard of soldiers around the tomb—cf. MATT. 27:62-66.

7. What is the story of Christ's Resurrection?

Early Sunday morning several women, followers of Christ,
went to the tomb with the intention of anointing the body of
Jesus. When they arrived they were amazed to find the stone

rolled away and the tomb empty. An angel announced to them that Jesus had risen and instructed them to tell Peter and the other apostles that he would meet them in Galilee—cf. LUKE 24:1-13.

Peter and John, upon hearing the news, ran to the tomb to see for themselves. They, too, found the tomb empty.

8. Did the friends of Christ expect that He would rise from the dead?

No. Despite our Lord's prediction that he would rise on the third day his friends did not expect the resurrection and at first refused to believe that Christ had risen.

Mary Magdelene, seeing the empty tomb, immediately concluded that the body had been stolen. When Christ appeared to her she thought he was the gardener—cf. JOHN 20:1-18.

That evening Christ entered the room where most of the apostles were gathered. Instead of rushing to meet him they cowered in a corner, believing him to be a ghost. Our Lord ate food in order to convince them that he was alive—cf. LUKE 24:36-43.

That same evening Christ appeared to two of his disciples on a road outside of Jerusalem. They had not believed the rumors of the Resurrection either and did not recognize Christ until he had vanished out of their sight—cf. LUKE 24:13-35.

One of the apostles, Thomas, who had not been present the first time Jesus appeared to the others, refused to believe that Christ had risen. He said that unless he could examine the wounds in Christ's body he would not believe. Later Jesus again appeared and insisted that Thomas see for himself—cf. JOHN 20:24-29.

9. What did Christ's Resurrection teach the apostles?

Christ's resurrection taught the apostles that Jesus was not only the promised Messiah but God himself, the eternal Son of God. After the Holy Spirit came upon them on Pentecost they fully understood the fact that Christ was God and grasped the meaning of his death as the act by which he redeemed the world.

10. How is the Resurrection of Christ the Source of our hope?

The resurrection of Christ shows us that Christ has conquered sin and death. He conquered sin by his death on the cross. He conquered death by his resurrection. Death is a result of original sin. Christ's victory over death is our pledge that he will raise as up on the last day.

> "For if we believe that Jesus died and rose again, so with him God will bring those also who have fallen asleep through Jesus. . . . For the Lord himself with cry of command, with voice of archangel, and with trumpet of God will descend from heaven; and the dead in Christ will rise up first . . ."
> —1 THESS. 4:14-16.

11. Where did the soul of Christ go after his death?

After his death the soul of Christ "descended into hell." This means that Christ's soul went where the souls of the just who had died before him were awaiting their entrance into heaven.

12. How long did Jesus remain on earth after his Resurrection?

Jesus remained after his Resurrection for forty days. Then on Ascension Thursday after instructing his apostles to return to Jerusalem to await the coming of the Holy Spirit on Pentecost, he gave them the commission to teach, sanctify and rule in his name and to spread the Church throughout the world. Thereupon he ascended out of their sight into heaven.

13. Will Christ ever return to earth?

At the end of time Christ will come again to judge the living and the dead. Meanwhile, true to his promise, "I will not leave you orphans," he remains in the world in his Church, through which he continues to act in the world. And, although visible only to the eyes of faith, he is present under the appearances of bread and wine in the Eucharist.

Liturgy

The Resurrection of Christ and its profound meaning in our lives is brought home to us in the liturgy of Easter. The Easter services begin with the Easter Vigil, which is held on Holy Saturday night, preferably late in the night, so that the first Easter Mass may begin about midnight. This service is one of the most beautiful and meaningful in all the liturgy. In it we enact in word, ceremony and song the story of our redemption, our passage from death to life by means of water and the Holy Spirit. Christ, the Light of the World, represented by the new Easter fire, comes among us once more, risen from the dead, a guarantee of our future resurrection, provided we live in him and by him. The ceremony begins with the dramatic blessing of the new fire. This is followed by the lighting of the paschal candle, which represents Christ, and the singing of a glorious hymn praising this holy night and the wonder of our redemption. A series of instructions or readings are then sung. This provides an instruction for all, but particularly for those who are to be baptized during the ceremony. The blessing of the baptismal water follows, and then the baptism of those who are prepared to be baptized. All present then renew their baptismal vows while holding a lighted candle in their hands. After the recitation of the Litany of the Saints the first Mass of Easter is celebrated with fullest solemnity.

The Masses of the Easter season are full of the joy of the Resurrection. We follow the risen Christ as he appears to the apostles and the other disciples. On Ascension Thursday we celebrate our Lord's triumphal Ascension into heaven, and begin a nine day's period of prayer to the Holy Spirit in preparation for the glorious feast of Pentecost.

Practice

Read the account of our Lord's Resurrection and of his appearances to his apostles and disciples:

—John 20: entire chapter, Luke 24:1-49

> *Pilate therefore again entered into the praetorium, and he*
> *summoned Jesus, and said to him, "Art thou the king of*
> *the Jews?" Jesus answered, "Dost thou say this of thyself,*
> *or have others told thee of me?" Pilate answered, "Am I a*
> *Jew? Thy own people and the chief priests have delivered*
> *thee to me. What hast thou done?" Jesus answered, "My*
> *kingdom is not of this world. If my kingdom were of this*
> *world, my followers would have fought that I might not*
> *be delivered to the Jews. But, as it is, my kingdom is not*
> *from here." Pilate therefore said to him, "Thou art then*
> *a king?" Jesus answered, "Thou sayest it; I am a king.*
> *This is why I was born, and why I have come into the*
> *world, to bear witness to the truth. Everyone who is of the*
> *truth hears my voice"*—JOHN 18:33-37.

THE PROPHETS of the Old Testament had
described the Messiah as a ruler who would establish a kingdom.
Jesus Christ fulfilled these prophecies, but in a way different
from that which his disciples expected. "My kingdom," he said,
"is not of this world"—JOHN 18:36. His kingdom is a spiritual
one, founded on God's great mercy and love. Christ is the king
who now rules over the spiritual kingdom of God on earth, the
Church, and who sits at the right hand of the Father, reigning
triumphantly in heaven. One day he will come to earth again as
king to judge all men. Then, gathering his subjects, he will reign
gloriously in heaven over a kingdom that will have no end.

1. By what right is Christ king?

As God, Christ is king of heaven and earth, because all
things belong to him as God.

> *In the beginning was the Word, and the Word was with God;*
> *and the Word was God. He was in the beginning with God.*

All things were made through him, and without him was made nothing that has been made—JOHN 1:1-3.

As man, Christ is king. The Father has given all men to him as his subjects.

Its measure is the working of his mighty power, which he has wrought in Christ in raising him from the dead, and setting him at his right hand in heaven above every Principality and Power and Virtue and Domination—in short, above every name that is named, not only in this world, but also in that which is to come. And all things he made subject under his feet . . .—EPH. 1:20-22.

Christ is king of all men because he has redeemed them. As members of a fallen race we had been under the domination of Satan. Christ has paid the price for us, has purchased us with his blood. Therefore we are his.

2. How does Christ exercise his kingship?

a. Christ is king of the angels and saints in his eternal kingdom in heaven.

b. Christ rules as king in his kingdom on earth, his Church, through the pope and bishops.

c. Christ is content to allow his rule of the temporal order to be exercised by lawfully constituted civil authority. Here, although he is king over all things, he chooses not to exercise his rule directly.

3. How did Jesus acknowledge his kingship during his life on earth?

Even as an infant Jesus received the homage of the Wise Men, who came from the East and sought him as the "newly born king of the Jews"—cf. MATT. 2:2.

On Palm Sunday, at his triumphal entry into Jerusalem, he was hailed "king of Israel"—JOHN 12:13.

At his trial before Pilate he publicly acknowledged that he was king—JOHN 18:37.

Shortly before his ascension into heaven Jesus ascribed to himself kingly powers: "All power in heaven and on earth has been given to me"—MATT. 28:18.

4. How did Jesus exercise his office of king during his life on earth?

Jesus not only taught as "one having authority"; he also enacted laws for his kingdom.

He frequently urged his followers to keep his commandments:

> To observe all that I have commanded you—MATT. 28:20.
> If you love me, keep my commandments—JOHN 14:15.

In the Sermon on the Mount he quoted the Old Law, which was of divine origin, and on his own authority changed it, saying repeatedly:

> You have heard that it was said to the ancients, . . . but I say to you . . .—MATT. 5:21-22.

5. What did Jesus teach about his kingdom?

Jesus used many parables in an effort to teach the people what his kingdom really was, a spiritual kingdom, one that extended beyond the Jewish people into the whole world. In speaking of the kingdom of heaven and the kingdom of God, Jesus speaks of his Church, with himself as the head and men throughout the world as the members, and of its completion in heaven.

cf. The parable of the sower—MATT. 13:3-9, 18-23

The parable of the wheat and the cockle
—MATT. 13:24-30, 37-43

The parable of the mustard seed—MATT. 13:31-32

The parable of the leaven—MATT. 13:33

The parable of the fishing net—MATT. 13:47-50

The parable of the laborers in the vineyard
—MATT. 20:1-16

The parable of the vine-dressers—MATT. 21:33-41

The parable of the marriage of the king's son
—MATT. 22:1-14

6. Did Jesus delegate his powers to anyone?

Yes. Jesus delegated his powers to his apostles and their successors. As he was about to ascend into heaven he told his apostles:

> . . . All power in heaven and on earth has been given to me. Go, therefore, and make disciples of all nations, baptizing them in the name of the Father, and of the Son, and of the Holy Spirit, teaching them to observe all that I have commanded you; and behold, I am with you all days, even unto the consummation of the world—MATT. 28:18-20.

7. What did Jesus mean by these words, addressed to the apostles?

With these words Jesus was giving the apostles the commission to teach, sanctify and rule in his kingdom, the Church. He was giving them and their successors a share in his threefold office of prophet, priest and king.

For three years Jesus had lived with these men, teaching them about the kingdom. At the Last Supper he had ordained them priests. After his resurrection he had placed Peter over all the members of his Church and over the other apostles as well, making Peter the visible head of his Church.

After his resurrection Jesus gave the apostles the power to forgive sins. Now, at the moment of his ascension into heaven, he was giving them the commission to teach, sanctify and rule the members of his Church.

8. Did the apostles begin their work immediately after the Ascension of Jesus?

No. The apostles did not begin their work immediately. Jesus had instructed them to remain in Jerusalem in prayer for nine days. He had promised them that on the ninth day the Holy Spirit would come to strengthen them and give them understanding of all he had taught.

9. What do we call the day on which the Holy Spirit descended upon the apostles?

We call that day Pentecost Sunday. The Church, which was

born from the pierced side of Christ as he died on the cross, was made manifest to the world on that day.

10. What was the effect of the coming of the Holy Spirit upon the apostles?

After the Holy Spirit had come upon them the apostles were no longer timid or uncertain. They then understood the teachings which Jesus had patiently taught them for three years. They went forth fearlessly, preaching and administering the sacraments in the name of Jesus Christ.

11. How did the apostles fulfill their mission to spread the Church throughout the world?

The apostles remained for a time in their own country, using Jerusalem as a base. Later they went forth to the various parts of the world. Saints Peter and Paul eventually made their way to Rome, of which city St. Peter became bishop.

Liturgy

The feast of Christ the King is celebrated on the last Sunday of October. The glorious kingship of Christ is expressed in a beautiful song of thanksgiving and praise, the Preface of the Mass on the feast of Christ the King:

> Right indeed it is and just, proper and for our welfare, that we should always and everywhere give thanks to thee, holy Lord, almighty Father eternal God, who didst anoint thy only-begotten Son, Jesus Christ our Lord, with the oil of gladness to be a priest forever and king of the whole world, so that he might offer himself as an unblemished victim and peace offering upon the altar of the cross, thereby performing the sacrificial rite of man's redemption, and by subduing all creation to his sway, he might deliver to thy boundless sovereignty a

universal and eternal kingdom: a kingdom of truth and life, of holiness and grace, of justice, love and peace . . .
(Preface from the Feast of Christ the King)

Practice

▶ Having studied the lessons on the life of our Lord, and having read some selections from the Gospels, we should now try to see the life of Christ as a whole.

Read straight through one of the first three Gospels (Matthew, Mark, or Luke). Afterwards, read straight through the Gospel according to St. John.

RECOMMENDED READING—PART II

Christ, Our Brother, ADAM. New York, Macmillan, $2.75.
    A classic on the humanity of Jesus Christ. Not difficult to read.

The Lord, GUARDINI. Chicago, Regnery, 535 pp., $6.50.
    Not a biography of Christ, but a book of essays on the mysteries and events in the life of our Lord. It is a book to be read slowly, bit by bit, and reread and reread. A masterpiece.

In the Likeness of Christ, LEEN. New York, Sheed & Ward, 361 pp., $3.50.
    This highly readable book draws lessons from the life of our Lord. Very good for spiritual reading.

Only Son, FARRELL. New York, Sheed & Ward, $3.50.
    A short, one-volume life of Christ. Easy to read.

    See appendix on page 280 for readings on the Bible.

PART III

THE CHURCH THE BODY OF CHRIST

section **13** | **The Mystical Body**

Now you are the body of Christ, member for member
—I COR. 12:27.

And he himself gave some men as apostles, and some as prophets, others again as evangelists, and others as pastors and teachers, in order to perfect the saints for a work of ministry, for building up the body of Christ, until we all attain to the unity of the faith and of the deep knowledge of the Son of God, to perfect manhood, to the mature measure of the fullness of Christ. And this he has done that we may be now no longer children, tossed to and fro and carried about by every wind of doctrine devised in the wickedness of men, in craftiness, according to the wiles of error. Rather are we to practice the truth in love, and so grow up in all things in him who is the head, Christ. For from him the whole body (being closely joined and knit together through every joint of the system according to the functioning in due measure of each single part) derives its increase to the building up of itself in love—EPH. 4:11-16.

JESUS CHRIST is our high priest, teacher and king. It was to sanctify, teach and rule men that he became man and lived and died among men. He lived 2,000 years ago, and died in a remote corner of the world, surrounded by only a handful of his friends. How then does he remain among us even though he has ascended into heaven? How does he extend himself into time and space? How does he continue to sanctify, teach and rule men at all times and everywhere in the world?

Christ might have chosen any number of ways to continue his work in the world. He might have chosen to draw each man to himself separately by some sort of illumination from heaven. He might have chosen merely to leave a record of his life and teachings, so that all who read it and accepted those teachings might learn to love and imitate him from afar. As a matter of fact, however, Jesus Christ chose to distribute his graces and to continue his work in the world by taking to himself a new Body, his Church. As Head of the Body, he continues to give life and direction to his members. The Church, therefore, is not merely an organization established by Christ; it is Christ, the fullness of Christ, the Mystical Body of Christ.

1. How does Jesus Christ share the divine life with men?

Jesus Christ shares the divine life with men by joining them to himself in a living union.

Christ said:

I am the vine, you are the branches. He who abides in me, and I in him, he bears much fruit; for without me you can do nothing—JOHN 15:5.

2. How does Jesus Christ unite men to himself in this life-giving union?

As he died on the cross Christ took to himself another Body. This second Body of Christ is called his Mystical Body, and is the Catholic Church. By being baptized into that Body we become united to Christ, who is its Head, and thus become adopted sons of God and sharers of the divine nature.

3. How did Jesus Christ speak of his Church?

Jesus spoke of his Church,

a. *As his bride,* referring to himself as the bridegroom.

. . . Can the wedding guests mourn as long as the bridegroom is with them? But the days will come when the bridegroom shall be taken away from them, and then they will fast—MATT. 9:15.

b. *As his flock,* of which he is the shepherd.

I am the good shepherd, and I know mine and mine know me, even as the Father knows me and I know the Father; and I lay down my life for my sheep. And other sheep I have that are not of this fold. Them also I must bring,

*and they shall hear my voice, and there shall be one fold
and one shepherd*—JOHN 10:14-16.

c. *As his kingdom*, calling it the kingdom of heaven (kingdom of God), and the kingdom of his Father, a spiritual kingdom in which he teaches, rules and gives life through the men he empowers to act in his name. Many of the parables of Christ taught of his Church under this aspect.

*Again, the kingdom of heaven is like a net cast into the
sea and gathering in fish of every kind*—MATT. 13:47.

d. *As a vine and its branches*, a living organic union between himself and the members of his Church.

I am the vine, you are the branches . . .—JOHN 15:5.

4. How did St. Paul speak of the Church?

The union between himself and his members which Jesus described as his bride, his flock, his kingdom and as the union of vine and branches was described by St. Paul as the union of a living body. "Christ," says St. Paul, "is the head of the body of the Church . . . though many we are one body in Christ." That the Church is the Body of Christ is the theme which is dominant in the teachings of St. Paul.

*If we would define and describe this true Church of Jesus
Christ—which is the one, holy, catholic, apostolic, Roman
Church—we shall find no expression more noble, more
sublime or more divine than the phrase which calls it "The
Mystical Body of Jesus Christ." This title is derived from
and is, as it were, the fair flower of the repeated teaching of
sacred Scripture and the holy fathers*—Encyclical on the
Mystical Body 13.

5. Is it true to say that the Church is Christ?

Yes. The Church is "the Mystical Christ." Jesus Christ as he exists today is the God-Man, inseparably linked to his new Body, the Church.

6. How is the Church a body?

A body has many members, which are joined together in such a way as to help one another. So it is with our own body; when one part of the body suffers, all the other parts share its pain, and the healthy parts come to the assistance of the parts which are ailing. Such is the case too, in the Church. The individual members of the Church do not live for themselves alone; they also help their fellow members. All work together for their common good and for the perfect building up of the whole body.

Our bodies, moreover, are not formed by any haphazard grouping of members. They are made up of organs, i.e., members which have different functions, but which work together in such a way that the body lives and acts as a whole. So, too, it is with the Church. In the Church there are many members, millions of men, women and children. As members of the Church, they occupy special positions and exercise special functions; the pope, as the visible head, teaching, sanctifying and ruling in the name of Christ; the bishops—exercising the same functions in union with the Holy Father; the clergy—assisting the bishops in the work of teaching and sanctifying; laymen—each performing some special function; teachers—teaching; parents—forming the youngest members of Christ; doctors, lawyers, farmers, workers— all cooperating, each in his own way, according to his calling in the work of worshipping God, extending the Body of Christ throughout the world and increasing its inner holiness.—cf. Enc. on the Mystical Body.

> It is thus the Apostle describes the Church when he writes: "As in one body we have many members, but all members have not the same office: so we being many are one body in Christ, and everyone members of one another"—Enc. on the Mystical Body 16.

7. Why is the Church called the Mystical Body of Christ?

The Church is called the *Mystical* Body of Christ:

a. To distinguish it from the physical body of Christ, his human body, which is present in heaven and in the Eucharist under the appearances of bread and wine.

b. To express the uniqueness of this second Body of Christ. The Church is not a physical body (one in which the members are joined physically to one another, as is the case with our own bodies). Neither is it *merely* a moral body (an organization, such as a club, a labor union, or a corporation). It is a unique body, having all the elements of a moral body plus a living soul. This soul, the one unifying life-giving principle which unites all the members to one another and to Christ, the Head, is the Third Person of the Blessed Trinity, the Holy Spirit.

The word *Mystical* must not be taken to mean vague, shadowy or unreal. Rather, it means mysterious, something which is real, but beyond the powers of our intellect fully to understand. The Church is, indeed, a sublime mystery, visible in her external organization but capable of being known only by faith in her inner life.

8. *What does the Holy Spirit do as soul of the Mystical Body?*

As soul of the Mystical Body the Holy Spirit joins the members of the Church to one another and to Christ, their Head. He is entire in Christ, the Head, entire in the Body, and entire in each of the members. Through his grace he is the cause of every supernatural act in all parts of the Body. He is personally present and active in all the members. He also acts in the members through the ministry of the higher members. He provides for the constant growth of the Church.—cf. Enc. on the Mystical Body 61-63.

9. *Is the Mystical Body of Christ visible?*

Yes. Like Christ, the Head, who has both an invisible divine nature and a visible human nature, the Church, his Body, has both an invisible inner life (our union with Christ and one another through the Holy Spirit) and a visible, external structure, the hierarchical organization of the Church.

10. *How is the union between Christ and his members manifested externally?*

The union between Christ and his members is manifested externally by the fact that all the members of Christ profess the same faith, share the same sacred rites, participate in the same sacrifice, observe the same laws and, above all, recognize as visible head of the Mystical Body the pope, the vicar of Christ.

As the divine Redeemer sent a Paraclete, the Spirit of Truth, who in his name should govern the Church in an invisible way; similarly he commissioned Peter and his successors, to be his personal representative on earth and to assume the visible government of the Christian community—Enc. on the Mystical Body 69.

11. Is there another bond of union between Christ and the members of his Mystical Body?

Yes. Besides the visible union which is realized by submission to the Church and the invisible bond of union, the Holy Spirit, there is yet another bond of union, "those three virtues which link us so closely to each other and to God: Christian faith, hope and charity"—Enc. on the Mystical Body 70.

12. What work does Christ do in the Church?

Christ continues the work of redemption which he began in his physical body; now, however, he accomplishes this work through the members of his Mystical Body.

The work of redemption has three phases:

I. While he was on earth in his physical body Christ won grace once and for all for all men.

II. After his death on the cross, he began the second phase of redemption, the distribution and application of those graces through the Mystical Body. Christ teaches and rules through the pope and the bishops. Christ makes men holy through the sacraments. Christ worships the Father through the sacrifice of the Mass, which is continually offered by the whole Mystical Body. Christ still suffers, no longer in his physical body, but in his Mystical Body. Though the sufferings of Christ gained grace for men, this grace must be applied to individual souls. The prayers, the sufferings and the works of the members of the Church bring this about.

... what is lacking of the sufferings of Christ I fill up in my flesh for his body which is the Church—COL. 1:24.

III. After the end of the world, Christ and those who have accepted his graces of redemption will begin the third phase, when they form one body in heaven, to praise and glorify God for all eternity.

13. Is it possible to be united to Christ without being united to the Church?

No. Just as we cannot go to God except through Christ, so we cannot go to Christ except through the Church, because Christ and the Church are one.

Those outside the Catholic Church who have the divine life have received that life only through the Church, even though they do not realize it.

14. Since it is possible to be saved through the Church without realizing it, what is the advantage of belonging to the Church in the fullest sense?

Salvation, sanctification and the peace and joy which come from intimacy with God are surely far easier and more certain of attainment for those who are consciously and fully joined to Christ in his Mystical Body. Membership in the Church is our greatest privilege on earth.

> For nothing more glorious, nothing nobler, nothing surely more honorable can be imagined than to belong to the holy, Catholic, apostolic and Roman Church, in which we become members of one Body as venerable as it is unique; are guided by one supreme Head; are filled with one divine Spirit; are nourished during our earthly exile by one doctrine and one heavenly Bread, until at last we enter into the one, unending blessedness of heaven—Enc. on the Mystical Body 91.

15. Are there any distinguishing marks by which the Mystical Body of Christ can be identified?

Yes. In order to make it possible for men of all ages to recognize his Church, Christ has given it four identifying marks. The Church is one; the Church is apostolic; the Church is holy; the Church is universal (catholic).

Practice

▶ All the members of the Church have a share in the great work of building up and perfecting the Mystical Body of

Christ. It would be a great mistake to think that only the clergy have the responsibility for the growth of the Church and the dissemination of her teachings. One of the important developments in modern times is the growth of the lay apostolate in the Church. Pope Pius XII in an address to the Second World Congress for the Lay Apostolate said:

> It would be a misunderstanding of the Church's real nature and her social character to distinguish in her a purely active element, Church authorities, and a purely passive element, the laity. All the members of the Church, as we ourselves said in the encyclical "Mystici Corporis Christi" are called upon to cooperate in building up and perfecting the Mystical Body of Christ. . . .
>
> History shows that from the Church's earliest days laymen have taken part in the activity which the priest carries out in the service of the Church, and today more than ever they must cooperate with greater and greater fervor "for building up the body of Christ" in all forms of the apostolate, especially by making the Christian spirit penetrate all family, social, economic, and political life.

In most places there are not enough priests to accomplish the vast work which the Church has to do in the world. The influence of one priest must be multiplied by the cooperation of laymen who work with him in the apostolate of the Church.

However, the layman must never think that his cooperation is necessary only because of a shortage of priests. The layman has a work to do which is indispensably his, a work which the priest cannot do. The lay members of the Mystical Body must share in the Church's work of carrying Christ's message to the world. Their words carry particular weight because of the fact that they are living under the same circumstances as those whom they teach. Laymen can be experts in many fields, too, in which the priest ordinarily is not, fields such as the social sciences, psychology, medicine, law, the physical sciences. Here the Church needs laymen who are deeply Christian and who are imbued with the spirit of the apostolate, men and women who by their lives and their work will Christianize the field in which they work, will be apostles to others who work in that field, will do the work of the Church in that place where Christ has placed them.

The Church needs artists, writers, philosophers to apply the teachings of Christ in the great fields of art, literature and architecture. One of the Church's most effective means of teaching, inspiring and ennobling men is by means of art and literature. This vital part of the Church's work will not and cannot be done by priests. It will be done by apostolic lay members of Christ or it will not be done at all.

☖   ☖

section 14 | **The Church, the Family of God**

For as the body is one and has many members, and all the members of the body, many as they are, form one body, so also is it with Christ.

For in one Spirit we were all baptized into one body, whether Jews or Gentiles, whether slaves or free; and we were all given to drink of one Spirit. For the body is not one member, but many. If the foot says, "Because I am not a hand, I am not of the body," is it therefore not of the body? And if the ear says, "Because I am not an eye, I am not of the body," is it therefore not of the body?

If the whole body were an eye, where would be the hearing? If the whole body were hearing, where would be the smelling? But as it is, God has set the members, each of them, in the body as he willed. Now if they were all one member, where would the body be? But as it is, there are indeed many members, yet but one body. And the eye cannot say to the hand, "I do not need thy help"; nor again the head to the feet, "I have no need of you." Nay, much rather, those that seem the more feeble members of the body are more necessary; and those that we think the less honorable

99

members of the body, we surround with more abundant honor, and our uncomely parts receive a more abundant comeliness, whereas our comely parts have no need of it. But God has so tempered the body together in due portion as to give more abundant honor where it was lacking; that there may be no disunion in the body, but that the members may have care for one another. And if one member suffers anything, all the members suffer with it, or if one member glories, all the members rejoice with it— 1 Cor. 12:12-26.

THROUGH JESUS CHRIST we have been made members of the family of God. We are joined to Christ and to one another in a union which is far closer than any union on earth. Our Lord himself compared it to the sublime union of the Blessed Trinity, ". . . that all may be one, even as thou, Father in me and I in thee; that they also may be one in us. . . ."

Because we belong to the family of God we are never alone. We are one with Christ and one with one another in the union of the Mystical Body of Christ here on earth. So close is this union that whatever we do or fail to do to one another we do or fail to do to Christ himself.

Because of our union with Christ we are united, too, with all those who share his life in the larger family of God, the Communion of Saints. We on earth, members of the Church Militant, still fighting the good fight as soldiers of Christ, still journeying on our way to our Father's house, are helped by the prayers and encouragement of the victorious and blessed members of the family, the Church Triumphant in heaven. We, who are still able to increase the divine life within us, still able to win God's favors by our cooperation with the grace of Christ, can help the suffering members of the family, those who are being purified in purgatory. They, in turn, although unable to help themselves, can and do pray for us. Thus, through the Communion of Saints we are one with those . . . " 'who rest in Christ, who have gone before us with the sign of faith and repose in the sleep of peace;' for whether we live or whether we die still we are not separated from the one and only Christ"—Enc. on the Sacred Liturgy.

1. How do we manifest the love and unity which is ours in the communion of saints?

We manifest the love and unity which is ours in the communion of saints:

a. By praying to the saints in heaven as our patrons and intercessors with God, and by honoring them and imitating them in our daily lives.

b. By praying for our brothers who are undergoing purification in purgatory. They cannot help themselves, cannot shorten their period of purification. But we can help them reach heaven, our common home, more quickly by our prayers and sacrifices, if we offer them to God in their behalf.

c. By praying for, helping and cooperating with our fellow members of the Mystical Body on earth.

2. Why must we have special love for our fellow members in the Mystical Body of Christ?

We must have special love for our fellow members in the Mystical Body of Christ because in loving the members of his Body we are loving Christ.

> *Amen, I say to you, as long as you did it for one of these, the least of my brethren, you did it for me*—MATT. 25:40.
> *By this will all men know that you are my disciples, if you have love for one another*—JOHN 13:35.

In practice, of course, we must treat all men, whether or not they are Catholics, as we would treat Christ himself. Christ died for all men. Those outside the Church are to be considered as potential members of the Body of Christ.

> *Therefore, while we have time, let us do good to all men, but especially to those who are of the household of faith*
> —GAL. 6:10.

3. How do we manifest the love and unity which is ours in the Mystical Body of Christ?

We manifest that love and unity:

a. By offering together the great act of worship of the family of God, the Mass.

b. By praying for each other.

c. By helping each other in need.

d. By supporting with our prayers and alms our fellow members of Christ who are laboring in the missions.

e. By working together in the lay apostolate to "restore all things in Christ."

f. By associating and cooperating with one another in the work of the diocese and the parish to which we belong, and in social, economic and civic life.

4. What is a diocese?

A diocese is a territory which is cared for and ruled by a bishop who has been appointed by the Holy Father, the supreme bishop of the Church. The bishop, who is Christ among us, is our spiritual father. It is he who teaches, rules and sanctifies in the name of Christ. The bishop performs these functions both directly and through his representatives and assistants, the pastors of parishes.

5. What is a parish?

A parish is a territory within a diocese, which is administered by the pastor, who has been appointed by the bishop. The parish is the center of our worship and sanctification, and is the community in which we usually manifest our union with one another in the Church.

6. What is the role of the parish?

The role of the parish is the same as that of the Church itself:

a. To worship God. This is accomplished above all through the Mass and through the sacraments.

b. To sanctify its members and through them the whole community. This work of sanctification is accomplished by Christ acting through the sacraments and through the Mass and by the prayers and example of priests and people.

c. To teach its members and the whole community. This work of teaching the word of God is accomplished by the liturgy, by instructions, classes for Catholics, convert and inquiry classes, by the parish school, by the organizations of Catholic Action and by the general efforts of priests and people to witness Christ in their neighborhood.

d. To guide and rule its members. This work is accomplished through the pastor, the shepherd of that portion of Christ's flock which makes up his parish.

7. What is the role of the pastor in a parish?

The role of the pastor in a parish is the role of Christ. The pastor is the representative of the bishop, who is the chief shepherd and spiritual ruler of the diocese.

8. What is the role of the people in a parish?

The role of the people in a parish is that of the members of Christ's kingdom. Theirs is the role of cooperating with the pastor in the total life of the parish, of taking an active part in the worship of the parish, of belonging to and working together in the various parish organizations, of supporting the parish financially, and of carrying the teaching and sanctifying action of the Church into the community in which they live and work.

9. Who is the center of the parish?

The center of the parish and the source of its life is Christ. He is physically present in the Eucharist. He is present in the individuals who possess the divine life. He is present, too, among the community of Christians who meet with him in their midst. Through their meeting with one another in a spirit of fraternal charity the people of the parish give evidence of Christ's presence among them, the sign by which the world can recognize them as members of Christ's kingdom.

> *For where two or three are gathered together for my sake, there am I in the midst of them*—MATT. 18:20.

10. What is the function of a parish in the community?

Since the parish is Christ in the community, its function is twofold: to feed and care for the sheep of the fold and to go out in search of the other sheep, both those who have strayed from the fold, and those who do not yet belong to it.

And other sheep I have that are not of this fold. Them also I must bring, and they shall hear my voice, and there shall be one fold and one shepherd—JOHN 10:16.

In its task of caring for its members one of the functions of the parish is to help build a better community, one in which people can more easily lead Christian lives.

11. What means does a parish possess for its missionary activity in the community?

The organization of its lay members in movements of the lay apostolate is the means by which a parish can most effectively perform its missionary work in the community. The Christian Family Movement, the Young Christian Workers, the Legion of Mary, the Confraternity of Christian Doctrine and other apostolic organizations, working with the pastor and priests of the parish, can extend and multiply the influence of the parish throughout the community in the work of restoring it in Christ.

Practice

▶ In the Mystical Body we are united not only with Christ, but with all the other members as well. Consequently, there is no escaping the fact that what we do to any member of his Mystical Body we do to Christ. This is the basis for the words of Jesus, spoken to St. Paul at his conversion, "Saul, Saul, why dost thou persecute me?"—ACTS 9:5. St. Paul did not protest that it was not Christ but the members of Christ's Church he was persecuting. He understood then and there, with the revelation that Christ gave him, that whatever he did to a member of Christ's Body he did to Christ. This, too, is the basis for the words which Jesus will say at the last judgment: "For I was hungry and you gave me to eat; . . . As long as you did it for one of these, the least of my brethren, you did it for me"—MATT. 25:35-40.

The things which separate us from one another, wealth,

social position, color of skin, difference in nationality, etc., are all minor compared to the bond which unites us as members of Christ and of one another.

Try to keep in mind this week the important fact that whatever we do to any man we do to Christ.

Make an effort to see Christ in your neighbor, and check up on your success or failure in doing so.

section **15** | The Church Is One

Yet not for these only do I pray, but for those also who through their word are to believe in me, that all may be one, even as thou, Father, in me and I in thee; that they also may be one in us, that the world may believe that thou has sent me. And the glory that thou has given me, I have given to them, that they may be one, even as we are one: I in them and thou in me; that they may be perfected in unity, and that the world may know that thou hast sent me, and that thou hast loved them even as thou hast loved me
—JOHN 17:20-23.

THIS PRAYER OF CHRIST is realized today in the marvelous oneness which exists within his Church. It is a oneness which is present amid a remarkable diversity. The members of Christ live in all the various countries of the world. They belong to every race on earth. They speak different languages. They have different cultures, different tastes, different political opinions. But they are one in the great unity of the Body of Christ.

There are, however, millions of men and women who love Christ and worship him as their Saviour and their God, who are

105

separated from the unity of the Body of Christ. The prayer of Christ for unity among his members is a prayer also for re-union with his Body.

1. What do we mean when we say that the Church is one?

When we say the Church is one we mean that:

All the members of the Mystical Body believe the same doctrines.

All accept the same sources of life, the seven sacraments.

All worship together in the sacrifice of the Mystical Body, the Mass.

All submit to the same divine authority, that of Christ the Head, who rules the Body through the visible head, our Holy Father the Pope, and the bishops who are in communion with him.

2. Can there be more than one true Church of Christ?

No. There cannot be more than one true Church of Christ because the Church *is* Christ. Christ cannot be divided.

> *. . . one body and one Spirit, even as you were called in one hope of your calling; one Lord, one faith, one Baptism; one God and Father of all, who is above all, and throughout all, and in us all—*EPH. 4:4-6.

3. There are, in fact, many churches. Does it make any difference to which one belongs?

Yes. Jesus Christ took to himself one Mystical Body. That Body is the Catholic Church. In the course of history, disputes, misunderstandings, the pride and greed of men, weaknesses and abuses within the Church itself have resulted in the rending and tearing of the Body of Christ. Millions have been separated from the unity of the Body. Many good people today are deprived, through no fault of their own, of the life-giving sacraments and of participation in Christ's sacrifice. Christ wants all of them to be re-united in his Mystical Body, the Catholic Church.

> *And other sheep I have that are not of this fold. Them also I must bring, and they shall hear my voice, and there shall be one fold and one shepherd—*JOHN 10:16.

106

4. Can those who belong to other churches be saved?

Yes. God does not deny the means of salvation to anyone. He wants all men to belong to the unity of the Body of Christ. Nonetheless, many through no fault of their own remain outside the Church. God offers these people the grace necessary to save their souls.

Even though these people are not aware that the Church is the one true Church of Christ, it is through the Church that they receive their divine life and their salvation.

5. Are all Catholics bound by the same Church laws and customs?

No. Some of the Church laws and customs in the various rites differ. There are two great bodies of law in the Church, one for the Western rite and one for the Eastern rites.

6. What is a rite?

A rite is a system of ritual and prayer used in the worship of God and the administration of the sacraments.

The Latin rite, the one used by Rome and all the West, is the largest, numbering about 450,000,000 people. The next largest rite is the Byzantine, which has many national subdivisions. There are also Armenian, Syrian, Chaldean, Malabar, Maronite, Coptic and Egyptian rites, which are used in various countries. In all the Eastern rites, there are about 8,000,000 people.

7. How did these various rites originate?

Originally each bishop said Mass and administered the sacraments in his own way. Gradually the customs of certain important cities influenced the surrounding countryside. Rome was the most influential in Italy, Constantinople in Greece, Antioch in Asia Minor, Jerusalem in the Holy Land, and Alexandria in North Africa. In the course of centuries the liturgies of these cities became the basic part of a "rite," although sub-rites developed and still exist. Even in the Latin rite there are variations peculiar to the Dominican and Calced Carmelite orders, and to such cities as Milan, Braga, Lyons and Toledo.

8. What are some of the differences between the Eastern and Western Rites?

a. The ceremonies used at Mass and in the administration of the sacraments are different. The Eastern rites usually use an ancient form of the language of the people (Mass is said in fourteen or fifteen different languages). In the West only Latin is used.

b. In some of the Eastern rites a married man may become a priest (no man may marry after ordination; bishops and monks are unmarried or widowers). In the Western rite the clergy is unmarried.

c. Some of the Eastern rites have Communion under both species, and use leavened instead of unleavened bread. In the Western rite Holy Communion is now distributed under only one species, and only unleavened bread is used.

d. In the Eastern rite the people do not genuflect, but bow profoundly. They also make the sign of the cross from right to left instead of from left to right, as is the practice in the Western rite.

e. Eastern rites have some Church laws different from those of the Western Church.

f. In some of the Eastern rites the people are baptized by immersion, and are confirmed by the priest immediately after Baptism.

There are many other variations. The Church is a wise mother, who takes all of her children's customs to herself. The Eastern rites are as old or older than the Western rite. Hence they are not the exception in the Church, but part of her normal way of worshipping God.

9. Did all these rites remain within the Church?

No. In the course of time various groups either fell into heresy or went into schism, as did the Orthodox Eastern Churches (Greek, Russian, Georgian, etc.). Throughout the centuries groups of these peoples have returned to union with Rome. When they did so they were allowed to keep their own particular rite. The

Church is very solicitous about preserving these rites. Ordinarily one must obtain permission from Rome to change from one rite to another, but a woman may transfer to the rite of her husband without any special permission.

10. What other peoples have separated themselves from the unity of the Church?

At various times in history men have taught heretical doctrines and led others out of the Church. Next to the Eastern Schism, the greatest split occurred in the sixteenth century when Martin Luther broke with the Church and began the Protestant Reformation.

11. Why did the Protestants leave the Church?

The conditions which brought about the revolt of the Protestants were very complex. No adequate treatment of the subject could possibly be given here. The following points, however, can be noted:

a. There were real and serious evils in the Church in the sixteenth century. Many of the clergy were not faithful to their vows. There was an over-emphasis on externals and a neglect of the inner religious spirit. Responsible elements in the Church had long been calling for a real reformation to correct these abuses.

b. The spirit of nationalism was growing at that time. There was a strong desire in many countries to rebel against any authority higher than that of the individual state.

c. Martin Luther, whose revolt spearheaded other revolts which resulted in the establishment of many different Protestant churches, did not at first intend to rebel against the Church itself, but merely to cry out against abuses.

d. Luther's opposition to certain abuses ended in his opposition to the thing which had been abused, and finally to the very idea of a visibly organized church.

For example: Luther objected to what he termed the sale of indulgences; he ended up denying the validity of indulgences themselves and the existence of purgatory. He objected to the idea of having Masses said for the dead; he ended up objecting to the Mass itself. He objected to abuses among the clergy; he ended up by declaring that there was no need for priests, bishops or pope. He insisted that the entire revelation of God was contained in the Bible, and that no priest, no pope, no church was needed to interpret the Bible, that any man with good intentions would be guided by the Holy Spirit in reading the scriptures and would be kept from misinterpreting them.*

e. The end result was that an effort to reform the Church, to return to what Luther conceded to have been the true Church (the Church as it had been for the first 11 centuries) resulted in a Church which lacked the very essentials of the Church from apostolic times, a Church without a priesthood, without most of the sacraments, without the sacrifice of the Mass.

12. What effect did the Protestant Reformation have on the Church?

The Protestant Reformation divided Europe, taking millions away from the unity of the Body of Christ, just as the Eastern Schism had done earlier.

On the other hand, the revolt of the Protestants forced the Church to reform herself from the inside. Great saints were raised up within the Church. The Church emerged weaker in numbers but stronger internally.

The division among Christians which exists today is deeply distressing to all who love Christ. Men of good will both within the Catholic Church and among the separated Eastern and the Protestant Churches, pray for the reunion of all the believers and followers of Christ. Within Protestantism there is a great movement towards unity. The Catholic Church, on her part, is willing to make whatever concessions she can without sacrificing anything which is essential. We can only hope and pray that through charity and mutual understanding, the day will come when all men who follow Christ will once more be re-united in the one Body of Christ.

---

* This complete repudiation of tradition as a guide in interpreting the Scriptures is not adhered to by many Protestant Churches today. The Lutheran Church soon modified this teaching of Luther and insisted that the Bible be interpreted in the light of Christian tradition.

Practice

▶ 1. It is an interesting and rewarding experience to assist at Mass in a Catholic church of the Eastern rite. Anyone who does so cannot help but be impressed; the ceremonies are so different from those of the Western rite, yet the essentials are the same.

A Latin rite Catholic may fulfill his Sunday obligation by assisting at Mass in a Catholic Eastern rite church. In some of the rites Holy Communion is distributed under the appearances of both bread and wine. A Latin rite Catholic may, of course, receive Holy Communion in one of these rites. One note of warning, however. Be sure that the Eastern Rite church you plan to visit is a Catholic church, not a schismatical one.

2. A great deal is being written today about the tension which exists between Catholics, Protestants and Jews. Much of this tension is the result of misunderstanding, which in turn is the result of lack of contact between those of various faiths. While Catholics may not associate in worship with Protestants and Jews, they may and should do so on other levels. Civic projects, social works of various kinds, discussions in which men of good will combine in a common effort can do much to bring about a better understanding among Catholics, Protestants and Jews.

Pray that all men may be joined to the one Body of Christ.

Pray for the gift of faith for someone in particular, a relative or a friend.

*Therefore, you are now no longer strangers and foreigners,
but you are citizens with the saints and members of God's
household: you are built upon the foundation of the apostles
and prophets with Christ Jesus himself as the chief corner
stone*—EPH. 2:19-20.

AT THE VERY beginning of his public life
Jesus personally selected twelve men who were to be his apostles.
During the three years he spent in preaching, teaching and working miracles these twelve were always at his side. Christ spared
no effort in instructing and training the apostles, for they were
the men on whom he was to rely to extend his kingdom throughout the world. It was on these apostles that Christ founded his
Church. He said to Peter, whom he chose to be the head of the
apostles, "Thou art Peter, and upon this rock I will build my
Church"—MATT. 16:18. The Church of Christ, even in its in-
fancy, was the Church of the apostles. The apostles are among
us today in the person of their legitimate successors, the bishops
of the Catholic Church. Peter, the first pope, is among us in the
person of his successor, our Holy Father the Pope. Christ is
among us, teaching, sanctifying and ruling us through the hierarchy of the Catholic Church.

1. What do we mean when we say that the Church is apostolic?

When we say that the Church is apostolic we mean that
Christ founded his Church upon the apostles and that the Church
in every age is ruled by the successors of the apostles, and teaches
the doctrine of the apostles.

2. Who were the apostles?

The apostles were the twelve men whom Jesus chose and called to the work of teaching, ruling and sanctifying in his name. These were the men to whom he gave the mission of extending his Mystical Body throughout the world. They were the first bishops of the Church.

The apostles were simple men; most of them were fishermen; one was a tax gatherer. One of them, Judas Iscariot, betrayed Jesus to his enemies and hanged himself in despair. The other apostles, under the guidance of the Holy Spirit, chose Matthias to replace him. After his ascension into heaven Jesus himself called Saul of Tarsus, whose name he changed to Paul, to be the great Apostle to the Gentiles.

Christ sent the apostles

> **To Teach**—*Go into the whole world and preach the gospel to every creature*—MARK 16:15.

> **To Rule**—*He who hears you, hears me; and he who rejects you, rejects me; and he who rejects me, rejects him who sent me*—LUKE 10:16.

> **To Sanctify**—*He therefore said to them again, "Peace be to you! As the Father has sent me, I also send you." When he had said this, he breathed upon them, and said to them, "Receive the Holy Spirit; whose sins you shall forgive, they are forgiven them; and whose sins you shall retain, they are retained"*—JOHN 20:21-23.

3. What is a bishop?

A bishop is a successor of the apostles. Through the sacrament of Holy Orders and jurisdiction granted by the pope, he has the power not only of administering the sacraments, but also of teaching and ruling the portion of Christ's flock committed to his care.

4. Why is the pope called the head of the bishops?

The pope is called the head of the bishops because he is the successor of St. Peter, who was the head of the apostles. He is, therefore, the visible head of the Church, the one who acts for Christ, the Invisible Head.

5. Where in Scripture do we read that Christ made Peter the visible head of his Church?

Christ, first of all, promised that he would make Peter the visible head of the Church. Later he actually conferred this office upon him.

a. At the time he promised the primacy to Peter, Christ said to him:

> *And I say to thee, thou art Peter, and upon this rock I will build my Church, and the gates of hell shall not prevail against it. And I will give thee the keys of the kingdom of heaven; and whatever thou shalt bind on earth shall be bound in heaven, and whatever thou shalt loose on earth shall be loosed in heaven—MATT. 16:18-19.*

It is to be noted that Christ changed Peter's name from Simon to Peter, which means "rock."

b. At the Last Supper, in warning Peter of his coming temptation and denial, Christ said to him:

> *But I have prayed for thee, that thy faith may not fail; and do thou, when once thou hast turned again, strengthen thy brethren—LUKE 22:32.*

c. In conferring on Peter the primacy among the apostles, which he had earlier promised to him, Jesus told him, "Feed my lambs." Then he said to Peter, "Feed my sheep." The meaning of these words in the language our Lord was speaking gives Peter a clear commission to "feed," i.e., "teach and rule" not only the people (the lambs) but also the leaders of the flock, the bishops, the other apostles (the sheep).

> *When, therefore, they had breakfasted, Jesus said to Simon Peter, "Simon, son of John, dost thou love me more than these do?" He said to him, "Yes, Lord, thou knowest that I love thee." He said to him, "Feed my lambs." He said to him a second time, "Simon, son of John, dost thou love me?" He said to him, "Yes, Lord, thou knowest that I love thee." He said to him, "Feed my lambs." A third time he said to him, "Simon, son of John, dost thou love me?" Peter was grieved because he said to him for the third time, "Dost thou love me?" And he said to him, "Lord, thou knowest all things, thou knowest that I love thee." He said to him, "Feed my sheep"—JOHN 21:15-17.*

6. Why is the pope the successor of St. Peter?

St. Peter was the first bishop of Rome. The man who succeeds to the See of Rome and becomes bishop of Rome, therefore becomes the successor of St. Peter, and pope.

7. What special guarantee did Christ give the apostles to help them teach in his name?

In order to help them teach in his name Christ guaranteed the apostles infallibility, i.e., he promised that they could not err in teaching his doctrine.

8. How is infallibility found in the Church?

a. The Church as a whole is infallible, that is, the entire Church will never accept a doctrine which is contrary to faith.

b. The bishops as a whole are infallible when they are gathered in an ecumenical council or when they separately all teach the same doctrine.

c. The pope speaking "ex cathedra" is infallible.

9. Where do we read in Scripture that Christ gave the apostles the promise of infallibility?

As he prepared to ascend into heaven, Christ gave to all the apostles the commission to teach, rule and sanctify in his name, saying:

I am with you all days even unto the consummation of the world—MATT. 28:20.

The words, "I am with you" always mean, in the language of Scripture, "success in your endeavor." Christ says he will be "with them" in their endeavor, which includes teaching his doctrine. This is a guarantee of success. To teach error in so important a matter would not be success, but failure.

The words, "all days even unto the consummation of the world," prove that Jesus gave this guarantee not only to the apostles but also to their successors.

10. What is meant by the infallibility of the pope?

The infallibility of the pope means that by a special protection which Jesus Christ promised to St. Peter and his successors

115

God will not permit the pope to teach error when he is speaking as pope to the whole world on matters of faith or morals.*

In making Peter the supreme pastor of his flock Christ conferred upon him infallibility in matters of faith and morals. If Peter could teach erroneous doctrines to the Church, he would actually be poisoning the flock rather than feeding it. Since Peter is the foundation and rock upon which the Church of Christ rests and has the keys by which he can allow men to enter or be excluded from the kingdom of heaven, it follows necessarily that he must be infallible.

11. Must we accept the teachings of the pope even when he does not explicitly use his infallible authority?

Yes. We must accept the teaching of the pope at all times. When the pope speaks he is giving the ordinary teaching of the Church. This teaching is found in papal decrees and encyclicals. We must not only show outward compliance, but also give internal assent, at least out of obedience to the teaching Church.

> Nor must it be thought that what is expounded in encyclical letters does not of itself demand consent, since in writing such letters the popes do not exercise the supreme power of their teaching authority. For these matters are taught with the ordinary teaching authority, of which it is true to say: "He who heareth you, heareth me"; and generally what is expounded and inculcated in encyclical letters already for other reasons appertains to Catholic doctrine. But if the supreme pontiffs in their official documents purposely pass judgment on a matter up to that time under dispute, it is obvious that that matter, according to the mind and will of the same pontiffs, cannot be any longer considered a ques-

---

* Infallibility must not be confused with inspiration. The writers of Scripture were inspired to write what they wrote by God himself. Infallibility is rather a negative thing—consisting of a protection which prevents the pope from defining as an article of faith something which was not taught by the apostles. The public revelation of God ceased with the death of the last apostle. Nothing new will be revealed to mankind as a whole. Papal infallibility merely assures that the revelation given to the world by Christ will come down to all generations undistorted and entire. Although nothing new has been revealed to the whole world since the death of the last apostle, there is, of course, an "evolution of dogma." This means that, through study by theologians, more and more can be brought to light which is contained in that revelation. Neither does infallibility mean that the pope cannot sin nor make a mistake in judgment.

tion open to discussion among theologians—Enc. Humani Generis 20.

Liturgy

On the great feast of Pentecost we celebrate the manifestation of the birth of the Church, the coming of the Holy Spirit. In the liturgy of Pentecost Sunday the Church prays for a new outpouring of the Holy Spirit, an increase of his gifts.

Send forth thy Spirit, and they shall be created and thou shall renew the face of the earth. Alleluia. Come, O Holy Spirit, fill the hearts of thy faithful, and kindle in them the fire of thy love—Alleluia verse.

The Pentecost cycle, the longest of the liturgical year, lasts until the beginning of Advent. During this season we are urged by the liturgy to live the life of grace. The Epistles of the Masses for the Sundays after Pentecost give us directions for the development of the interior life; the Gospels show us Christ teaching and manifesting himself to the people.

Practice

▶ The oldest Christian profession of faith, one which comes down to us from the time of the apostles, is the Apostles' Creed:

I believe in God, the Father Almighty, Creator of heaven and earth. And in Jesus Christ, his only Son, our Lord: who was conceived by the Holy Ghost, born of the Virgin Mary, suffered under Pontius Pilate, was crucified, died and was buried; he descended into hell; the third day he rose again from the dead; he ascended into heaven, sitteth at the right hand of God the Father Almighty. From thence he shall come to judge the living and the dead. I believe in the Holy Ghost, the Holy Catholic Church, the Communion of Saints, the forgiveness of sins, the resurrection of the body, and life everlasting. Amen.

Memorize the Apostles' Creed, and say it frequently as a profession of faith.

117

| # The Sources of Revelation, Tradition and Scripture

But an angel of the Lord spoke to Philip, saying, "Arise and go south to the road that goes down from Jerusalem to Gaza." (This road is desert.) And he arose and went. And behold, an Ethiopian, a eunuch, a minister of Candace, queen of Ethiopia, who was in charge of all her treasures, had come to Jerusalem to worship and was returning, sitting in his carriage and reading the prophet Isaias. And the Spirit said to Philip, "Go near and keep close to this carriage." And Philip, running up, heard him reading the prophet Isaias, and he said, "Dost thou then understand what thou art reading?" But he said, "Why, how can I, unless someone shows me?" and he asked Philip to get up and sit with him.

Now the passage of Scripture which he was reading was this: *"He was led like a sheep to slaughter; and just as a lamb dumb before its shearer, so did he not open his mouth.*

In humiliation his judgment was denied him;
Who shall declare his generation?
for his life is taken from the earth."

And the eunuch answered Philip and said, "I pray thee, of whom is the prophet saying this? Of himself or of someone else?"

Then Philip opened his mouth and, beginning from this Scripture, preached Jesus to him. *And as they went along the road, they came to some water; and the eunuch said, "See, here is water; what is there to prevent my being baptized?" And Philip said, "If thou dost believe with all thy heart, thou mayest." And he answered, and said, "I believe Jesus Christ to be the Son of God." And he ordered the carriage to stop; and both Philip and the eunuch went down into the water, and he baptized him. But when they came out of the water, the Spirit of the Lord took Philip away, and the eunuch saw him no more, but he went on his way rejoicing*—ACTS 8:26-39.

JESUS CHRIST spent his life on earth teaching the truths which lead men to eternal life. Although only a relatively few heard his voice, his message was meant for all men. Christ relied upon the apostles, the first bishops of the Church, to bring his teachings to the whole world. It was they and their successors whom he empowered to teach his word. Even the early successors of the apostles had no written account of the teachings of Jesus Christ. The various parts of the New Testament were written at different times and were not assembled until the end of the second century. It was not until the end of the fourth century that the Church officially declared which books belonged to the New Testament. From the beginning, therefore, there were two sources of revelation, the sacred books of the Jews—the Old Testament, the written word of God—and the oral teachings of the apostles and their successors, called tradition. Later, as the New Testament came to be written, the written source of revelation was, of course, greatly enriched.

There are, therefore, two sources of revelation, the Bible and tradition. It is the same Holy Spirit who speaks to us through each source. Never for a moment was it expected that the written tradition was to be interpreted apart from the living teachings of the apostles and their successors, the pope and the bishops of the Catholic Church.

1. What is tradition?

Tradition is the handing down of revealed truths by word of mouth. Christ commanded the apostles to go and *teach* all nations. This they did. The Gospel was *preached* before there were any written Gospels. St. Paul says, "Faith then depends on hearing . . ."—ROM. 10:17. and . . . "So then, brethren, stand firm, and hold the teachings that you have learned, whether by word or by letter of ours"—2 THESS. 2:15.

2. Is there any written record of oral tradition?

Yes. The truths of oral tradition have found their way into books. The written records of tradition can be found in the decrees of popes and councils, in the liturgy, and in the writings of the fathers and doctors of the Church.

3. Who are the fathers and doctors of the Church?

The fathers of the Church are certain writers of the early centuries of Christianity who were characterized by orthodoxy of doctrine and holiness of life.

St. Hilary, St. Athanasius and St. Augustine are examples of the fathers. St. Gregory the Great, who died in 604 A.D. is generally considered to be the last of the fathers in the Western Church, St. John Damascene, who died about the middle of the eighth century, the last in the Eastern Church.

The doctors of the Church are theologians and teachers of later centuries who possess the same qualities, orthodoxy and holiness. St. Thomas Aquinas, who lived in the 13th century, is considered by many the greatest of the doctors.

4. What is the Bible?

The Bible is the written word of God. It is made up of a collection of books written at various times by different men who wrote under God's inspiration. The real author of the Bible is God himself, since it was he who inspired the authors of the various books.

5. How is the Bible divided?

There are two main divisions of the Bible—the Old Testament and the New Testament.

The Old Testament is the collection of inspired writings which comprise the sacred books of the Jewish religion. (For fuller treatment of the Old Testament—cf. pp. 43-49.)

The New Testament is a collection of inspired writings which were written in apostolic times after the ascension of Christ into heaven. The New Testament is composed of:

a. Four Gospels, i.e., accounts of the life of Jesus, which embody many of his words and teachings. The first three Gospels, written by Sts. Matthew, Mark and Luke, treat mostly of the same incidents in the life of Christ. The fourth Gospel, that of St. John, was written expressly to prove the divinity of Christ.

b. The Acts of the Apostles, a history of the early Church, written by St. Luke.

c. Twenty-one letters, called Epistles, written by various apostles—fourteen by St. Paul, three by St. John, two by St. Peter, one by St. James and one by St. Jude.

d. The Apocalypse (Revelations) a book of prophecy, written by St. John.

6. Is the entire revelation which Jesus Christ gave to the apostles contained in the New Testament?

No. The New Testament contains most of the teachings of Christ, but not all of them. The Gospel according to St. John was written to supplement the other three Gospels. Most of the incidents narrated in St. John's Gospel are not to be found in the other three. Yet St. John concludes his Gospel with these words:

> There are, however, many other things that Jesus did; but if every one of these should be written, not even the world itself, I think, could hold the books that would have to be written. Amen—JOHN 21:25.

The entire revelation of Jesus Christ is found in the teachings of the Catholic Church, which draws on both Scripture and tradition.

7. When were the books of the New Testament assembled?

The work of assembling the writings of the New Testament was not completed until about 150 A.D. Until that time the Church in different cities had various parts of the New Testament. St. Paul's Epistle to the Romans was in Rome, that to the Corinthians in Corinth, etc. Gradually, copies were made of these various books and sent to the Church throughout the world.

8. How do we know which writings belong in the Bible?

By the end of the second century the books of the New Testament had all been gathered together. In the year 397 A.D., the bishops of northern Africa came together in Carthage and drew up a list of the true books of the Bible. This list was sent to Rome and approved by the pope. At this time other books, which had been considered by some to have a sacred character, were set aside as not belonging to the Holy Scriptures.

Thus it is to the infallible teaching authority of the Church that we must appeal for proof of the makeup of Holy Scripture and of the fact of its inspiration.

9. How is the Bible to be interpreted?

The Bible is to be interpreted in the light of the teachings of the Catholic Church. This does not mean, of course, that we should be afraid to read the Bible privately. Anyone who knows and believes the teachings of the Church will interpret the Bible as the Church does.

10. Why are Catholics allowed to read only those editions of the Bible approved by the Church?

Our Lord has given the Church the commission to teach all nations. The Church, then, is the custodian of the word of God. She alone has the right to interpret the Bible and to make sure that the editions her children read contain no error.

Some people have the mistaken notion that there were no bibles in the language of the people before the time of Martin Luther. Actually, before the time of Luther, there were printed in Europe one hundred and thirty-four Latin editions of the whole Bible, fifteen German editions, thirteen Italian editions, eleven French, two Bohemian, one Dutch, and one Spanish edition, a total of one hundred and seventy-seven editions of the whole Bible, all approved by the Church. The first Protestant Bible was produced by Luther in 1534.

11. What is the difference between Catholic and Protestant bibles?

The difference consists mainly in the fact that Protestant bibles do not contain all the books which the Church teaches are inspired. It is true that differences in translation are to be found, but these are also to be found in the various editions of Catholic bibles.

Practice

▶ The Acts of the Apostles gives us the history of the Church in the earliest days. In this book of Scripture we read of the struggles and the triumphs of the apostles and the other early Christians. In it, too, we see how the Holy Spirit guided the Church in the earliest days, even as he does today.

Read the Acts of the Apostles, all 28 chapters, just as you would read any other short book.

section **18** | **The Church Is Catholic**

All power in heaven and on earth has been given to me. Go, therefore, and make disciples of all nations, baptizing them in the name of the Father, and of the Son, and of the Holy Spirit, teaching them to observe all that I have commanded you; and behold, I am with you all days, even unto the consummation of the world—MATT. 28-18-20.

IN THE Old Testament the people of God were the people of only one nation, Israel. Even though God wills the salvation of all men, in the Old Law he made his covenant only with the Jews. With the coming of the Redeemer, however, the kingdom was extended to include the whole world. The covenant Christ made on Calvary was with all mankind.

The Mystical Body of Christ is not confined in its membership to only one race, only one nation, only one class of men. Jesus Christ died for all men. All men are meant to be incorporated into his Body, the Church. The Church, therefore, is catholic (universal). Its universality is one of the essential marks by which the Body of Christ may be recognized.

1. What do we mean when we say that the Church is catholic?

We mean that the Church is for all men, having received from Christ the commission to "make disciples of all nations." The Church was catholic, therefore, even in the earliest days when she numbered only the apostles and a handful of others. True to her mission, the Church is to be found in all parts of the world and in every kind of civilization, and includes among her members all races and classes of men. She must gather within herself all mankind. She must not only make converts of all peoples. She must also transform their civilizations so as to make them truly Christian.

2. What is the mission of the Church?

The mission of the Church is clear from many Gospel texts:

Go, therefore, and make disciples of all nations
—MATT. 28:19.

Go into the whole world and preach the gospel to every creature—MARK 16:15.

. . . but you shall receive power when the Holy Spirit comes upon you, and you shall be witnesses for me in Jerusalem and in all Judea and Samaria and even to the very ends of the earth—ACTS 1:8.

And this gospel of the kingdom shall be preached in the whole world, for a witness to all nations; and then will come the end—MATT. 24:14.

The mission of the Church is as broad as the work of Christ himself. All humanity is the object of the Church's work.

3. Why does the Church send missionaries to other lands, when there are many who are not Catholic where the Church is already established?

a. The Church must be established in every country in the world. Christ told his apostles, "Go into the whole world and preach the gospel to every creature"—MARK 16:15. At present, five out of every six people in the world are not Catholics, and two out of every three are not Christians.

b. The Church is missionary because those who possess the divine life must wish to share it with others as God has so freely shared it with them. The members of the Church must be eager to spread the "good news" of salvation to all men throughout the world.

4. *How is the catholicity of the Church manifested in the world today?*

a. The Church sends missionaries—priests, brothers, sisters and lay people to pagan lands.

b. In countries where the Church is already established she continues to grow in numbers and to increase the holiness of her members.

c. In answer to the call of the popes and bishops lay people are trained in the movements of Catholic Action to apply the teachings of the Church to every phase of human life.

Part of the Church's task is to form the conscience of the individual Christian in order that he might bring the principles of Christ into the realms of education, marriage, recreation, business, etc. The layman lives in two worlds, as it were; one the spiritual (and this is the Church's direct and first care), the other the temporal (and this is the responsibility of laymen themselves). In this second field the Church merely guides and gives principles; she animates this world, but does not organize it or control it.

Catholic laymen have a part in the mission of the Church. They are not passive members of the Church. By the very fact of their membership in the Mystical Body of Christ they have a share in the apostolate of the Church. Theirs is a contribution which only a layman can make.

Practice

Pray this week that the kingdom of Christ may spread throughout the world.

. . . just as Christ also loved the Church, and delivered himself up for her, that he might sanctify her, cleansing her in the bath of water by means of the word; in order that he might present to himself the Church in all her glory, not having spot or wrinkle or any such thing, but that she might be holy and without blemish—EPH. 5:25-27.

CHRIST is the Anointed of the Lord, the Holy One of God. In his person he is holiness itself. During his life on earth his constant concern was to do the will of his Father and to impart holiness to men. But Christ was not content merely to exhort men to strive for holiness. He forgave sins; he strengthened souls; he filled men with his graces; he made men holy.

So it is, too, with the Mystical Christ. The Church is holy in itself and possesses all the means for the sanctification of men.

The history of the Church has been the history of the sanctification of the world. Not only has she preserved the holiness of Christ deep down within her; not only has she given life and holiness to her members; but to whatever extent she has been able to influence a culture or a civilization, to that extent she has elevated it, sanctified it, Christianized it. Like Christ her Head, she is often misunderstood, hated and falsely accused. But wherever there has been failure in her work of sanctifying the world, that failure has been due not to her teachings and her means of sanctification, but to a refusal on the part of the world and of her own members to heed those teachings, to avail themselves of those means.

One of the chief glories of the Church and one of the strongest evidences of her holiness is the glorious army of saints to which she has given birth. In every age of her history the Church has produced men and women of heroic sanctity. She is still

126

producing them and will go on producing them, not only canonized saints, who come to the attention of the whole world, but also holy persons whose sanctity is known only to those whose privilege it is to live and work in their company. These holy persons are the truest children of the Church, a living proof that the Body of Christ possesses and communicates the holiness of her Head.

1. What do we mean when we say that the Church is holy?

We mean that the Church, whose Head is Christ and whose Soul is the Holy Spirit, is holy and sacred in her very being.

> *The Church is called holy, because she is consecrated and dedicated to God. . . . The Church is holy because she is the Body of Christ, by whom she is sanctified, and in whose blood she is washed*—Catechism of the Council of Trent.

We mean, moreover, that the Church, as the Mystical Body, continues Christ's priestly work of sanctifying his members and the world through his teachings, the seven sacraments, the holy sacrifice of the Mass and the sacramentals.

2. Besides the Mass, the sacraments and the sacramentals, what other means does the Church offer for the sanctification of men?

a. The teachings of the Church are a powerful means of sanctification. The Church gives us the recipe for holiness in her doctrine. Anyone who lives according to the teachings of the Church is bound to lead a holy life.

b. The examples of holiness which the Church holds out to us provide an incentive for imitation. In every age there have been great saints whom the Church presents to us as models.

c. In addition to liturgical services Catholic parishes conduct devotions which are an added means of sanctification.

d. The laws of the Church, also, are a means of sanctification, because they oblige us to perform necessary acts of worship, penance and mortification, which we might otherwise neglect. This is why the Church obliges us to assist at Mass on certain days, to fast and abstain at certain times, and to receive the sacraments of Penance and the Eucharist at least once a year.

> *Those who fear the* Lord *seek to please him,*
> *those who love him are filled with his law.*
> *Those who fear the* Lord *prepare their hearts*
> *and humble themselves before him*—Sir. 2:16-17.

e. The religious orders and apostolic movements within the Church provide a way of life which leads to holiness.

The Church has always held up as the ideal the evangelical counsels of poverty, chastity and obedience. Men and women who belong to religious orders take vows which bind them in a special way to the practice of these virtues. In the Church, too, there are many apostolic movements for lay people, movements which have as one of their ends the sanctification of their members.

3. How has the holiness of the Church imprinted itself upon the world?

The Church transformed pagan civilization. It was her teaching and influence which brought about the eventual disappearance of slavery, a new respect for women, marriage and virginity, and a spirit of mercy and compassion for the poor, the sick and the aged.

Today, when pagan thinking has invaded every sphere of life, the Church refuses to yield to demands that she modify the teachings of God on marriage and birth control. Thus she protects the family and society in an age in which powerful forces are attempting to destroy them.

4. Is the Church free from faults?

The Church is free from faults in its Head, who is Christ and in its Soul, who is the Holy Spirit. But in its members the Church is not free from faults. Its members are men, who even though made holy by grace and fortified by the sacraments, still have human faults and weaknesses.

5. How is the Church perfect in its Head and Soul?

Because the Church is Christ it cannot fail to teach the doctrines of Christ, undiluted and undistorted, with infallible

128

correctness in every age, even though the men who teach these doctrines are imperfect human beings.

Because the Church is Christ it cannot fail to bring holiness to men through the sacraments and the sacrifice of the Mass, even though the men who administer these holy things are frail human beings.

6. Should we not expect perfection in the members of the Church also?

It would be unrealistic to expect that all members of the Church measure up to what the Church desires to make of them.

Christ, in taking a human body, did not dispense it from the weaknesses which are natural to a human body, the need for sleep, food, etc. He made himself subject to suffering and death. Nor did Christ, in taking to himself his Mystical Body, dispense it from the weaknesses which are natural to a body whose members are men.

> *And if at times there appears in the Church something that points to the weakness of our human nature, put it down not to the juridical constitution, but rather to that regrettable inclination to evil found in everyone, which its divine founder permits even at times in the most exalted members of his Mystical Body, for the purpose of testing the virtue of flock and shepherds, and that all may increase the merit of their Christian faith. For, as We said above, Christ did not wish to exclude sinners from his Church; hence if some members of the Church are spiritually ill, that is no reason why we should lessen our love for the Church, but rather a reason why we should increase our devotion to her members. Oh, the loving Mother is spotless in the sacraments, by which she gives birth to her children and nourishes them, she is spotless in the faith, which she has preserved inviolate always, in her sacred laws imposed on all, in the evangelical counsels which she recommends, in those heavenly gifts and extraordinary graces through which, with inexhaustible fecundity, she generates hosts of martyrs, virgins and confessors.*
>
> *But it cannot be laid to her charge if some members fall weak or wounded. In their name she prays to God daily: "Forgive us our trespasses"; and with the brave heart of a mother turns at once to nurse them back to spiritual health.*

When therefore we call the Body of Jesus Christ "mystical," we hear a solemn warning in the very significance of the word. It is a warning that echoes these words of St. Leo: "Recognize, O Christian, your dignity, and being made a sharer of the divine nature, go not back to your former worthlessness along the way of unseemly conduct. Keep in mind of what Head and of what Body you are a member"

—Enc. on the Mystical Body, 66.

Liturgy

The liturgical season of Lent is the time of the year when the Church lays particular stress on fasting and penitential prayer. Lent is a period of forty days set aside by the Church as a preparation for Easter. If we would rise with Christ to a new life of holiness on Easter we must die to sin, must practice mortification and self-denial. The Church obliges us to fast during Lent; she also urges us to abstain from amusements and entertainments, and to deepen our prayer-life. All the liturgical services during Lent are full of encouragement and inspiration for those who are trying to keep the spirit of the season. The chants and readings in the Mass and the office extol the merits of fasting and penance. Later, as Lent deepens into Passiontide, the suffering Saviour himself speaks to us, inviting us to suffer with him. Passiontide reaches its climax in Holy Week, when we re-live the awful suffering and death of Christ.

section 20 | # Mary, the Mother of Christ and the Church

Now there were standing by the cross of Jesus his mother and his mother's sister, Mary of Cleophas, and Mary Magdalene. When Jesus, therefore, saw his mother and the disciple standing by, whom he loved, he said to his mother, "Woman, behold thy son." Then he said to the disciple, "Behold thy mother." And from that hour the disciple took her into his home—JOHN 19:25-27.

WITH THESE WORDS, "Behold thy son— behold thy mother," Jesus was not merely providing for the care of his mother. He was explicitly confirming Mary's position as spiritual mother of the whole human race. Her right to that title was won at the moment she conceived the Son of God in her virginal womb. It had been through a woman that sin had entered the world, when Eve tempted Adam to sin. Christ, the new Adam, who brought redemption to the world, chose to come into the world through a woman. Mary, therefore, is the new Eve, the spiritual mother of mankind.

It was Mary whom the Father chose to be the mother of his Son. But Mary's work did not end even with this most exalted of roles. God chose, also, to use her cooperation in the work of redeeming us. As she stood at the foot of the cross Mary was not merely a mother suffering the agony of seeing her beloved Son die. She, as the new Eve, had to offer him, as he was offering himself, for the sins of men. God required of her that she freely and whole-heartedly join in the sacrifice of her Son. And, as always, she complied perfectly with the will of God. Thus, Mary not only gave Christ to the world, she also gave him back to his Father, receiving in exchange the whole sinful race which had been the cause of his death. By this heroic act of surrender Mary received an added right to the title Mother of Man, Mother of the Mystical Body of Christ.

1. What is the place of Mary in the Mystical Body of Christ?

Mary, as the mother of Christ, is the mother of the Mystical Body of Christ.

2. Why does our Lady merit the title, Mother of the Mystical Body of Christ?

This title, as well as most of Mary's other titles, stems from three basic facts:

a. It was she from whom the Second Divine Person took his human nature. She is the mother of Christ, our brother, and therefore the mother of all men.

b. By her complete identification with and acceptance of the offering Christ made of himself on the cross Mary cooperated in our redemption, thereby acquiring an added right to the title of mother of all men.

c. All the graces which Christ won for us by his death on the cross and which he as Head applies to the members of his Mystical Body are distributed through her maternal intercession.

3. What other titles of our Lady stem from these three facts?

Mary is called "Queen of Heaven and Earth."

Certainly, in the full and strict meaning of the term, only Jesus Christ, the God-Man, is king; but Mary, too, as mother of the divine Christ, as his associate in the redemption, in his struggle with his enemies and his final victory over them, has a share, though in a limited analogous way, in his royal dignity—Enc. on the Queenship of Mary.

She is also called "Co-Redemptrix."

Thus she who corporally was the mother of our Head, through the added title of pain and glory became spiritually the mother of all his members. She it was who through her powerful prayers obtained the grace that the Spirit of our Divine Redeemer, already given to the Church on the cross, should be bestowed through miraculous gifts on the newly founded hierarchy on Pentecost. Bearing with courage and confidence the tremendous burden of her sorrows and desolation, truly the Queen of Martyrs, she more than all the faithful "filled up those things that are wanting of the suffering of Christ . . . for His Body, which is the Church;" and she continues to show for the Mystical Body of Christ, born from the pierced heart of the Saviour, the same mother's care and ardent love with which she clasped the Infant Jesus to her warm and nourishing breast

—Enc. on the Mystical Body, 128.

She is also called "Mediatrix of All Graces."

For from her union with Christ she attains a radiant eminence transcending that of any other creature; from her union with Christ she receives the royal right to dispose of the treasures of the Divine Redeemer's kingdom; from her union with Christ, finally, is derived the inexhaustible efficacy of her maternal intercession before the Son and his Father. . . .

For if through his humanity the Divine Word performs miracles and gives graces, if he uses his sacraments and saints as instruments for the salvation of men, why should he not make use of the role and the work of his most holy mother in imparting to us the fruits of the redemption?

—Enc. on the Queenship of Mary.

4. Why do we call Mary, the Mother of God?

Mary is the Mother of God because it was from her that the Second Divine Person took his human nature. Mary gave to Jesus what every mother gives her child. But the Person who is her son is not a human person but a Divine Person. The Person whose mother she is is God; therefore she is, in very fact, the Mother of God.

5. What do we mean by the Immaculate Conception?

By the Immaculate Conception we mean that, by a privilege which was granted to no other human being, our Lady was preserved from original sin from the very first instant of her conception in the womb of her mother.

We declare, pronounce and define that the Most Blessed Virgin Mary, at the first instant of her conception was preserved immaculate from all stain of original sin, by the singular grace and privilege of the omnipotent God, in virtue of the merits of Jesus Christ, the Saviour of mankind,

and that this doctrine was revealed by God, and therefore, must be believed firmly and constantly by all the faithful
—Bull, INEFFABILIS DEI, Pius IX, Dec. 8, 1854.

6. What is meant by the Assumption of our Lady?

By the Assumption of our Lady is meant that Mary was taken, body and soul, into heaven. God did not allow the body from which his Son took his body to suffer corruption, the fate of all those who have been affected by original sin.

We pronounce, declare and define it to be a divinely revealed dogma that the immaculate Mother of God, the ever virgin Mary, having completed the course of her earthly life, was assumed body and soul into heavenly glory

—Apostolic Constitution, Munificentissimus Deus, Pius XII, Nov. 1, 1950.

Devotion

The devotion to our Lady which is especially dear to her and to her children is the one which is called the rosary. It is predominantly a mental prayer, a meditation on various mysteries in the life of our Lord and our Lady. The Hail Marys which we recite as we meditate on the mysteries in saying the rosary are meant to be a sort of chant in the background. In other words, while we say the various decades of the rosary we should attend to the mystery we are contemplating rather than to the words of the Hail Mary.

The entire rosary is composed of fifteen decades, a decade here means a series of ten beads, corresponding to fifteen mysteries. The five decade rosaries which one commonly sees are really one-third of the rosary itself.

The mysteries on which we meditate in the rosary are divided into three sets:

a. The Joyful Mysteries:

1. The Angel Gabriel announces to Mary that she is to be the Mother of God.

2. Our Blessed Lady visits her cousin Elizabeth, the mother of St. John the Baptist.

3. Our Lord is born in Bethlehem.

4. Our Lord is presented in the temple.

5. The boy Jesus is found in the temple after he had been lost for three days.

b. The Sorrowful Mysteries:

1. Our Lord suffers his agony in the garden of Gethsemani.

2. Jesus is scourged by the Roman soldiers.

3. Jesus is crowned with thorns.

4. Jesus carries his cross to Calvary.

5. Jesus is crucified.

c. The Glorious Mysteries:

1. Jesus rises from the dead.

2. Jesus ascends into heaven.

3. The Holy Spirit descends upon the infant Church.

4. Our Lady is assumed into heaven.

5. Our Lady is crowned Queen of Heaven.

The rosary begins with the recitation of the Apostles' Creed. This prayer is followed by an Our Father, three Hail Marys and the Glory Be to the Father, said on the beads preceding the decades. Each decade is preceded by an Our Father and concludes with the Glory Be to the Father. After the last decade the Hail Holy Queen is said.

> Hail, Holy Queen, Mother of mercy! our life, our sweetness, and our hope! To thee do we cry, poor banished children of Eve; to thee do we send up our sighs, mourning and weeping in this valley of tears. Turn then, most gracious advocate, thine eyes of mercy towards us; and after this our exile, show unto us the blessed fruit of thy womb, Jesus. O clement, O loving, O sweet Virgin Mary.
>
> Pray for us, O holy Mother of God.
> That we may be made worthy of the promises of Christ.

Practice

Begin the practice of saying the rosary. Make an effort to say it every day.

RECOMMENDED READING—PART III

Encyclical of Pius XII on the Mystical Body of Christ. Washington, D. C., NCWC, 10¢.

> The definitive work on the Mystical Body. Despite its official character it is not too difficult to read, and it expresses with great beauty this pivotal doctrine.

The Church and the Catholic, GUARDINI. New York, Sheed & Ward, $2.50.

> A brilliant and inspiring presentation of the real meaning of the Church. A deep book, and one which demands serious attention on the part of the reader.

The Church Today, SUHARD. Chicago, Fides, 371 pp., $4.75.

> Two pastoral letters of Cardinal Suhard, The Parish Community and Growth and Decline, both included in this book, give an inspiring picture of the Church in the modern world.

The Spirit of Catholicism, ADAM. N. Y. Image Books, 242 pp., 75¢ (paper)

> An excellent exposition of the life and history of the Church. Not easy reading, but most rewarding.

Many Are One, TRESE. Chicago, Fides, 99 pp., $1.00 (paper)

> A book on the Mystical Body which is inspiring and informative, yet easy to read.

One with Jesus, DE JAEGHER. Westminster, Md. Newman, 75¢ (paper)

> An excellent application of the doctrine of the Mystical Body to life. Easy to read.

PART IV

GROWTH IN THE DIVINE LIFE

part **IV** : *GROWTH IN THE DIVINE LIFE*

section **21** | ## The Sacred Liturgy

In obedience, therefore, to her Founder's behest, the Church prolongs the priestly mission of Jesus Christ mainly by means of the sacred liturgy. She does this in the first place at the altar, where constantly the sacrifice of the cross is re-presented and, with a single difference in the manner of its offering, renewed. She does it next by means of the sacraments, those special channels through which men are made partakers in the supernatural life. She does it finally by offering to God, all good and great, the daily tribute of her prayer of praise. "What a spectacle for heaven and earth," observes our predecessor of happy memory, Pius XI, "is not the Church at prayer! For centuries without interruption, from midnight to midnight, the divine psalmody of the inspired canticles is repeated on earth; there is no hour of the day that is not hallowed by its special liturgy; there is no stage of human life that has not its part in the thanksgiving praise, supplication and reparation of this common prayer of the Mystical Body of Christ which is his Church

—Enc. on the Sacred Liturgy 3.

THE FIRST function of the Mystical Body of Christ is to worship God. The second is to teach and sanctify her members. The third is to teach and sanctify the world. In this threefold work of the Church her liturgy plays the vital role. It is through the liturgy that Christ and his members give unceasing worship to God. It is through the liturgy that the members of Christ receive the divine life which flows from Christ, the Head. The liturgy of the Church does more than sanctify; it also teaches, teaches most effectively because it appeals to the whole man, to the heart as well as the mind.

The feasts of the Church year are more suitable for instructing people in the faith and for bringing the fullness of interior joy to their souls than the solemn expositions of the Church's teaching office

—Enc. Pius XI, on the Feast of the Kingship of Christ.

The Church's work in the world, too, stems from the liturgy. The liturgy is essentially a social thing; the inspiration, enlightenment and strength which the laity need in order to apply Christian solutions to the problems of the social order must come from the liturgy.

1. What is the sacred liturgy?

The sacred liturgy is the official public worship of God by the Mystical Body of Christ.

The sacred liturgy is the public worship which our Redeemer as Head of the Church renders to the Father as well as the worship which the community of the faithful renders to its Founder, and through him to the heavenly Father. It is, in short, the worship rendered by the Mystical Body of Christ in the entirety of its Head and members

—Enc. Pius XII, on the Sacred Liturgy 20.

2. What is included in the sacred liturgy?

The sacred liturgy includes:

    a. The eucharistic sacrifice, the Mass.

    b. The sacraments.

    c. The divine office.

    d. The sacramentals.

3. What is the divine office?

The divine office is the daily prayer of the Church. It is composed mainly of the psalms, inspired poems of the Old Testament. The office, which is recited every day by all clerics in major orders and by monks and other religious in choir, follows the cycles of the liturgical year and is divided into hours corresponding to various periods of the day and night.

The divine office, with its wealth of psalms, prayers, hymns, and readings from Scripture and the Fathers is a great treasure. The laity, although not officially deputed to pray the Office, may say part or all of the Church's daily prayer with great profit to themselves. Vernacular translations of the various hours are easily obtainable.

4. What is the liturgical year?

The liturgical year is the means by which the Church re-lives the life of Christ, her Head, by celebrating throughout the year the mysteries of his life, death and resurrection.

> *Throughout the entire year, the Mass and the divine office center especially around the person of Jesus Christ. This arrangement is so suitably disposed that our Saviour dominates the scene in the mysteries of his humiliation, of his redemption and triumph*—Enc. on the Sacred Liturgy 151.

5. How does the Church teach and sanctify us during the liturgical year?

Throughout the liturgical year the Church not only presents to us the mysteries of Jesus Christ, she strives to make us take part in them and thereby share more fully in the life of Christ, our Head.

> *While the sacred liturgy calls to mind the mysteries of Jesus Christ, it strives to make all believers take their part in them so that the divine Head of the Mystical Body may live in all the members with the fullness of his holiness*
>
> —Enc. on the Sacred Liturgy 152.

In the period of *Advent* the Church arouses in us the consciousness of our sins and urges us to long for a deeper union with God through prayer and mortification.

At *Christmas* she brings us to the stable at Bethlehem and there teaches us that we must be born again and undergo a complete reformation by being more intimately united to the Word of God made man.

At the solemnity of the *Epiphany*, in putting before us the call of the gentiles to the Christian faith, she exhorts us to give thanks for the blessings of the faith and to seek a deeper faith through prayer and meditation.

During the days of *Septuagesima* and *Lent* the Church strives to make us consider our misery, so that we may amend our lives, detest our sins and expiate them by prayer and penance.

In *Holy Week*, when the sufferings of Christ are put before us by the liturgy, the Church invites us to follow in the blood-stained footsteps of our Lord, to carry the cross willingly with him, to reproduce in our hearts the spirit of atonement and to die together with him.

At the *Easter Season,* which commemorates the triumph of our Saviour, the Church reminds us that we should rise with him from our cold and slothful life to one of greater fervor and holiness, aspiring only to the things of heaven.

During the time of *Pentecost* the Church urges us to be more docile to the action of the Holy Spirit, so that we may become holy as Christ and his Father are holy.

During the course of the liturgical year besides the mysteries of Jesus Christ the feasts of the saints are celebrated. Even though these feasts are of a lower and subordinate order, the Church strives to put before us examples of sanctity in order to move us to cultivate in ourselves the virtues of Christ—cf. Enc. on the Sacred Liturgy, 154-166.

✠　　　✠

section 22 | # The Mass, the Christian Sacrifice

Christ the Lord, Eternal Priest according to the order of Melchisedech, loving his own who were in the world, at the last supper, on the night he was betrayed, wishing to leave his beloved spouse, the Church, a visible sacrifice, such as the nature of men requires, that would represent the bloody sacrifice offered once on the cross, and perpetuate its memory to the end of time, and whose salutary virtue might be applied in remitting those sins which we daily commit, . . . offered his body and blood under the species of bread and wine to God the Father, and under the same species allowed the apostles, whom he at that time constituted the priests of the New Testament, to partake thereof; commanding them and their successors in the priesthood to make the same offering—Enc. on the Sacred Liturgy 67.

As LOVING children we long to offer gifts to God, our Father. But what gift can we find which would be worthy to offer to the Almighty? The food we eat, the clothes we wear, our most precious possessions, even our very lives are his already. Moreover, we were once disinherited children of God, a fallen race, estranged from our Father by sin. Men before the time of Christ longed to offer gifts to God; but all they could offer were the fruits of the land and the beasts of the field. How could these gifts atone for sin? The priests, too, who offered these gifts in the name of the people were members of the same fallen race. There was no gift worthy to be offered to God. There was no priest worthy to offer a gift to God. Yet God did accept the offerings made by his people in the Old Testament. He was pleased to accept these offerings because they foreshadowed the perfect gift which would one day be offered to him by the perfect priest, the gift of Christ himself which his Son, as priest, would offer to him on the cross.

Christ offered himself to his Father once on the cross. He continues to offer himself, day after day, minute after minute in that re-offering of his sacrifice of Calvary in which we now have a part, the eucharistic sacrifice of the Mass.

> . . . by baptism men are plunged into the paschal mystery of Christ: they die with Him, are buried with Him, and rise with Him; they receive the spirit of adoption as sons "in which we cry: Abba, Father" (Rom. 8:15), and thus become true adorers whom the Father seeks. In like manner, as often as they eat the supper of the Lord they proclaim the death of the Lord until He comes. For that reason, on the very day of Pentecost, when the Church appeared before the world, "those who received the word" of Peter "were baptized." And "they continued steadfastly in the teaching of the apostles and in the communion of the breaking of bread and in prayers . . . praising God and being in favor with all the people" (Acts 2:41-47). From that time onwards the Church has never failed to come together to celebrate the paschal mystery: reading those things "which were in all the scriptures con-

cerning him" (Luke 24:27), *celebrating the Eucharist in which "the victory and triumph of his death are again made present", and at the same time giving thanks "to God for his unspeakable gift" (2 Cor. 9:15) in Christ Jesus, "in praise of his glory" (Eph. 1:12), through the power of the Holy Spirit.*

—Constitution on the Sacred Liturgy 6

1. What is sacrifice?

Sacrifice is the public offering of a gift to God. It requires: a priest, who makes the offering, and a gift, which is called the "victim." It often includes, also, the eating of the gift as a sign of participation and unity among those who make the offering.

2. Why do we offer gifts to God?

We offer gifts to God in an attempt to give ourselves to him. The gift we offer represents us. We offer it as a sign that we acknowledge God's supreme ownership of us and of all things.

3. What was the perfect offering which was made to God?

The perfect offering which was made to God was the offering which Jesus Christ made when he offered himself to the Father in perfect love and obedience.

4. When did Jesus Christ offer Himself to the Father?

Jesus Christ offered himself to the Father as he died on the cross. He began that offering by offering himself in a sacrifical meal at the Last Supper.

5. What was the significance of the Last Supper?

The Last Supper was the living memorial of the death and resurrection of Christ. At the Last Supper Jesus told the apostles that they were to celebrate this sacrificial meal in memory of him. This we do in the Mass. The Mass in the re-offering of that sacrificial meal which makes Christ's death and resurrection present again among us.

144

"At the Last Supper, on the night when He was betrayed, our Savior instituted the Eucharistic sacrifice of His body and blood. He did this in order to perpetuate the Sacrifice of the Cross throughout the centuries until He should come again, and so to entrust to His beloved spouse, the Church, a memorial of His death and resurrection: a Sacrament of love, a sign of unity, a bond of charity, a Paschal Banquet in which Christ is eaten, the mind is filled with grace, and a pledge of future glory is given to us."

—Constitution on the Sacred Liturgy 47

6. How are the Last Supper and the Mass the fulfillment of the ancient Jewish Passover?

The Passover was the meal which celebrated the covenant which God had made with the Israelites through Moses on Mt. Sinai. The Last Supper and its re-offering, the Mass, celebrate the new, perfect and everlasting covenant which God made with mankind through Christ, that covenant which was sealed in the blood of Christ as he died on the cross.

7. What did the death of Christ as a sacrifice accomplish?

a. It gave infinite worship to God.

b. It redeemed us by atoning for our sins, thereby restoring divine life to the human race.

c. It gave perfect thanks to God for all his favors to man.

8. Why is the Mass called the Eucharistic celebration?

The word "eucharist" means "thanksgiving". The Mass is the great act of praise and thanksgiving which Christ and the whole Church offer in loving thankfulness to God for the saving death and resurrection of Christ.

145

Practice

1. We should take our full part in the Eucharistic Celebration by enacting fully the role which is ours in the Mass.

Mother Church earnestly desires that all the faithful should be led to that full, conscious, and active participation in liturgical celebrations which is demanded by the very nature of the liturgy. Such participation by the Christian people as "a chosen race, a royal priesthood, a holy nation, a redeemed people" (1 Pet. 2:9; cf. 2:4-5), is their right and duty by reason of their baptism.

In the restoration and promotion of the sacred liturgy, this full and active participation by all the people is the aim to be considered before all else; for it is the primary and indispensable source from which the faithful are to derive the true Christian spirit;—Constitution on the Sacred Liturgy 11

a. Readers, commentators and leaders of song fulfill their role by performing these functions reverently and carefully.

Servers, lectors, commentators, and members of the choir also exercise a genuine liturgical function. They ought, therefore, to discharge their office with the sincere piety and decorum demanded by so exalted a ministry and rightly expected of them by God's people.

Consequently they must all be deeply imbued with the spirit of the liturgy, each in his own measure, and they must be trained to perform their functions in a correct and orderly manner. —Constitution on the Sacred Liturgy 29

b. The congregation performs its role by listening to the readings and the homily with a mind and heart open to the Holy Spirit and by saying and singing their parts of the Mass together in a spirit of prayer.

N.B. 1. We should *listen* to the Scripture readings rather than read them in our missal as they are being read to us.

146

To promote active participation, the people should be encouraged to take part by means of acclamations, responses, psalmody, antiphons, and songs, as well as by actions, gestures, and bodily attitudes. And at the proper times all should observe a reverent silence.

—Constitution on the Sacred Liturgy 30

2. The most basic and important participation in the Eucharistic celebration is taking part in the Eucharistic meal, Holy Communion. We should always take part in Communion at Mass. We should do so with the realization that we are partaking of a family meal as members of God's great family, who are united into one by Christ.

The Church, therefore, earnestly desires that Christ's faithful, when present at this mystery of faith, should not be there as strangers or silent spectators; on the contrary, through a good understanding of the rites and prayers they should take part in the sacred action conscious of what they are doing, with devotion and full collaboration. They should be instructed by God's word and be nourished at the table of the Lord's body; they should give thanks to God; by offering the Immaculate Victim, not only through the hands of the priest, but also with him, they should learn also to offer themselves; through Christ the Mediator, they should be drawn day by day into ever more perfect union with God and with each other, so that finally God may be all in all.

—Constitution on the Sacred Liturgy 48

3. We should realize that we pray when we sing, not only when we speak words. We should sing the hymn which is sung at Communion time in a spirit of true prayer, rather than saying private prayers silently at that time. We should recall the words of St. Augustine, "He who sings well prays doubly well."

The musical tradition of the universal Church is a treasure of inestimable value, greater even than that of any other art. The main reason for this pre-eminence is that, as sacred song united to the words, it forms a necessary or integral part of the solemn liturgy.

147

Holy Scripture, indeed, has bestowed praise upon sacred song, and the same may be said of the fathers of the Church and of the Roman pontiffs who in recent times, led by St. Pius X, have explained more precisely the ministerial function supplied by sacred music in the service of the Lord.

Therefore sacred music is to be considered the more holy in proportion as it is more closely connected with the liturgical action, whether it adds delight to prayer, fosters unity of minds, or confers greater solemnity upon the sacred rites. But the Church approves of all forms of true art having the needed qualities, and admits them into divine worship.

—Constitution on the Sacred Liturgy 112

section 23 | # The Structure of the Mass

EVERY IMPORTANT event requires a suitable preparation. The Mass, the most sublime act of worship, is no exception. At the Last Supper our Lord surrounded the moment of sacrifice with ceremonies, the supper itself, the washing of feet, a sermon and a hymn. The Church does likewise. In the earliest days the Mass followed the same pattern as the Last Supper. For centuries it was preceded by a meal. Later conditions brought about changes. The Mass today in the Latin rite is divided into two main parts, the Liturgy of the Word and the Liturgy of the Eucharist. The Liturgy of the Word is composed of an entrance rite, a service of Scripture reading, a homily on the Word of God from Scripture and the Prayer of the Faithful. The Liturgy of the Word prepares us for the Liturgy of the Eucharist. The Liturgy of the Eucharist is composed of three parts, the preparation and offering of gifts for the sacrifice, the sacrificial act itself and the sacrificial meal, the Eucharistic banquet.

An understanding of the ceremonies of the Mass will aid in our appreciation of the Mass itself and will enable us to participate more fully.

1. What is the origin of the Liturgy of the Word?

In the earliest days of the Church, the Mass began just as the Last Supper did, with a meal. It was celebrated in the evening in the homes of the people. Later the Mass was separated from the meal and came to be celebrated in the morning. In place of the preparatory meal there was substituted an adaption of the Jewish synagogue service, which the earliest Christians had continued to hold, at first with the Jews in the synagogue and later by themselves. This service of prayer and instruction is the basis of our present Liturgy of the Word. In the course of the centuries other parts have been added.

2. What is the structure of the Liturgy of the Word today?

The Liturgy of the Word includes the following parts:

a. The prayers at the foot of the altar: a confession of sinfulness by the priest and servers.

b. The Introit: the remnant of a psalm which was once sung by the people as the procession entered the church at the beginning of Mass on solemn occasions. Now it may be regarded as a sort of short overture setting the theme of the Mass for that day.

c. "Lord have mercy", "Christ have mercy" repeated nine times to intensify our plea for mercy.

d. The Gloria: a hymn of praise to the Holy Trinity, which is said only in Sunday and feast day Masses.

e. The Collect: a prayer of petition. The name "collect" derives from the fact that it was said in the station church, i.e., where the people assembled (collected) to form a procession to the church where the solemn Mass was to be celebrated, in the days when this custom was practiced.

f. The Lesson: (first scriptural reading). This is often called the Epistle, because usually it is a selection from one of the lettters of the apostles, called Epistles.

g. The Gradual: a chant interposed between the two readings. Sometimes other chants (Tract, Alleluia, Sequence) are added.

h. The Gospel: (second scriptural reading). Here Christ speaks to us. This is always a selection from one of the four Gospels.

i. The Homily: an instruction drawn from the Mass texts for the day.

j. The Creed: an act of faith in the word of God to which we have just listened.

k. Prayer of the Faithful: a series of petitions for the needs of the Church and the people.

3. What is the structure of the Liturgy of the Eucharist?

The Liturgy of the Eucharist is divided into three parts:

a. The Offertory: the offering of gifts as a preparation for the sacrifice at the Consecration. The Offertory was originally a procession; the people brought to the altar gifts of bread and wine, food, clothing, money, alms for the poor. At the Offertory we should realize that we are offering ourselves with the bread and wine.

The collection taken up at this time is the modern substitute for the Offertory procession. We should regard what we offer in the collection as part of the gift for the sacrifice.

b. The Canon: this, the most important part of the Mass, is introduced by a song of thanksgiving, called the Preface. During the canon, or Eucharistic prayer, Jesus offers the sacrifice of his body and blood to his Father. Once again he renews the offering he made of his life on the cross. The Consecration occurs in the center of the Canon. Everything that goes before leads up to it; everything that follows leads away from it.**

** Immediately after each Consecration, the priest holds Christ aloft for the adoration of the people. This action is called the "elevation." Because it is such a prominent gesture, this moment in the Mass is sometimes taken to be the most important. Actually it is not. The all-important moment in the Mass is the Consecration. The elevation did not appear in the Mass until the eleventh century.

Before and after the moment of sacrifice the Church prays for various people, the pope, the bishops, the faithful, the living, the dead, sinners, and for the things of earth we use.

The Canon has a beautiful ending. Christ, our high priest, mediator between God and man, drawing all things to himself, presents them to his Father. "Through him, with him, and in him is to thee who art God the Father almighty, in the unity of the Holy Spirit, all honor and all glory, world without end." The people answer "Amen", which signifies their thankful commitment in faith to the act which Christ has just performed.***

c. The Communion, the sacrificial meal: the Communion service begins with the Lord's prayer. In this prayer we ask for the bread which is our Lord, and we forgive those who have offended us, as we wish God to forgive us. During the prayers which follow, the accent is on that peace which only Christ can bring.

The priest receives Communion under the appearances of both bread and wine, the people under the appearance of bread alone. After the Communion the priest says the Communion Verse, a remnant of the psalm the people used to sing as they came to receive Communion. Then follows another prayer, the Postcommunion. After this prayer the priest dismisses and blesses the people.

4. What is the importance of Communion in the Mass?

Communion is the great family meal of the people of God. It is the part of the Mass in which our union with one another and with Christ is most deeply symbolized and increased. The Mass, the Eucharistic Celebration, is a sacrifice-meal. Every member of the congregation should take part in Communion at Mass. Not to do so would be to fail to participate fully in the Mass.

*** In contrast to the practice of the Eastern rites the Canon in the Latin rite is said in silence. This practice came about because the singing of the Sanctus consumed so much time that the priest continued with the Canon instead of waiting for the choir to finish. Gradually the custom became fixed as it is today.

5. What is the language of the Mass?

In Catholic churches of the Eastern rites the Mass is celebrated in various languages. Latin is the language of the Mass in the Roman rite, but a suitable place is also allowed for the vernacular, the language which the people speak.

6. Which parts of the Mass of the Roman rite are said or sung in the vernacular?

In the Roman rite Mass those parts are said or sung in the vernacular which are addressed to the people or said by the people, e.g., the Scripture readings, most of the Entrance Rite—i.e., Entrance Song, Lord have mercy, the Gloria,—the response to the first Scripture reading, the Creed, the Prayer of the Faithful, the Offertory antiphon, the Sanctus, the Agnus Dei, the Lord's Prayer.

7. What is meant by the different roles which are fulfilled in the celebration of Mass?

By the different roles is meant the different actions and prayers which different members of the congregation perform and say during Mass.

a. The celebrant presides at the assembly. He sums up the petitions of the people in the Collect. He preaches the homily after the reading of the Gospel. He prepares the bread and wine and offers them at the Offertory. He says the great sacrificial prayer of the Mass, the Canon and the words of consecration. He leads the people in the prayers of the Communion Service.

b. The commentator assists the congregation by announcing the parts of the Mass and giving brief explanations of their meaning.

c. The readers proclaim the word of God to the whole congregation in the Scripture readings.

d. The choir assists the whole congregation in singing their parts of the Mass and provides music which helps the people to pray and meditate.

e. The people sing and say together the people's parts of the Mass.

8. *What are the different kinds of Masses?*

The different kinds of Masses are:

a. the low Mass: this is a Mass in which the priest does not sing;

b. the high Mass, or the sung Mass: this is a Mass in which the priest sings certain parts and the people or choir sing others;

c. the solemn Mass: this is a high Mass celebrated by a priest who is assisted by a deacon and a subdeacon.

9. *Why are vestments of different colors used in the Mass?*

Vestments of different colors are used to indicate the spirit of the Mass or the season of the liturgical year, e.g., during Advent and Lent violet vestments are worn, during the Christmas and Easter season white vestments, during the Pentecost season red vestments. On the Sundays after Pentecost green vestments are worn. On the feasts of other saints, our Lord and our Lady, white vestments are worn.

Practice

▶ Even while we are attending instructions we should join in the prayers of the congregation at Mass. We should learn and say the prayers which the people sing and we should learn the songs which the people sing at Mass.

'And it came to pass as he was praying in a certain place, that when he ceased, one of his disciples said to him, "Lord, teach us to pray, even as John also taught his disciples." And he said to them, "When you pray, say:

'Father, hallowed be thy name.
Thy kingdom come!
Give us this day our daily bread,
And forgive us our sins,
for we also forgive everyone who is indebted to us.
And lead us not into temptation' "—LUKE 11:1-4.

THROUGH the liturgy the Church prays to God. As members of the Mystical Body of Christ we pray with and through the Church by taking part in the liturgy.

We must also pray privately. Our response to God for all the gifts he has given us must be to converse lovingly with him through prayer and meditation. Only if we cultivate the spirit of prayer in our lives through private prayer will we be able to pray with the Church as we should in liturgical prayer and deepen our life in Christ.

There are many different ways of praying privately. We can pray by using words which someone else has composed; we can pray by speaking to God in our own words. But however and whenever we pray, we should pray as Christ taught us.

1. How should we pray?

a. "Our Father, who art in heaven . . ."

We should pray with *simplicity* and *trust,* as a child speaks to its father. We should pray with the realization that God knows and loves us individually and personally, but always mindful of the fact that we are members of the family of God, united to our brothers.

154

And as for clothing, why are you anxious? See how the lilies of the field grow; they neither toil nor spin, yet I say to you that not even Solomon in all his glory was arrayed like one of these. But if God so clothes the grass of the field, which is alive today and tomorrow is thrown into the oven, how much more you, O you of little faith!—MATT. 6:28-30.

b. "Hallowed be thy name . . ."

We should, first of all, *adore God* in our prayer. We should think of his goodness and his mercy and express our adoration and love in acts of faith, hope, love, and adoration.

More than this we need not add;
  let the last word be, he is all in all!
Let us praise him the more, since we cannot fathom him,
  for greater is he than all his works;
Awful indeed is the LORD'S majesty,
  and wonderful is his power—SIR. 43:28-30.

c. "Thy kingdom come. Thy will be done on earth as it is in heaven."

We should pray *as members of the Body of Christ,* conscious of our duty of witnessing Christ to the world and of extending his kingdom.

Even so let your light shine before men, in order that they may see your good works and give glory to your Father in heaven—MATT. 5:16.

d. "Give us this day our daily bread."

We should *ask God for the things we need,* first of all for spiritual gifts for ourselves and for others.

But seek first the kingdom of God and his justice . . .
                                                      —MATT. 6:33.

We should also ask God for the needs of everyday life and even for special favors, praying for these latter things on the condition that it is the will of God that we have them.

Ask, and it shall be given you; seek, and you shall find; knock, and it shall be opened to you. For everyone who asks, receives; and he who seeks, finds; and to him who knocks, it shall be opened. Or what man is there among you, who, if his son asks him for a loaf, will hand him a stone; or if he asks for a fish, will hand him a serpent? Therefore, if you, evil as you are, know how to give good gifts to your children, how much more will your Father in heaven give good things to those who ask him!—MATT. 7:7-11.

e. "And forgive us our trespasses as we forgive those who trespass against us."

We should pray for *forgiveness of our sins*, resolving to avoid sin in the future, and mindful of our Lord's words:

And his master, being angry, handed him over to the torturers until he should pay all that was due to him. So also my heavenly Father will do to you, if you do not each forgive your brothers from your hearts—MATT. 18:34-35.

f. "And lead us not into temptation, but deliver us from evil."

We should pray for *help in time of temptation* and for strength to avoid the occasions of sin, humbly admitting that without such help from God we would not be able to remain faithful to him.

2. What should be the qualities of our prayer?

a. We should pray with *reverence and sincerity*, remembering that it is God to whom we are speaking.

Again, when you pray, you shall not be like the hypocrites, who love to pray standing in the synagogues and at the street corners, in order that they may be seen by men. Amen I say to you, they have received their reward. But when thou prayest, go into thy room, and closing thy door, pray to thy Father in secret; and thy Father, who sees in secret, will reward thee—MATT. 6:5-6.

b. We should pray with childlike *humility* and with *confidence* that our Father will hear and answer us.

But in praying, do not multiply words, as the Gentiles do; for they think that by saying a great deal, they will be heard. So do not be like them; for your Father knows what you need before you ask him—MATT. 6:7-8.

c. We should pray with *faith* and *perseverance*, refusing to give up in discouragement because God does not seem to answer our prayer immediately.

But Jesus answered and said to them, "Have faith in God. Amen I say to you, whoever says to this mountain, 'Arise, and hurl thyself into the sea,' and does not waver in his

heart, but believes that whatever he says will be done, it shall
be done for him. Therefore I say to you, all things whatever
you ask for in prayer, believe that you shall receive, and
they shall come to you"—MARK 11:22-24.

d. We should pray with *submission* to the will of our Father,
who alone knows whether what we ask is really good for us. We
should pray as our Lord prayed: "Father . . . not as I will, but
as thou willest"—MATT. 26:39.

3. Does God always answer our prayers?

Yes. Our Lord said, "If you ask the Father anything in my
name, he will give it to you"—JOHN 16:23. Our prayers are always answered, but not always in the way we expect.

4. When should we pray?

We should pray every day:

In the morning, as we begin our day we should greet God
first of all and offer ourselves and our day to him.

In the evening before retiring we should thank God for the
blessings of the day and ask his pardon for the faults we have
committed.

Before and after meals we should ask God's blessing on the
food he has provided for us and thank him for it.

In time of temptation we should ask God for help. Frequently during the day we should elevate our hearts and minds to God
with short prayers such as, "My Jesus, mercy," "All for thee,
most Sacred Heart of Jesus," "My God I love thee."

5. To whom should we pray?

a. We should pray to God, through Christ, our mediator.
Thus the Church prays most frequently in her liturgy: to God
the Father, through Christ, in union with the Holy Spirit.

b. We should pray to each of the Divine Persons individually: e.g., we pray to the Holy Spirit for light and inspiration.

c. We should pray to our Lord Jesus Christ as man: e.g.,
we pray to the Sacred Heart as the symbol of Christ's humanity;
we pray to Christ in the Eucharist.

157

d. We should pray to the Blessed Virgin Mary, the Mother of God and our mother.

e. We should pray to the saints, to St. Joseph, Patron of the universal Church, to the saints whose names we bear, to other saints to whom we have a special devotion, and to our guardian angel.

6. With whom should we pray?

We should pray with Christ and our fellows members in Christ by participating in the public worship of the Church, the liturgy.* We should pray with others by taking part in devotions such as the way of the cross, May and October devotions, common recitation of the rosary, holy hours, etc. We should pray as families, e.g., the family rosary, grace before and after meals. We should pray by ourselves.

7. Why should we pray to the saints?

The doctrine of the Communion of Saints teaches us that there is a union between the faithful on earth, the souls in heaven and the souls in purgatory. The saints in heaven can know our needs and intercede for us with God. The souls in purgatory are unable to earn any help for themselves, but can be aided by our prayers. The faithful on earth, too, can aid one another by their prayers.

8. Why should we pray to the Blessed Virgin Mary?

We should pray to the Blessed Virgin Mary because she is the Mother of God and our mother. Our Lady intercedes with God for us at all times. God is certainly pleased when we pray to her and honor her in a special way. In honoring her we are only imitating what God himself has done, since he has blessed her above all his other creatures.

---

* The term "public prayer" is used officially for liturgical prayer (the Mass, the sacraments, the divine office). Services which are non-liturgical, such as the way of the cross and the recitation of the rosary, even when they involve a large group of people, are called "private devotions."

Liturgy

During the course of the liturgical year the feasts of the various saints are celebrated day by day. The great feasts of our Lady brighten the year, the Immaculate Conception in the midst of Advent on December 8th, the Assumption on August 15th, as well as her lesser feasts throughout the year. Special feasts of our Lord, too, are celebrated at regular times, such as the feast of Christ the King in October and the Sacred Heart in June. All the saints are honored together on November 1st, and all the souls in purgatory remembered especially on All Souls Day, November 2nd.

Practice

▶ Suggested morning prayer:

The morning offering.—cf. pg. 21.

Grace before meals:

Bless us O Lord and these thy gifts which we are about to receive from thy bounty through Christ our Lord. Amen.

Thanksgiving after meals:

We give thee thanks for all thy benefits, Almighty God, Who livest and reignest forever. May the souls of the faithful departed, through the mercy of God, rest in peace. Amen.

Suggested evening prayer:

A short examination of conscience to discover the faults we have committed during the day.

An Act of Contrition:

O my God, I am heartily sorry for having offended thee, and I detest all my sins, because of thy just punishments, but most of all because they offend thee, my God, who art all good and deserving of all my love. I firmly resolve with the help of thy grace, to sin no more and to avoid the near occasion of sin. Amen.

We should make sure now that we are acquiring the habit of daily prayer, if we have not already done so. The minimum should be:

A short offering of ourselves and our day to God, made in the morning, and a brief examination of conscience and an act of contrition at night.

We should remind ourselves again that it is highly desirable to add the rosary and grace before and after meals to our daily prayers.

section 25 | **The Sacraments**

He came, accordingly, to a town of Samaria called Sichar, near the field that Jacob gave to his son Joseph. Now Jacob's well was there. Jesus therefore, wearied as he was from the journey, was sitting at the well. It was about the sixth hour. There came a Samaritan woman to draw water.

Jesus said to her, "Give me to drink"; for his disciples had gone away into the town to buy food. The Samaritan woman therefore said to him, "How is it that thou, although thou art a Jew, does ask drink of me, who am a Samaritan woman?" For Jews do not associate with Samaritans.

Jesus answered and said to her, "If thou didst know the gift of God, and who it is who says to thee, 'Give me to drink,' thou, perhaps, wouldst have asked of him, and he would have given thee living water." The woman said to him, "Sir, thou hast nothing to draw with, and the well is deep. Whence then hast thou living water? Art thou greater than our father Jacob who gave us the well, and drank from it, himself, and his sons, and his flocks?" In answer Jesus said to her, "Everyone who drinks of this water will thirst again. He, however, who drinks of the water that I will give him

160

shall never thirst; but the water that I will give him shall become in him a fountain of water, springing up unto life everlasting—JOHN 4:5-14.

OUR LORD JESUS CHRIST is the source of the "living water," the divine life. He gives us this life and increases it within us by means of the seven channels of grace which are called the sacraments. Through the sacraments Jesus Christ unites us to himself, ever deepening our union with him, ever increasing our holiness. Through the sacraments Chirst is with us throughout our lives to provide us with all the help and strength we need to grow in the divine life. At the very beginning of our life our Lord is there to join us to his Mystical Body and give us the divine life. At the end, he is there to forgive our sins, strengthen us for our last battle with the enemy and prepare us for heaven. All throughout our lives he is there to strengthen us, to forgive us, to nourish us, and to fit us for the vocation in which we serve him in the Church.

1. What is a sacrament?

A sacrament is a sacred sign instituted by Christ to give grace.

2. How many sacraments are there?

There are seven sacraments:

Baptism, Confirmation, Penance, Holy Eucharist, Anointing of the Sick, Holy Orders and Marriage.

3. In what way are the sacraments sacred signs?

Signs are things or actions which convey an idea. A smile or a frown is a sign of one's feelings. A flag is a sign of a nation. Words are signs which convey an idea. In the sacraments the words together with the action constitute the sacred sign.

The sacraments are signs which not only communicate an idea but also produce what they signify. The sacraments not only make us aware of the divine life; they actually produce this life within us.

Water, since it is so necessary for life, can be used as a sign of life; hence water is an appropriate sign of the divine life. But in the sacrament of Baptism it not only signifies that life; it actually produces it. Oil is used to strengthen the body. In Confirmation it is used to signify the strength we receive from this sacrament and to give us that strength. Oil is also used as a medicine. In the sacrament of the Anointing of the Sick it is used both to signify and to impart health of soul and body.

The Sacrament	The Sign	
Baptism	Pouring of water	I baptize you in the name of the Father, and of the Son, and of the Holy Spirit.
Confirmation	Anointing with oil	I sign you with the sign of the cross and I confirm you with the chrism of salvation; in the name of the Father, and of the Son and of the Holy Spirit.
Penance	The confession of the sinner and the absolution of the priest	I absolve you from your sins in the name of the Father, and of the Son, and of the Holy Spirit. Amen.
Holy Eucharist	Bread and wine	This is my body; This is my blood.
Anointing of the Sick	Anointing with oil	May the Lord forgive you by this holy anointing whatever sins you have committed. Amen.
Holy Orders	The imposing of the bishop's hands	Bestow, we beseech thee, almighty Father, on this thy servant the dignity of the priesthood. Renew in his heart the spirit of holiness so that he may keep the office of second rank that he has received from you, O God, and gently reproach the conduct of others by the example of his holy life.
Marriage	The exchange of marriage vows	

4. What do we mean when we say that the sacraments were instituted by Christ?

We mean that Christ himself determined the signs to be used in the sacraments, and that the sacraments are the instruments which Christ uses here and now to produce grace in us.

5. How do we know that Christ determined the signs to be used?

There are references in the Bible to Christ's institution of Baptism, Penance, Holy Eucharist and Holy Orders. The Church infallibly teaches that he also instituted the others.

6. How does Christ act in the sacraments?

Even though it is a man who administers the sacraments, we can truthfully say that it is Christ who baptizes, Christ who confirms, Christ who forgives sin, etc. Christ acts in and through the one who administers the sacrament. This person must have power from Christ to do so, and must intend to do what Christ intends. But because the sacraments are Christ's actions the holiness of the one administering them does not essentially affect them.

All the sacraments are administered by a priest or bishop, except Marriage—and, in certain cases, Baptism.

7. Has the Church the power to change the sacraments?

No. Christ determined both the number and the essential elements of the sacraments. The Church may change only the ceremonies which she herself has added to the administration of the sacraments.

8. Do the sacraments always produce grace?

If the sacrament is properly received it will always produce grace, provided we do not place an obstacle in the way. An example of such an obstacle would be mortal sin in one who receives Confirmation, Holy Orders or Marriage. In such a case the grace which should have been given, but was impeded by the obstacle of mortal sin, will be given when the sinner repents.

9. What kind of grace do the sacraments produce?

All the sacraments produce the divine life. In addition, each sacrament gives its own particular actual graces and a right to future actual graces.

10. What part do the sacraments play in the life of the Church?

Each of the sacraments plays an indispensable part in the life of the Church. Baptism, Confirmation, Marriage and Holy Orders confer an office in the Mystical Body. Baptism makes us members of the Body and gives us a share in the priesthood of Christ. Confirmation makes us mature and responsible Christians and increases our participation in Christ's priesthood. Holy Orders confers the actual powers of the priesthood and provides for the continuation of the Church. Marriage makes a man and woman one and provides for the growth of the Body of Christ by conferring the vocation of parenthood and guaranteeing the graces which enable parents to guide the youngest members of Christ.

Anointing of the Sick restores the sick member of Christ's Body to health, so that he can re-join the other members in celebrating the Eucharist. If it is the sick person's time to die, this sacrament prepares him for entrance into the ranks of the Church Triumphant in heaven. Two other sacraments are at our disposal at all times to provide for our everyday spiritual needs; the sacrament of Penance to give us pardon for sin and strength to resist temptation, and the sacrament of the Eucharist to nourish our souls and give us an increase of the power to love God and our neighbor.

11. What other effects do the sacraments produce?

Three of the sacraments, Baptism, Confirmation and Holy Orders, produce in the soul a mark which can never be lost. This mark or character is a badge of our membership in Christ, a participation in his eternal priesthood, by which we are dedicated to sacred worship. These sacraments may be received only once.

Practical Points

1. Confirmation, Holy Eucharist, Anointing of the Sick, Holy Orders and Marriage are called sacraments of the living, because we must be in possession of the divine life, in the state of grace, in order to receive them lawfully. One who knowingly received

any of these sacraments in mortal sin would thereby commit a very serious sin of sacrilege.

2. The more faith and love we have when we receive the sacraments the more grace they will confer on us. It is true that the sacraments worthily received always give grace, even if they are received without due preparation. But it is also true that the better prepared we are to receive them the more fruitful will be our reception.

section **26** | **Baptism**

*For how shall we who are dead to sin still live in it? Do you not know that all we who have been baptized into Christ Jesus have been baptized into his death? For we were buried with him by means of Baptism into death, in order that, just as Christ has arisen from the dead through the glory of the Father, so we also may walk in newness of life. For if we have been united with him in the likeness of his death, we shall be so in the likeness of his resurrection also—*Rom. 6:2-6.

IN THE early days of the Church, people were baptized by immersion. When they entered the pool, stripped of their clothes, and were submerged in its waters, they understood that they were dying to their former sinful selves and were being buried in the waters to rise as Christ did to a new life. When they left the water they put on white garments to show that they were alive with the new life of Christ.

This practice symbolized most strikingly what our Lord does for us in Baptism. Through the waters of Baptism he washes away sin and gives us a new life in God. By Baptism Christ unites

165

us to himself and gives us the grace he merited by his life, death and resurrection.

1. What is Baptism?

Baptism is the sacrament of rebirth through which Jesus Christ gives us the divine life and joins us to his mystical body.

2. What did Christ say about the necessity for Baptism?

Speaking to Nicodemus, who came to him by night to inquire about his teaching, Our Lord told of the necessity for Baptism in these words;

> *Amen, amen, I say to thee, unless a man be born again, he cannot see the kingdom of God. . . . Amen, amen, I say to thee, unless a man be born again of water and the Spirit, he cannot enter into the kingdom of God*—JOHN 3:3-6.

3. When did Jesus Christ institute Baptism?

Jesus Christ instituted Baptism after the resurrection when he sent his apostles into the world to bring to all people the "good news" of the redemption, telling them:

> *. . . All power in heaven and on earth has been given to me. Go, therefore, and make disciples of all nations, baptizing them in the name of the Father, and of the Son, and of the Holy Spirit, teaching them to observe all that I have commanded you*—MATT. 28:18-20.

4. What does Jesus Christ accomplish in us through Baptism?

a. Christ gives us a new life, the divine life, and makes us adopted children of God. He welcomes us into a life of intimacy with the Persons of the Blessed Trinity, Father, Son and Holy Spirit.

> *Behold what manner of love the Father has bestowed upon us, that we should be called children of God; and such we are*—1 JOHN 3:1.

Along with the divine life Christ also gives us powers which enable us to act as children of God and grow in the divine life. Among these powers are faith, hope and charity.

b. Christ removes our sins.

> *. . . for sin shall not have dominion over you, since you are*

166

not under the Law but under grace—ROM. 6:14.

The grace received at Baptism remedies the "graceless" condition of the soul called original sin.

He also takes away personal sins and the punishment due to them, when the recipient is properly disposed.

c. Christ unites us to himself and to the members of his Mystical Body.

> . . . *one body and one Spirit, even as you were called in one hope of your calling; one Lord, one faith, one Baptism; one God and Father of all, who is above all, and throughout all, and in us all*—EPH. 4:4-6.

After Baptism we can no longer pray or suffer alone. When we pray we pray to a common Father in heaven, and our prayers are heard because of our union with Christ. Our sufferings have value for the entire Church. St. Paul says, "And what is lacking of the sufferings of Christ I fill up in my flesh for his body, which is the Church"—COL. 1:24.

d. Christ gives us a share in his priesthood through the baptismal character. It is by means of this sharing in Christ's priesthood that we participate in the Mass, unite our prayers and sacrifices with those of Christ, and obtain the right to receive the other sacraments.

5. *What actual graces does Christ give in Baptism?*

In Baptism Christ gives us not only the divine life; he gives us also the right to all the actual graces we will need to live a life befitting a child of God. A person newly sanctified by Baptism still retains the inclination to sin. The actual graces given in Baptism help him to overcome this inclination.

But more than that, the Christian is expected to rise above a mere observance of the law. He is expected to imitate Christ and become holy. Baptism gives us the actual graces which enable us to do this day by day.

> *Wherefore, put away lying and speak truth each one with his neighbor, because we are members of one another. "Be angry and do not sin": do not let the sun go down upon your anger: do not give place to the devil. He who was wont to steal, let him steal no longer; but rather let him labor, working with his hands at what is good, that he may have something to share with him who suffers need. Let no ill*

speech proceed from your mouth, but whatever is good for supplying what fits the current necessity, that it may give grace to the hearers. And do not grieve the Holy Spirit of God, in whom you were sealed for the day of redemption. Let all bitterness, and wrath, and indignation, and clamor, and reviling, be removed from you, along with all malice. On the contrary, be kind to one another, and merciful, generously forgiving one another, as also God in Christ has generously forgiven you—EPH. 4:25-32.

6. What is the sign used in Baptism?

The sign used in Baptism is washing with water and the saying of the words:

I baptize you in the name of the Father, and of the Son, and of the Holy Spirit.

Water is a most appropriate symbol of the effects of Baptism.

a. Water is used for cleansing. The flowing waters of Baptism symbolize the cleansing of the soul of sin.

b. Water is also life-giving. Irrigation makes a desert bloom. In the book of Genesis water is described as one of the elements from which the life of the world came.

In the beginning God created the heavens and the earth; the earth was waste and void; darkness covered the abyss, and the spirit of God was stirring above the waters
—GEN. 1:1-2.

7. Who administers the sacrament of Baptism?

Baptism normally is administered by a priest. In case of necessity, however, anyone can baptize, even an unbeliever, provided he performs the actions, says the proper words and has the intention of doing what Christ intends.

8. Is Baptism the only way of receiving the divine life for the first time?

Baptism is the normal way of receiving the divine life. But the mercy and love of Christ is so great that he gives the divine life in an extraordinary manner whenever a person, through no fault of his own, cannot receive Baptism.

a. One who has sorrow for his sins out of love of God and

sincerely desires Baptism, receives the divine life by virtue of his desire.

b. One who does not know of the necessity of Baptism but who has such sorrow and desires to do the will of God receives the divine life by virtue of his implicit desire for Baptism.

c. An unbaptized person who gives his life for his belief in God is baptized, as it were, in his own blood, thereby receiving the divine life.

9. *What happens to unbaptized infants?*

As far as we know, the only way in which an infant can receive the divine life is through Baptism. An infant who dies without Baptism, therefore, is unable to reach heaven. On the other hand, being without personal sin, he is not liable to hell. The usual explanation of theologians is that such an infant goes to a place of natural happiness, called limbo.

The salvation of one who does not have the use of reason depends upon the efforts of others. Therefore, parents have a serious obligation to see that their children are baptized soon after birth.

10. *Why does it sometimes happen that a person who had been baptized a Protestant is baptized again when he becomes a Catholic?*

Because of the importance of Baptism for salvation the Church must make certain that we are validly baptized. Some non-Catholic baptisms are doubtfully valid because of a possible defect in the words, actions or intention. Thus, although a person can be validly baptized only once, anyone doubtfully baptized is baptized conditionally with these words, "If you are not baptized, I baptize you in the name of the Father, and of the Son, and of the Holy Spirit."

RITE OF BAPTISM

A study of the rite of Baptism is one of the best ways of learning the true meaning of the sacrament. The present rite is the result of telescoping several services which in the ancient

Church were separated by weeks, months or even years. (The Roman numerals indicate the sections which took place on different days. The italicized words are the first words of the various prayers said during the baptismal ceremony. One studying these notes should have a complete copy of the ceremony.)

i. Reception of the Candidate

The priest meets the candidate for Baptism at the door of the church. Formerly this meeting was the beginning of a long period of instruction for the person who wished to become a Christian. The sponsor was usually the person of whom the candidate made his first inquiry, and who would be responsible for his instruction.

Peace be with you, etc.

The candidate is questioned regarding his motives for Baptism. Then he is told he must love God and his neighbor in order to enter into everlasting life.

Depart from him, etc.

Throughout the service there are several exorcisms to free the candidate from the power of Satan. If the candidate is an infant, he is subject to the devil because of original sin. If he is an adult, his own personal sins have increased his enslavement. Through these exorcisms the Church teaches us that much of the evil in the world today is the result of a living person, Satan. As Christ overcame him in the desert, so too, he now overcomes him in Baptism. But we shall have to fight him all our lives.

The priest not only orders the devil to leave; he breathes upon the face of the candidate as if he were blowing the devil away.

Receive, etc.

After driving out the devil, the priest takes possession of the candidate by making the sign of the cross on his forehead and laying his hands on his head. The one to be baptized is marked by the cross to show that he now belongs to Christ, who upon the cross defeated the devil. The grace won upon the cross is applied through Baptism. By Baptism, too, we undertake to carry his cross daily in imitation of Christ. The imposition of hands is a solemn rite of the Church by which she takes possession of the candidate in the name of Christ and places him under her protection.

Receive the salt, etc.

Salt is used to preserve food and to give it flavor. It was given to one who was beginning instructions as a symbol of the relish he should have for the things of God and of his preservation from corruption.

Peace be to you, etc.

The kiss of peace ended the enrollment ceremony.

ii. Preparatory Purifications

The candidate for Baptism attended during Lent a series of seven meetings or "Scrutinies," which consisted primarily of prayers and exorcisms. The prayers in this part of the rite are taken from those of the Scrutiny which took place on the Wednesday of the third week in Lent. The exorcism, the signing with the cross and the laying on of hands were repeated.

I exorcise you, unclean spirit, etc.

iii. Admittance to the Church

This section is a remnant of the "Great Scrutiny" which took place on the Wednesday of the fourth week in Lent.

Enter the Temple, etc.

The priest puts his stole on the candidate's shoulder and leads him into the Church. This entrance symbolizes leaving the realm of Satan to enter the kingdom of God. The Church on earth is the vestibule of the heavenly kingdom for which the candidate longs, but in order to possess that kingdom, he must be made one with Christ in the Mystical Body.

Apostles' Creed and Our Father

The candidate recites the Apostles' Creed and the Our Father. Formerly Christians were forbidden to commit these prayers to writing or to teach them to pagans, lest they be mocked. At this Scrutiny, therefore, the candidates heard these prayers explained for the first time.

iv. Final Preparation

I exorcise, etc.

On Holy Saturday morning there was a ceremonial examination and a final exorcism.

Ephphetha

The last exorcism, which precedes the renunciation of Satan and his works and the solemn profession of faith recalls our Lord's action in curing the deaf and dumb man. The candidate, who was, as it were, deaf to the word of God and unable to proclaim his praises, can now hear that word and proclaim those praises.

Do you renounce, etc.

This is a solemn public renunciation of the devil and his wiles. Formerly it was followed by a swearing of allegiance to Christ. Nowadays at the Easter Vigil service the entire congregation repeats these vows, thereby manifesting their continued resolve to live for Christ.

I anoint, etc.

The candidate is anointed with oil on the chest and between the shoulders. Formerly the candidates disrobed at this point before descending into the pool. This action showed that they were putting off the old man of sin. Then their entire bodies were anointed with oil. Like the athletes of old, who before entering the arena anointed their bodies with oil, the candidate for baptism thus prepares himself for the continual battle with the evil spirit. When the oil of the catechumens is blessed on Holy Thursday there is a reference to the fact that the devil can have nothing to do with one who is touched by this oil.

v. The Baptism

During the Easter Vigil service the candidates were baptized. Now that this service has been restored, Baptism may again take place during it.

Do you believe, etc.

The candidates make a profession of faith.

I baptize, etc.

The actual Baptism transforms the candidate into a Christian, a child of God, a member of the Mystical Body of Christ.

May almighty God, etc.

Formerly the newly baptized person was immediately confirmed by the bishop. The anointing with chrism remains to remind Christians of this ceremony and to symbolize their sharing in the priesthood of the Anointed One, Christ.

Receive this white robe, etc.

The new Christians were clothed in a white garment, which they wore for eight days. Today a baptismal cloth is placed on the candidate's head as a symbol of the shining purity of his soul, and as a reminder that he is one with Christ, who when he was transfigured, wore garments white as snow.

Receive this lighted candle, etc.

Carrying lighted candles, the newly baptized marched from the baptistry into the church singing the "Vidi Aquam." At the Easter Vigil service today the procession with lighted candles takes place before the baptismal ceremony. Candles are a symbol of Christ who is the light of the world. The candle given at Baptism was lighted from the Paschal candle, to show that the Christian receives his illumination from Christ.

Go in peace, etc.

This was the dismissal. The new Christian then for the first time, joined the Christian community in offering Mass.

Almighty, etc.

This prayer has been recently added, and is optional. It explains how the divine life will grow (through the Holy Eucharist) and how it should culminate in eternal life with God in heaven.

Practical Points

1. Everyone should be given a saint's name at Baptism. The saint, then, is the special protector and model for the person to imitate.

2. One godparent is required, but two are allowed. Godparents must be baptized, practicing Catholics who are at least fourteen years of age. The parents of the child may not be godparents.

3. A dying infant may be baptized by anyone who pours natural water over the child's head and says, "I baptize you in the name of the Father, and of the Son, and of the Holy Spirit." A dying adult should express some desire to be baptized and should believe at least that there is one God in three Persons, who rewards the good and punishes the evil, and that Christ is the Son of God.

4. The baptism of an infant should never be put off for more than a month.

5. Converts should prepare for Baptism by an act of contrition. They should go to Communion as soon as possible after Baptism. Converts and all who are baptized absolutely do not go to confession immediately after Baptism, because their sins are forgiven by Baptism. Converts who are conditionally baptized must make a profession of faith before Baptism and afterwards go to confession and receive conditional absolution.

Practice

If you are preparing for Baptism it is time to select a patron saint, either the one whose name you already bear or one of your own choosing. Perhaps you can find out something about the life of your patron saint.

And when the days of Pentecost were drawing to a close, they were all together in one place. And suddenly there came a sound from heaven, as of a violent wind coming, and it filled the whole house where they were sitting. And there appeared to them parted tongues as of fire, which settled upon each of them. And they were all filled with the Holy Spirit and began to speak in foreign tongues, even as the Holy Spirit prompted them to speak.

Now there were staying at Jerusalem Jews, devout men from every nation under heaven. And when this sound was heard, the multitude gathered and were bewildered in mind, because each heard them speaking in his own language. But they were all amazed and marveled, saying, "Behold, are not all these that are speaking Galileans? And how have we heard each his own language in which he was born? Parthians and Medes and Elamites, and inhabitants of Mesopotamia, Judea, and Cappadocia, Pontus and Asia, Phrygia and Pamphylia, Egypt and the parts of Libya about Cyrene, and visitors from Rome, Jews also and proselytes, Cretans and Arabians, we have heard them speaking in our own languages of the wonderful works of God—ACTS 2:1-11.

THE MARK of maturity is responsibility. All the actions of a new-born child center about himself. Not for years does he begin to do things for others. Gradually, however, he assumes more and more responsibility as he becomes more mature. A similiar growth from childhood to maturity takes place in the supernatural life. Here, however, the growth is not gradual; it comes about instantaneously through the sacrament of Confirmation.

The Church was born from the pierced side of Christ on Good Friday; but it was not until the Holy Spirit descended upon her on Pentecost that she manifested herself to the world and assumed the responsibility of bearing witness to Christ. Somewhat the same thing happens in the life of a Christian. He is born into a new life at Baptism. He reaches his supernatural maturity, assumes his full responsibilities to bear witness to Christ when the Holy Spirit comes upon him in Confirmation.

1. What is the sacrament of Confirmation?

Confirmation is the sacrament in which Jesus Christ confers upon us spiritual adulthood through the graces of the Holy Spirit, especially those which enable us to profess and spread our faith courageously. Through Confirmation Christ confers on us the Holy Spirit, making us full-fledged and responsible members of the Mystical Body.

2. When did Christ institute Confirmation?

The Scriptures do not give us the scene of the actual institution. But Christ's institution of the sacrament of Confirmation is proved from Scripture by the fact that he promised to send, and actually did send the Holy Spirit to strengthen the apostles, and by the fact that the apostles did administer the sacrament soon after the Resurrection.

And Philip went down to the city of Samaria and preached the Christ to them. . . . Now when the apostles in Jerusalem heard that Samaria had received the word of God, they sent to them Peter and John. On their arrival they prayed for them, that they might receive the Holy Spirit; for as yet he had not come upon any of them, but they had only been baptized in the name of the Lord Jesus. Then they laid their hands on them and they received the Holy Spirit
—ACTS 8:5, 14-17.

3. What does Jesus Christ accomplish in us through the sacrament of Confirmation?

Christ gives us:

   a. an increase of the divine life.

   b. the sacramental mark or character of Confirmation.

   c. an increase of the strength to profess, defend and spread the faith.

176

4. What is the sign of the sacrament of Confirmation?

The sign of the sacrament of Confirmation is the imposition of hands and anointing with chrism. These actions are performed together as the bishop says:

I sign you with the sign of the cross and I confirm you with chrism of salvation in the name of the Father, and of the Son, and of the Holy Spirit.

The imposition of hands signifies the conferring of full and perfect manhood. This is an ancient ceremony, which signifies the giving of a special power.

Chrism, the oil used in Confirmation, is a mixture of olive oil and a perfume called balm, consecrated by the bishop.

5. What is the effect of the distinctive character given in Confirmation?

The character is a spiritual power, a sharing in the priesthood of Christ. The baptismal character admits us to the Church and enables us to receive the sacraments and participate in the Mass. The character given in Confirmation consecrates a Christian for the defense of the faith and the winning of others to Christ.

6. What are the powers which enable us to profess, defend and spread the faith?

These powers are the gifts of the Holy Spirit and the actual graces of the sacrament of Confirmation. These actual graces enable us to meet the challenges to our faith and to take advantage of the possibilities of spreading the faith in our every-day life.

And when they bring you before the synagogues and the magistrates and the authorities, do not be anxious how or wherewith you shall defend yourselves, or what you shall say, for the Holy Spirit will teach you in that very hour what you ought to say—LUKE 12:11-12.

7. What are the gifts of the Holy Spirit?

The gifts of the Holy Spirit are: wisdom, understanding, knowledge, counsel, fortitude, piety and fear of the Lord. They render us docile to the inspirations of the Holy Spirit. In Baptism we receive these gifts in embryo. Through Confirmation they become more fully developed.

8. How does a Christian profess and spread his faith?

A Christian professes and spreads his faith by:

a. praying for all men,

I urge therefore, first of all, that supplications, prayers, intercessions and thanksgivings be made for all men

—1 Tim. 2:1.

b. participating in the apostolate of suffering,

And our hope for you is steadfast, knowing that as you are partakers of the sufferings, so will you also be of the comfort

—2 Cor. 1:7.

c. giving good example,

You are the light of the world. . . . Even so let your light shine before men, in order that they may see your good works and give glory to your Father in heaven

—Matt. 5:14-16.

d. professing belief in Christ,

Therefore, everyone who acknowledges me before men, I also will acknowledge him before my Father in heaven. But whoever disowns me before men, I in turn will disown him before my Father in heaven—Matt. 10:32-33.

e. doing the works of mercy,

Then the just will answer him, saying, "Lord, when did we see thee hungry, and feed thee; or thirsty, and give thee drink? And when did we see thee a stranger, and take thee in; or naked, and clothe thee? Or when did we see thee sick, or in prison, and come to thee?" And answering the king will say to them, "Amen I say to you, as long as you did it for one of these, the least of my brethren, you did it for me"—Matt. 25:37-40.

f. aiding the foreign missions by prayers, alms, the encouragement of vocations to the missions, and by actually taking part in the work of the missions.

g. taking part in the work of the lay apostolate.

How then are they to call upon him in whom they have not believed? But how are they to believe him whom they have not heard? And how are they to hear, if no one preaches? And how are men to preach unless they be sent?

—Rom. 10:14-15.

9. What is the lay apostolate?

The lay apostolate is the collaboration of the laity with the hierarchy in the fulfillment of the mission of the Church, i.e., the redemptive work of Christ.

The apostolate of prayer and personal example might be called the lay apostolate in a wide sense. To belong to the lay apostolate in the *strict* sense a person or an organization must have been chosen or approved by the hierarchy.

10. Are all Catholics meant to belong to the lay apostolate?

All Catholics who have received Confirmation must take part in the lay apostolate in the wide sense, i.e., they must be missionaries in the sense that they try by prayer and good example to spread the kingdom of Christ.

Not all Catholics are called to engage in the lay apostolate in the strict sense. However, those who possess the apostolic spirit, tact and a willingness to undergo training are urgently needed by the Church today as lay apostles in the strict sense.

11. What is the scope of the lay apostolate?

Since the lay apostolate is the collaboration in the mission of the Church, its scope is as extensive as the mission of the Church itself. Lay apostles are needed in every field.

In accordance with the principle of "like to like," i.e., that the apostle to the worker must be a worker, the apostle to the student, a student, etc., lay apostles are receiving training and working in various fields. The Young Christian Workers, the Christian Family Movement, the Young Christian Students, are examples of organizations of the lay apostolate in the fields of youth work, the family and student life. Similar organizations are to be found among the various professions, such as law, medicine, nursing, etc.

The lay apostolate is active in the teaching of Christian doctrine. The Confraternity of Christian Doctrine is an example of an organization of the lay apostolate in this field.

Missionary work, such as reclaiming fallen-away Catholics and making contacts for convert work, is done by other organizations of the lay apostolate. An example of such an organization is the Legion of Mary.

In the field of foreign and home missions there are organizations which train laymen and laywomen (some of them married couples as well) who will devote either their whole life or several years of it to the missions. There are other organizations which do a similar work in other fields. Among such organizations in the lay apostolate are the Grail, International Catholic Auxiliaries, the Association for International Development, and Secular Institutes.

Many of the traditional organizations, associations and pious unions within the Church have enlarged their scope and adapted themselves to meet the needs of the Church today, thus becoming part of the lay apostolate. The Holy Name Society, the Sodality and Third Orders are examples of such organizations.

Practical Points

1. In ordinary cases it is the bishop who administers the sacrament of Confirmation. A priest may do so with permission from the pope. A pastor may do so if the bishop is not available when one of his parishioners who has never been confirmed is dying.

2. A sponsor is required at Confirmation. Qualifications: He must be at least fourteen years of age, a good Catholic who has been confirmed himself, of the same sex as the person to be confirmed, and a person other than the sponsor at baptism.

3. The usual age for the reception of Confirmation is about ten; but different rules may prevail in various localities.

4. A saint's name is given in Confirmation just as it is in Baptism. Thus the person confirmed acquires another patron, one of his own choosing.

5. Confirmation may be administered at any time or place, although it is usually given in church.

28

The Eucharist

'And while they were at supper, Jesus took bread, and blessed and broke, and gave it to his disciples, and said, "Take and eat; this is my body." And taking a cup, he gave thanks and gave it to them, saying, "All of you drink of this; for this is my blood of the new covenant, which is being shed for many unto the forgiveness of sins. But I say to you, I will not drink henceforth of this fruit of the vine, until that day when I shall drink it new with you in the kingdom of my Father"—MATT. 26:26-28.

THE LOVE OF GOD, our Father, knows no bounds. The greatest expression of the love of God for us is the gift he has given us, his own Son, Jesus Christ. "For God so loved the world that he gave his only-begotten Son, that those who believe in him might not perish, but may have life everlasting"—JOHN 3:16.

The love of Jesus Christ for us, too, is a love without limit. Christ proved that love by offering his life to his Father for our salvation. "Greater love than this no one has, that one lay down his life for his friends"—JOHN 15:13.

But Christ was not content even with offering himself once upon the cross. Such is his love for us that on the night before he died he gave us his greatest gift, himself in the Eucharist. By means of the Eucharist Christ continually re-offers himself to the Father through the ministry of his priests in the sacrifice of the Mass. By means of it, too, he comes to us to be the food of our souls and to unite us in Holy Communion. Finally, this greatest of gifts is Christ's continual and abiding presence among us in this, the most wonderful of all his sacraments.

". . . Compare the Eucharist to a fountain; the other sacraments to rivulets. For the Holy Eucharist is truly and necessarily to be called the fountain of all graces containing as it does . . . the fountain itself of celestial gifts and graces, and the author of the other sacraments, Christ our Lord . . ."—Council of Trent.

1. What is the Holy Eucharist?

The Holy Eucharist is the sacrament and the sacrifice in which Jesus Christ under the appearances of bread and wine is contained, offered and received.

2. What is the sign of the sacrament of the Eucharist?

The sign of the Eucharist is wheat bread and pure grape wine over which the words: "This is my body" and "This is my blood," are said.

3. When did Christ institute the Eucharist?

Christ instituted the Eucharist at the Last Supper.

And while they were at supper, Jesus took bread, and blessed and broke, and gave it to his disciples, and said, "Take and eat; this is my body." And taking a cup, he gave thanks and gave it to them, saying, "All of you drink of this; for this is my blood of the new covenant, which is being shed for many unto the forgiveness of sins"—MATT. 26:26-28.

4. How do we know that Christ is truly present in the Eucharist?

a. The words, "This is my body"; "this is my blood," were spoken in fulfillment of a promise Jesus had made that he would give his flesh to eat and his blood to drink. When he made this promise he said, "My flesh is food indeed and my blood is drink indeed"—JOHN 6:57. The people to whom Jesus spoke these words took them literally. Jesus, who could read their minds, did not correct them. Rather he let them go away in disbelief, and would have allowed even the apostles to leave unless they would accept his words literally—cf. JOHN 6:61-70.

b. St. Paul, speaking of the Holy Eucharist says:

This cup is the new covenant in my blood; do this as often as you drink it, in remembrance of me. For as often as you shall eat this bread and drink the cup, you proclaim the death of the Lord, until he comes, therefore whoever eats this bread or drinks the cup of the Lord unworthily, will be *guilty of the body and the blood of the Lord. But let a man prove himself, and so let him eat of that bread and drink of the cup; for he who eats and drinks unworthily, without distinguishing the body, eats and drinks judgment to himself. This is why many among you are infirm and weak, and many sleep—*1 COR. 11:25-31.

c. It has been the constant, infallible teaching of the Church that in the Eucharist the body and blood, soul and divinity of Jesus Christ are contained under the appearances of bread and wine.

5. To whom did Jesus give the power of changing bread and wine into his body and blood?

Jesus gave this power to the apostles at the Last Supper. He gives it to his priests in the sacrament of Holy Orders.

6. What happens when the priest pronounces the words, "This is my body; this is my blood," over the bread and wine?

At these words the actual bread and wine cease to exist. In their place is the body and blood, soul and divinity of Jesus Christ.

7. Does anything remain of the bread and wine after the words of consecration have been spoken?

Only the appearances of bread and wine remain; that is, the looks, taste, smell etc., remain, although the bread and wine themselves have been changed into Christ.

8. Are both the body and blood of Christ present under the appearances of bread alone?

Yes. It is the living Christ who is present in the Eucharist. Under the appearances of bread alone (and under the appearances of wine alone) both the body and blood of Christ are present.

Practice

► Our Lord is actually present in every Catholic church. We should not only pay him reverence each time we pass a church; we should stop in and visit him whenever we have the opportunity.

Adopt the practice of tipping your hat or bowing your head whenever you pass a Catholic church. Resolve that whenever you pass a church and have time to do so you will stop in for a short visit with our Lord in the Blessed Sacrament.

☩   ☩

section **29** | **The Eucharist, the Sacrificial Meal**

Then the Lord said to Moses, "I will now rain down bread from heaven for you. Each day the people are to go out and gather their daily portion;" . . . On seeing it, the Israelites asked one another, "What is this?" for they did not know what it was. But Moses told them, "This is the bread which the Lord has given you to eat." They so gathered that everyone had enough to eat . . . morning after morning they gathered it till each had enough to eat—Ex. 16:4-21.

Amen, amen, I say to you, he who believes in me has life everlasting. "I am the bread of life. Your fathers ate the manna in the desert, and have died. This is the bread that comes down from heaven, so that if anyone eat of it he will not die. I am the living bread that has come down from heaven. If anyone eat of this bread he shall live forever; and the bread that I will give is my flesh for the life of the world."

The Jews on that account argued with one another, saying, "How can this man give us his flesh to eat?" Jesus there-

fore said to them, "Amen, amen, I say to you, unless you eat the flesh of the Son of Man, and drink his blood, you shall not have life in you. He who eats my flesh and drinks my blood has life everlasting and I will raise him up on the last day. For my flesh is food indeed, and my blood is drink indeed. He who eats my flesh, and drinks my blood, abides in me and I in him. As the living Father has sent me, and as I live because of the Father, so he who eats me, he also shall live because of me. This is the bread that has come down from heaven; not as your fathers ate the manna, and died. He who eats this bread shall live forever—JOHN 6:47-59.

HOW PRIVILEGED were the men and women who lived in the Holy Land at the time of Christ. They could see his face, could hear his voice, could feel the touch of his hand as he blessed them. And yet we today enjoy an even greater intimacy with our Saviour. We cannot see him with the eyes of the body. But ours is the far greater privilege of receiving his sacred body into our own, of eating his flesh and drinking his blood. The marvel by which this intimacy is achieved is the precious legacy which Christ gave to his Church the night before he died, his greatest gift, the most Holy Eucharist. By means of the sacrament of the Holy Eucharist we have his continual and abiding presence among us. Jesus once told the apostles, "I will not leave you orphans." True to his promise, he has indeed remained among us, actually and physically present in the Holy Eucharist.

> *What other nation is there so honored as the Christian people? Or what creature under heaven so beloved as a devout soul, to whom God cometh, that he may feed her with his glorious flesh? O unspeakable grace; O wonderful condescension! O infinite love, singularly bestowed on man*
>
> —Thomas a Kempis, "The Imitation of Christ."

1. What is meant by the expression, Holy Communion?

Holy Communion is the expression used when speaking about receiving the Holy Eucharist.

This expression is very appropriate. It sums up the most important effect of the Holy Eucharist, the strengthening of the union between Christ and his members and of the union between the members themselves.

> *The cup of blessing that we bless, is it not the sharing of the blood of Christ? And the bread that we break, is it not the partaking of the body of the Lord? Because the bread is one, we though many, are one body, all of us who partake of the one bread*—1 COR. 10:16-17.

2. Why are bread and wine appropriate material for the Holy Eucharist?

Bread is the staple food in the diet of most people, and wine is the staple drink of a great part of mankind. Therefore, bread and wine are appropriate material for the Eucharist, which is the food of our soul.

Bread and wine, too, are wonderful symbols. The bread is made of many grains of wheat baked into one wafer; the wine is made up of many grapes, crushed into one draught of wine. Thus is symbolized the union of all the faithful with each other in Christ.

3. When may we receive Holy Communion?

We may receive Holy Communion every day. The Church encourages everyone to do so. Since Holy Communion is the sacrificial meal, it is most fitting to receive it in the Mass, not before, after, or outside of Mass, unless it is too difficult to do so.

4. What does Christ accomplish in us through Holy Communion?

Through Holy Communion Christ gives us:

a. an increase of the divine life, and consequently a deeper union with God,

b. an increase of faith, hope and charity,

c. a closer union with himself, and with every member of the Mystical Body,

d. a pledge of our resurrection and our future glory,

e. the forgiveness of our daily faults and the grace to overcome our inclination to sin,

f. the promise of actual graces to help us love God and others more.

5. How does Communion unite us with our neighbor?

Our Lord gave us Communion in the form of a banquet in which we all eat of the same food. Communion, therefore, both symbolizes and deepens our union with one another in the Mystical Body. It symbolizes our union, because eating and drinking together is a sign of love and friendship. It deepens that union, because it gives us an increase of the divine life and of the power to love one another.

. . . I pray, but for those also who through their word are to believe in me, that all may be one, even as thou, Father, in me and I in thee; that they also may be one in us, that the world may believe that thou has sent me. And the glory that thou hast given me, I have given to them, that they may be one, even as we are one—JOHN 17:20-22.

6. What effect does Communion have upon our bodies?

Holy Communion lessens the difficulty we experience in bringing the impulses of the body under control. Frequent and daily Communion is the greatest means we can use to become chaste, temperate, patient, etc.

7. How is the Eucharist a pledge of our future glory?

Our Lord promised,

He who eats my flesh and drinks my blood has life everlasting and I will raise him up on the last day—JOHN 6:55.

8. How does Communion remove our daily faults?

Our union with Christ in the Holy Eucharist is a union based on love. Because of this love Christ forgives us our venial sins; the love thus engendered in our hearts merits for us the forgiveness of part of the punishment due to sin.

St. Pius X in his decree on frequent Communion said,

The desire of Jesus Christ and of the Church that all Christians should daily approach the holy banquet is based chiefly on this, that Christians united to God through the sacrament should derive from there the strength to conquer concupiscence, and wash away light faults of daily occurrence, and should forestall more serious ones to which human frailty is exposed. . . .

9. What is required in order to receive Communion?

St. Pius X in his decree on frequent Communion said that only three things are necessary:

a. a good intention, i.e., the desire to love God more,

b. freedom from mortal sin,

c. the eucharistic fast.

10. How can we make our reception of Holy Communion more fruitful?

We can make our reception of Holy Communion more fruitful by a good preparation before and a good thanksgiving after receiving.

Preparation includes not only the desire to be united to Christ and an intelligent and active assistance at Mass, which is the immediate preparation for Holy Communion, but also an attempt to practice love of our neighbor in our daily lives and a desire for an increase of the gift of charity.

Thanksgiving includes not only some moments of private prayer after Communion, a practice which is highly recommended, but also an attempt to use the graces of the sacrament by practicing love of God and our neighbor.

11. Is it necessary to go to confession before receiving Communion?

No. It is not necessary to go to confession before receiving Communion unless we have committed a mortal sin. Many people who receive Communion daily or weekly go to confession once a month. If we have committed a mortal sin, however, even though we have made an act of perfect contrition, we must go to confession before Communion.

12. What is the Eucharistic fast?

The Eucharistic fast is the fast from food and drink which is to be observed before receiving Communion.

a. Water and medicine never break the fast. They may be taken at any time before receiving.

b. Solid food and alcoholic drinks in moderation may be taken up to an hour before receiving.

13. What kind of sin would it be to receive Communion in the state of mortal sin?

To receive Communion knowingly in the state of mortal sin would be a most serious sin of sacrilege.

To receive Communion knowingly without the proper fast would be a serious sin.

14. Why do Catholics of the Latin rite receive Holy Communion under the appearance of bread alone?

The Catholics of the Latin rite receive Holy Communion under the appearance of bread alone because, with the large numbers of people who receive Holy Communion, distribution under both appearances would prolong the service very greatly. As a matter of convenience the Western Church adopted the present custom. Since Christ is present, body and blood, under both the appearances of bread and of wine, when we receive under the appearances of bread alone we receive both the body and blood of the Lord.

If any one would like to receive under both appearances he may do so by attending one of the Catholic Churches of the Eastern rites which still distributes under both appearances.

15. How is the Eucharist Christ's abiding presence among us?

The Eucharist is reserved in the tabernacle of all Catholic churches. Jesus Christ is, therefore, actually present in our churches at all times. He is there just as truly as he is in heaven, except that here, under the appearances of bread, he can be seen only with the eyes of faith.

16. Why do we adore the Holy Eucharist?

We adore the Holy Eucharist because Christ, present in the Eucharist, is truly God.

We genuflect whenever we pass in front of the tabernacle as an act of adoration of Christ. It is the custom for men and boys to tip their hats and for women and girls to bow their heads when passing a Catholic church, as an act of adoration of Christ in the Eucharist.

17. What is the Forty Hours Devotion?

The Forty Hours Devotion is a devotion honoring Christ in the Eucharist, which is held each year in every parish. During the Forty Hours Devotion the Blessed Sacrament is exposed on the altar. Solemn ceremonies mark the beginning and the end of the Forty Hours Devotion.

18. What is Benediction of the Most Blessed Sacrament?

Benediction is a blessing given by Christ in the Blessed Sacrament. The service also includes incensing of the Blessed Sacrament, hymns and prayers.

Practical Points

1. Every Catholic is invited to receive Communion each time he assists at Mass. Of course, we may receive only once a day, even though we might assist at more than one Mass.

2. The goal of every Catholic should be to offer Mass and receive Communion daily, or at least frequently during the week.

> *Two classes of people should communicate often, the perfect because, being well prepared, they would be very wrong not to approach the fountainhead of perfection; and the imperfect, that they might acquire perfection; the strong that they might preserve their strength, the weak that they might become strong; the sick that they might find a cure; the healthy, that they might be preserved from sickness*
> —Introduction to a Devout Life, St. Francis de Sales.

3. Catholics are bound under penalty of mortal sin to receive Communion at least once a year during the Easter time, that is from the first Sunday of Lent until Trinity Sunday.

4. In addition to Holy Thursday we celebrate a great feast in

honor of the Blessed Sacrament on the Thursday after Trinity Sunday, the feast of Corpus Christi.

Practice

▶ When, for some reason, we are unable to receive Holy Communion we should make a "spiritual communion" at the Communion part of the Mass; that is, we should tell our Lord that we regret our inability to receive him in the Blessed Sacrament here and now, but desire to be united to him and to our neighbor in a deeper love.

If you are taking instructions and are as yet unable to receive Holy Communion, make such a spiritual communion every time you assist at Mass.

✠   ✠

section **30** | **Penance**

Now the Scribes and Pharisees brought a woman caught in adultery, and setting her in the midst, said to him, "Master, this woman has just now been caught in adultery. And in the Law Moses commanded us to stone such persons. What, therefore, dost thou say?" Now they were saying this to test him, in order that they might be able to accuse him. But Jesus, stooping down, began to write with his finger on the ground.

But when they continued asking him, he raised himself and said to them, "Let him who is without sin among you be the first to cast a stone at her." And again stooping down, he began to write on the ground. But hearing this, they went away, one by one, beginning with the eldest. And Jesus remained alone, with the woman standing in the midst.

And Jesus, raising himself, said to her, "Woman, where are they? Has no one condemned thee?" She said, "No one, Lord." Then Jesus said, "Neither will I condemn thee. Go thy way, and from now on sin no more"—JOHN 8:3-11.

THE STORY of the woman taken in adultery is only one of the many incidents in the Gospels which give us a glimpse of the love and tenderness of Jesus in his dealings with sinners. How often in the Gospel narrative do we not see Christ looking deep into the heart of a man or woman, seeing the frightful condition of that soul after a lifetime of sin, and then applying his healing with the words, "Thy sins are forgiven thee." Often the sinner approached our Lord in the hope of obtaining a cure of his bodily disease. But before healing the body Jesus healed the soul. Sometimes the sinner did not even ask for forgiveness. No matter; Jesus could see what was in the heart and mind, could see not only the sin but the sorrow for sin as well. And his unfailing response was, "Thy sins are forgiven thee."

Christ no longer walks the earth in his physical body. Nonetheless, he continues his work as healer of souls. He still pronounces those words which alone can bring peace and comfort, "Thy sins are forgiven thee." Now he does so through the sacrament of divine mercy, the sacrament of Penance. In his great love for sinners our Lord has provided a means whereby his healing action can penetrate to every corner of the earth. He has given to his priests the power of forgiving sins in his name. True, the priest cannot read the mind and heart of the sinner as Christ could. But after a confession of his sins and the absolution of the priest the sinner today can be just as assured as was the woman taken in adultery that the words of Christ, "Neither will I condemn thee," have been addressed to him.

Our Lord gloried in the title, friend of sinners. Nowhere did he better demonstrate his right to that title than in his institution of the sacrament of Penance, the sacrament of God's forgiveness.

1. What is the meaning of the word penance?

The word penance has three meanings:

a. the virtue by which we are sorry for and detest our sins because they offend God and separate us from him;

b. good works performed or prayers said in satisfaction for sin (such a penance is imposed on the sinner after he has confessed his sins);

c. the sacrament of Penance.

2. What is the sacrament of Penance?

Penance is the sacrament in which Jesus Christ through the absolution of the priest forgives sins committed after Baptism.

We also speak of the sacrament of Penance as "confession," although in reality the confession of sins is only part of the sacrament. The expressions "going to confession" and "receiving the sacrament of Penance" are popularly used interchangeably.

3. When did Jesus Christ institute the sacrament of Penance?

On Easter night when Jesus appeared to the apostles he said to them:

> *Peace be to you! As the Father has sent me, I also send you. . . . Receive the Holy Spirit; whose sins you shall forgive, they are forgiven them; and whose sins you shall retain, they are retained*—JOHN 20:21-23.

4. What is the sign of the sacrament of Penance?

The sinner's manifestation of sorrow by word or gesture, the sins confessed, the sinner's willingness to make satisfaction and the words of the priest, "I absolve you from your sins in the name of the Father, and of the Son, and of the Holy Spirit" constitute the sign of the sacrament of Penance.

5. What does Jesus Christ accomplish in us in the sacrament of Penance?

In the sacrament of Penance Christ forgives mortal sin, restores the divine life in even greater abundance, and removes the sentence of hell for those who had been guilty of serious sin.

He forgives all venial sins which we confess with contrition, and gives an increase of the divine life.

He gives us a pledge of the actual graces we need to atone for past sins and to avoid sin in the future.

He removes the temporal punishment due for sin, all or part of it, depending on the depth of our sorrow for sin and the strength of our purpose of amendment.

6. Why did Jesus make confession a part of the sacrament of Penance?

Christ made confession a part of the sacrament of Penance because of his understanding of the needs of the human heart. He realized that the confession of sins helps the sinner. Moreover, our Lord instituted the sacrament in such a way that the priest must act as a judge. For this reason the priest must have evidence, which can be obtained only through a confession on the part of the penitent.

7. How does confession help the sinner?

a. The urge to confess is natural to man. A sorrow or shame is lessened when shared with another.

b. Confession makes us conscious of our sinfulness. It forces us to think of our sins. We cannot bury them and forget about them. We have to face them time and time again. This has the effect of making us conscious of them and of helping us overcome them, and of helping us realize how weak we are and how merciful God is.

c. Man needs reassurance that God has actually forgiven him. He does not have this reassurance if he merely says in his heart that he is sorry. When Christ forgave sins he announced the fact, in order that the sinner would know that he was forgiven.

8. If the main purpose of the sacrament of Penance is to forgive mortal sin, should we receive it when we have no mortal sins?

We should receive the sacrament of Penance frequently, even

if we have no mortal sins. Pope Pius XII says in his Encyclical on the Mystical Body:

> To hasten daily progress along the path of virtue, we wish the pious practice of frequent confession to be earnestly advocated. Not without the inspiration of the Holy Spirit was this practice introduced into the Church. By it genuine self-knowledge is increased, Christian humility grows, bad habits are corrected, spiritual neglect and tepidity are countered, the conscience is purified, the will strengthened, a salutary self control is attained, and grace is increased in virtue of the sacrament itself—88.

9. How does the sacrament of Penance help us grow in the divine life?

The sacrament of Penance not only forgives sin; it also develops virtues which make us more Christ-like.

a. The virtue of penance is based on a sense of the holiness of God. The realization of the goodness of God must be the basis of all our sorrow. This realization should grow each time we say the act of contrition or go to confession.

b. Penance reminds us of the great love God has for us. Love must engender love; we should grow in the love of God each time we receive the sacrament.

c. The sacrament of Penance increases our hope. We realize that even though we are sinners we can obtain from God the help we need to reach heaven.

10. What is necessary for a worthy reception of the sacrament of Penance?

The five things necessary for a worthy reception of Penance are:

a. examination of conscience,
b. sorrow for sin,
c. resolution to avoid sin in the future,
d. confession,
e. acceptance of the penance.

11. What is an examination of conscience?

An examination of conscience is a reasonable effort to recall the sins committed since our last confession. In examining our conscience, we must avoid two dangers: on the one hand, carelessness and lack of effort to recall our sins, on the other, anxiety and excessive soul searching, which would make the sacrament of Penance a burden.

12. How do we make an examination of conscience?

First of all, we should pray to the Holy Spirit for light to know our sins and for the grace to be sorry for them. Then we should call to mind the commandments of God and of the Church and the obligations of our state in life. Then we should ask ourselves wherein we have failed to live up to them. If we go to confession frequently we can simply ask ourselves whether we have sinned in thought, word or deed against God, neighbor or self.

13. What is to be done if we find that we have no sins to confess, or if our confessions have become routine?

In the first case, we usually can discover sins and defects in ourselves if we examine our conscience more carefully on the subject of charity or one of the other virtues. The holiest people are always well aware of their shortcomings.

In the second case, we should select one or two faults for which we are truly sorry, instead of reciting a whole catalogue of "the usual venial sins," and make an effort to recall the number of times we have committed such faults.

In both cases it will help to seek the advice of our confessor.

14. What is contrition?

Contrition is sorrow for and detestation of our sins, together with the intention of not sinning in the future. Without this sorrow there can be no forgiveness. God himself cannot forgive a sin if we do not want to give it up.

15. What are the qualities of true contrition?

a. We must mean what we say. There must be a true resolve to reform our lives.

b. Our sorrow must be based on the love, or at least the fear of God. If we are sorry for our sins only because we are in disgrace, because we are disgusted with ourselves or for any other merely human reason, our sorrow is not true contrition.

c. We must hate sin more than any other evil. Our detestation for sin does not have to be felt to be sincere. Contrition is a matter of the will, not of the feelings.

d. We must be sorry for *all* our mortal sins. It is not enough to be sorry for one and not another. When we sin mortally we separate ourselves from God. To be reunited with God, we must give up *all* our mortal sins.

16. *Are there different kinds of contrition?*

Yes. There are two kinds of contrition, perfect and imperfect. They are different by reason of their motives. In each case we are sorry for our sins because they are an offense against God. In imperfect contrition the motive is fear of the justice of God and of the punishment which our sins deserve. In perfect contrition the motive is the goodness of God, which prompts us to love him above all else for his own sake.

Perfect contrition removes all sins, even mortal sins. Imperfect contrition by itself will remove only venial sins. However, in the sacrament of Penance, imperfect contrition suffices.

17. *What is the procedure in going to confession?*

We begin: "Bless me, Father, for I have sinned. It has been _____ weeks since my last confession." Then we tell our sins. At the conclusion of our confession we say, "I am sorry for these and all the sins of my past life." The priest then gives us a penance to perform and, perhaps, some advice. While we are saying the Act of Contrition aloud, the priest gives us absolution. After that we say, "Thank you, Father," and leave.

18. *What sins must we tell in confession?*

a. We must tell all our mortal sins;

—their number, as nearly as we can remember,
—their kind, e.g., "I stole $100" (it is not enough to say, "I broke the 7th commandment"),
—any circumstances which might change the nature of the sin, e.g., "I stole a *chalice.*"

b. We are encouraged to tell also our venial sins. However, this is not necessary. The reception of any of the other sacraments, an act of imperfect contrition, or any virtuous act will also remove venial sins.

If we forget to mention a mortal sin, the sin is forgiven nevertheless. We need not remain away from Communion nor go back to confession immediately. In our next confession we should say, "In my last confession I forgot to mention _____."

19. What is meant by a "bad confession"?

A "bad confession" is one in which the penitent deliberately conceals a mortal sin. This renders the confession invalid and sacrilegious and all future confessions invalid and sacrilegious until the sin is confessed.

20. What is meant by a "resolution not to sin again"?

By a resolution not to sin again is meant a sincere *intention* not to sin again. Even God will not forgive a sin unless the sinner intends not to commit it again. Unless a person is resolved not to repeat his offense he can hardly be said to be sorry for it. The resolution to avoid sin in the future, therefore, is necessary for the forgiveness of sin.

In the case of venial sin, unless we are sorry for those we confess, and intend not to commit them again, we would do better not to confess them, since they will not be forgiven. Only those venial sins which we intend to avoid in the future will be pardoned.

In the case of mortal sins, unless we are sorry for *all* our mortal sins and intend not to commit *any kind* of mortal sin in the future, none of our sins will be forgiven.

It is important to remember, however, that all God demands in the way of a resolution for the future is that *we intend to do our best*. No one may safely say: "I am certain that I shall never commit this sin." All we can say is: "With God's help I shall do my best. I intend never to commit this sin again, and shall keep away from anything which would cause me to fall again."

21. What is the penance given by the priest?

Usually the penance is the saying of a few prayers, the recitation of the rosary or attendance at Mass. The acceptance of the penance shows our willingness to make amends to God.

The performance of the penance is a most effective way of ridding ourselves of the temporal punishment due for our sins.

22. What is meant by "punishment due for sin"?

Mortal sin deserves eternal punishment in hell.

Depart from me, accursed ones, into the everlasting fire which was prepared for the devil and his angels
—MATT. 25:41.

Venial sin deserves some punishment, one which will last only for a time.

When God forgives mortal sin he takes away the eternal punishment due for it. But the sinner must still suffer something as a consequence of his sins, whether mortal or venial, even after forgiveness has been granted. This suffering is called temporal punishment.

23. How can we make payment for the temporal punishment due for our sins?

Besides the sacramental penance given by the priest the other means we have of making such payment are prayer, fasting, almsgiving, attendance at Mass, other good works, patience in suffering and indulgences.

If we die without having satisfied for all the temporal punishment due for our sins, we must make such satisfaction in the next world, in purgatory.

24. What is an indulgence?

An indulgence is the remission in whole or in part of the temporal punishment due for sin. It is called plenary if it is a full pardon. Otherwise it is called partial. Because we are all members one of another in the Mystical Body, the merits of our Lord, our Lady and the Saints are available to all. The pope has the power of applying these merits to us as a reward for certain good actions.

And I will give thee the keys of the kingdom of heaven; and whatever thou shalt bind on earth shall be bound in heaven,

199

and whatever thou shalt loose on earth shall be loosed in heaven—MATT. 16:19.

Indulgences may be applied to ourselves or to the souls in purgatory.

25. How do we gain indulgences?

To gain an indulgence we must have the necessary dispositions of soul and fulfill the conditions.

It is necessary to be in the state of grace to gain any indulgence. To gain a plenary indulgence for oneself it is necessary to be free from even venial sin and all attachment to it.

The conditions required for gaining an indulgence sometimes vary. For some indulgences, confession and Communion and prayers for the Holy Father are required.

Practical Points

1. We should go to confession frequently, certainly not less than once a month.

2. It is not necessary to go to confession each time we receive Communion unless we have committed mortal sin.

3. We are bound under pain of mortal sin to go to confession at least once a year.

4. If possible, we should have a regular confessor.

Practice

▶ We should not wait until the time of our first confession to begin the practice of examining our conscience. It is highly recommended that everyone examine his conscience every day. Just before retiring at night is a good time to do so. An effort to recall the sins we have committed during the day, followed by an act of contrition for these as well as all our past sins will help us to advance spiritually.

We should also begin to memorize the Act of Contrition, if we have not already done so. See page 159.

The Anointing of the Sick

Is any one among you sick? Let him bring in the presbyters of the Church, and let them pray over him, anointing him with oil in the name of the Lord. And the prayer of faith will save the sick man, and the Lord will raise him up, and if he be in sins, they shall be forgiven him—JAMES 5:14-15.

CHRIST OUR LORD is with us all through our life with his life-giving sacraments. When we fall ill and are in danger of death, he is with us in the sacrament of the Anointing of the Sick. Through this sacrament our Lord strengthens us to live a vigorous supernatural life. Such a restoration affects the whole person and has repercussions in his faculties, both spiritual and corporal. If it is our time to die, Christ prepares us through this sacrament for entrance into the home of our Father.

1. *What is the sacrament of the Anointing of the Sick?*

The Anointing of the Sick (Extreme Unction) is the sacrament in which Christ through the anointing and prayers of the priest strengthens the sick person in body and soul so that he may lead a vigorous spiritual life when we are in danger of death.

2. *What does Christ accomplish in us through the sacrament of the Anointing of the Sick?*

Through the sacrament of Anointing of the Sick:

a. Christ increases the divine life in the soul;

b. He brings relief to the body so that it no longer impedes the soul. Thus strengthened he is able to live an intense spiritual life despite illness.

c. He gives the actual graces which enable us to be resigned to death and so to bear our illness, etc.

d. he forgives sin and removes the temporal punishment due to sin. When confession is impossible, he forgives even mortal sin through this sacrament.

3. What is the sign of this sacrament?

The sign of this sacrament is the anointing with oil and the words of the priest: "May the Lord forgive you by this holy anointing and his most loving mercy whatever sins you have committed." The priest anoints the eyes, ears, nose, lips, hands and if convenient, the feet of the sick person. In case of necessity a simple anointing on the forehead is sufficient.

4. What are the prayers the priest says in anointing?

Extending his right hand over the head of the sick person, the priest says:

"In the name of the Father, and of the Son and of the Holy Spirit. May any power that the devil has over you be utterly destroyed, as I place my hands on you and call upon the help of the glorious and holy Mother of God, the Virgin Mary, and of her illustrious spouse, Joseph, and of all the holy angels, archangels, patriarchs, prophets, apostles, martyrs, confessors, virgins and all the saints. Amen."

Having moistened his thumb with holy oil, the priest anoints the eyes, ears, nostrils, mouth, hands and feet of the sick in the form of a cross as he prays:

"May the Lord forgive you by this holy anointing and his most loving mercy whatever sin you have committed by the use of your sight (hearing, etc.) Amen.

Let us pray. O Lord God, you said through your apostle James: 'Is anyone sick among you? Let him bring in the priests of the Church, and let them pray over him, anointing him with oil in the name of the Lord. And the prayer of faith will save the sick man, and the Lord will raise him up, and if he be in sins, they shall be forgiven him.' We implore you,

202

our Redeemer, that by the grace of the Holy Spirit you cure the illness of this sick man (woman) and heal his (her) wounds; forgive his (her) sins, and drive away from him (her) all pains of mind and body. In your mercy give him (her) health, inward and outward, so that he (she) may once more be able to take up his (her) work, restored by the gift of your mercy. You who live and reign with the Father and the Holy Spirit, God, forever and ever. Amen.

Let us pray. We implore you, O Lord, look with kindness on your servant, N, who is growing weak as his (her) body fails. Cherish the soul which you created, so that, purified and made whole by his (her) sufferings, he (she) may find himself (herself) restored by your healing. Through Christ our Lord. Amen.

Let us pray. Lord, Holy Father, almighty and eternal God, by pouring the grace of your blessing into the bodies of the sick, you watch with all-embracing care over your creatures. Be present in your kindness as we call upon your holy name. Free your servant from sickness, restore him (her) his (her) health, raise him (her) up by your right hand, strengthen him (her) by your power, protect him (her) by your might and give him (her) back to your holy Church, with all that is needed for his (her) welfare. Through Christ our Lord. Amen."

5. Should the Anointing of the Sick be administered only to one who is dying?

No. This sacrament should be administered to anyone who is seriously ill. The term "in danger of death" is not used here in the medical sense, i.e. that death is certain and imminent, but only in the sense that the person is seriously ill and death may result from the sickness. Thus, a person could be anointed even though it was much more probable that he would entirely recover from his illness. One of the effects of the sacrament is to strengthen the person in body and soul so he can lead an intense spiritual life despite his sickness. The sooner in his illness he receives the sacrament, the more he will profit by its invigorating effects. This fact is clear also from the prayers said by the bishop in the blessing of the oil.

"May all who have been anointed with this heavenly medicine have it as protection of mind and body; may all pains, all weaknesses, all sickness of mind and body be turned out through it."

6. How does the Anointing of the Sick prepare us for heaven?

The Anointing of the Sick not only forgives our sins; it also remedies the weaknesses which are in us as a result of our sins. In this sacrament Christ gives us graces which enable us to have deep sorrow for our sins, to bear the pain and distress of our illness with patience, and to give our lives freely back to God, accepting death with resignation as a consequence of sin. If we cooperate with these graces we can be so purified from sin and imperfection that we shall be ready to enter heaven immediately after we die.

7. What is included under the term "the last rites"?

The last rites include:

a. the sacrament of Penance,

b. the Anointing of the Sick,

c. Holy Communion, which is here called Viaticum.

d. the apostolic blessing, which imparts a plenary indulgence.

Practical Points

1. Those who have the care of a sick person should call the priest as soon as they discover that the illness is serious. To put off calling the priest for fear of frightening the person is false charity. The earlier in his illness a person receives the sacrament, the better can he prepare himself for death, and the better are his chances of being healed.

2. For a sick call have the following items handy: holy

water, a crucifix, two blessed candles, a glass of water, a spoon and some cotton. These articles should be on a table which is covered with a white linen cloth.

3. When the priest comes to the house on a sick call, the members of the family should remain in the sick room except while the priest is hearing the confession. If the priest is bringing the Blessed Sacrament, he should be met at the door with a lighted candle and led to the sick room.

4. Catholics should be careful to let the parish priest know whenever there is any serious illness in the family. The priest can judge what ought to be done. In the case of a prolonged illness the priest will bring Communion even when there is no danger of death.

5. If someone dies suddenly or is injured seriously, the priest should be called immediately. The priest should be called even though to all appearances death has already taken place.

6. When the last rites are given the family should join in saying the prayers. Booklets can be procured for this purpose. The prayers for the dying should be said aloud by the family in the absence of the priest.

7. The Church treats the bodies of her children, even after death, with the greatest reverence. The body, which was once the temple of the Holy Spirit and which is destined to rise again on the last day, is brought to the church, where Mass is offered. It is then incensed and sprinkled with holy water and carried to its burial in consecrated ground. Catholic cemeteries are holy places, consecrated as the abode of the bodies of the faithful. All Catholics are to be buried in a Catholic cemetery. Burial in consecrated ground is part of the burial service, which includes the Mass for the dead, the blessing after Mass and the services at the grave. Church law, therefore, requires burial in a Catholic cemetery. If you already own a lot in a non-sectarian cemetery, check the matter with your parish priest.

8. It is a pious custom to have Masses said for the dead.

For every high priest taken from among men is appointed for men in the things pertaining to God, that he may offer gifts and sacrifices for sins. He is able to have compassion on the ignorant and erring, because he himself also is beset with weakness, and by reason thereof is obliged to offer for sins, as on behalf of the people, so also for himself. And no man takes the honor to himself; he takes it who is called by God, as Aaron was. So also Christ did not glorify himself with the high priesthood, but he who spoke to him, "Thou art my son, I this day have begotten thee"

—HEB. 5:1-5.

JESUS CHRIST, mediator between God and man, is the eternal priest. In the crowning act of his priesthood he offered himself to the Father on the cross for our sake. But Christ was priest not only on the cross; in his very being he is *the* priest, and his priesthood is an eternal one: ". . . he, because he continues forever, has an everlasting priesthood. Therefore he is able at all times to save those who come to God through him, since he lives always to make intercession for them"—HEB. 7:24-25.

But Christ is not content to live his priesthood only in heaven. He desires to live on and exercise that priesthood here on earth until the end of time. Christ, the merciful priest who forgave sinners, the gentle priest who blessed the people, the zealous priest who sought out the lost sheep, the loving priest who offered himself and fed his disciples with his own flesh and blood, still lives and continues his priestly work in the world. He does so by means of the sacrament of Holy Orders, through which he shares his priesthood with men. Through this sacrament Christ gives to human beings the staggering power of changing bread and wine into his body and blood, the power of forgiving sins, the awesome powers of his priesthood.

Some people are shocked at the idea that a priest should claim to possess such powers. "How," they ask, "can an ordinary man forgive sin?" The answer is that a priest is not an ordinary man. He is a man who has been made "another Christ" through the sacrament of Holy Orders. It is Christ who has performed this wonder. It is Christ who will have it so. He desires to work through men. He desires to forgive sinners, to teach and preach, to give the divine life, to renew his sacrifice on the cross through human beings, the men whom he consecrates and empowers as his priests through this great sacrament.

> *The priest is like "another Christ" because he is marked with an indelible character, making him, as it were, a living image of our Saviour. The priest represents Christ who said, "As the Father has sent me, I also send you; he who hears you, hears me." Admitted to this most sublime ministry by a call from heaven, he is appointed for men in the things pertaining to God, that he may offer gifts and sacrifices for sins.*
>
> *To him must come anyone who wishes to live the life of the divine Redeemer and who desires to receive strength, comfort and nourishment for his soul; from him the salutary medicine must be sought by anyone who wishes to rise from sin and lead a good life. Hence all priests may apply to themselves with full right the words of the Apostle of the Gentiles: "We are God's helpers"*—Enc. on the Development of Holiness in Priestly Life, 7.

1. What is the sacrament of Holy Orders?

Holy Orders is the sacrament through which Christ gives to men the power and the grace to perform the sacred duties of bishops, priests and other ministers of the Church.

2. When did our Lord institute Holy Orders?

After changing bread and wine into his body and blood Jesus told his apostles, "Do this in commemoration of me." With these words he conferred the priesthood on the apostles.

3. What is the sign of the sacrament of Holy Orders?

The sign of this sacrament is the laying on of hands by the bishop and the essential words from the preface. (cf. pg. 162)

When the apostles ordained deacons, priests or bishops they did so by the laying on of hands

. . . I admonish thee to stir up the grace of God which is in thee by the laying on of my hands—2 Tim. 1:6.

4. What does Christ accomplish through the sacrament of Holy Orders?

Through the sacrament of Holy Orders our Lord—

a. increases the divine life of the one who is ordained,

b. gives a new character to the soul,

c. gives the right to all the actual graces needed to fulfill the sacred office.

d. gives the powers of the priesthood.

5. Who administers Holy Orders?

The bishop administers Holy Orders.

6. What are the degrees in Holy Orders?

The three major orders of deacon, priest and bishop, comprise the sacrament of Holy Orders. The order of subdeaconate and the four minor orders are not part of the sacrament, but sacramentals which consecrate a man to the service of the Church in a special way.

The *Major Orders* are those of bishop, priest and deacon.

A *bishop* has the fullness of the priesthood and ecclesiastical jurisdiction over a diocese.

A *priest* has the power to offer Mass and administer the sacraments.

A *deacon* may assist a priest or bishop at a solemn Mass, may preach, and, with permission, may distribute Communion and solemnly baptize.

A *subdeacon* may assist the deacon and the priest at a solemn Mass.

The *Minor Orders* are acolyte, exorcist, lector, and porter.

7. How is Holy Orders a social sacrament?

Holy Orders is given to a man primarily for the benefit of others. There are five sacraments for the salvation and personal growth in holiness of the individual. The other two, Marriage and Holy Orders, provide for the life of the community, the Church.

8. What is the work of a priest?

The work of a priest is the work of Christ, the teaching, and sanctifying (and in the case of bishops, who have the fullness of the priesthood, the ruling) of the members of the Mystical Body of Christ. The priest, as Christ among men, also has a missionary work, that of bringing Christ to all men and all men to Christ.

The work of the Church in the modern world is so extensive that her priests are to be found working in many fields.

Some priests are missionaries, carrying the Gospel to other lands, or doing missionary work in their own country.

Some priests are teachers in Catholic schools. Some are chaplains of Catholic students in secular universities. Some priests are engaged in administrative and specialized work.

Some priests are in monastic orders, living the life and doing the work which is special to the order or congregation to which they belong.

Some priests are working in parishes, as pastors or as assistants to pastors.

The primary function of all priests, whatever their field of special work, is to offer Mass and to pray the divine office. These functions they perform officially, in the name of the whole Church.

9. What is the work of a priest in a parish?

The work of a priest in a parish is a most varied work. It partakes of something of each of the special fields outlined above.

The parish priest does missionary work. He has the care not only of the healthy members of the parish, but also of those who have fallen away, those who have married outside the Church, and those who are lukewarm and weak in their faith. He must seek out, too, those who are not Catholics, and try to bring them into contact with Christ's Church.

The parish priest also teaches. He instructs converts, both privately and in classes. He teaches catechism in the parish school.

The parish priest has the care of the sick in the parish. He visits them in their homes and in the hospitals. He brings Holy Communion to the sick and anoints those who are in danger of death.

The priest in a parish administers the sacraments to the people; he baptizes, hears confessions, prepares couples for marriage and assists at the wedding.

The parish priest acts as chaplain for the various parish organizations. Many parish priests are chaplains of groups who are working in the lay apostolate, the Legion of Mary, the Young Christian Workers, the Christian Family Movement, and many other organizations of men, women, and youth.

The parish priest is in charge of the most important function of the parish, the worship of God. He must officiate at and provide for the ceremonies which are part of the liturgy.

Pastors of parishes have a great deal of administrative work to do. Theirs is the responsibility for the whole parish, the physical plant as well as the care of souls.

Practice

▶ Parents should consider it a great blessing to have a son who aspires to the priesthood, and they should do all in their power to foster his vocation.

The functions of an acolyte are performed by the altar boys. Parents should be proud to have their sons serve at the altar. Men should also be proud to perform such functions as acting as ushers, serving Mass and singing in the choir.

Make sure that you know the name of the bishop of the diocese in which you live. Pray for him at Mass at the beginning of the canon, where we pray for the pope and for our bishop. Pray, too, for priests, particularly the priest who is giving you instructions, and for the priests of your parish.

Be subject to one another in the fear of Christ. Let wives be subject to their husbands as to the Lord; because a husband is head of the wife, just as Christ is head of the Church, being himself Saviour of the body. But just as the Church is subject to Christ, so also let wives be to their husbands in all things.

Husbands, love your wives, just as Christ also loved the Church, and delivered himself up for her, that he might sanctify her, cleansing her in the bath of water by means of the word; in order that he might present to himself the Church in all her glory, not having spot or wrinkle or any such thing, but that she might be holy and without blemish. Even thus ought husbands also to love their wives as their own bodies. He who loves his own wife, loves himself. For no one ever hated his own flesh; on the contrary he nourishes and cherishes it, as Christ also does the Church (because we are members of his body, made from his flesh and from his bones).

"For this reason a man shall leave his father and mother, and shall cleave to his wife; and the two shall become one flesh."

*This is a great mystery—I mean in reference to Christ and to the Church. However, let each one of you also love his wife just as he loves himself; and let the wife respect her husband—*EPH. 5:21-33.

WITHIN THE Mystical Body of Christ each member has his function to perform: "And God indeed has placed some in the Church, first apostles, secondly prophets, thirdly teachers . . ."—1 COR. 12:28. Certain of the sacraments give us our vocation within the Body of Christ and guarantee us the graces to live up to that vocation. It is the sacrament of Marriage which confers the vocation of parenthood. Christian fathers and mothers, therefore, have a special sacrament which fits them for the very important office which is theirs, that of giving life and Christian education to the newest members of Christ, their children. The sacrament of Marriage sanctifies the natural love of man and woman, raises it from the natural order to the supernatural and makes it the vehicle of God's grace.

In the marriage ceremony the priest may address the following words from the ritual to the couple about to be married.

Dear friends in Christ: As you know, you are about to enter into a union which is most sacred and most serious, a union which was established by God himself. By it, he gave to man a share in the greatest work of creation, the work of the continuation of the human race. And in this way he sanctified human love and enabled man and woman to help each other live as children of God, by sharing a common life under his fatherly care.

Because God himself is thus its author, marriage is of its very nature a holy institution, requiring of those who enter into it a complete and unreserved giving of self. But Christ our Lord added to the holiness of marriage an even deeper meaning and a higher beauty. He referred to the love of marriage to describe his own love for his Church, that is, for the people of God whom he redeemed by his own blood. And so he gave to Christians a new vision of what married life ought to be, a life of self-sacrificing love like his own. It is for this reason that his apostle, St. Paul, clearly states that marriage is now and for all time to be considered a great mystery, intimately bound up with the supernatural union of Christ and the Church, which union is also to be its pattern.

1. What is the sacrament of Marriage?

Marriage is the sacrament in which Christ unites a Christian man and woman in a life-long union, making them two in one flesh.

2. What is the sign of the sacrament of Marriage?

The sign of the sacrament of Marriage is the expression on the part of the bride and groom of their consent to marriage.

3. When did Jesus Christ raise marriage to the dignity of a sacrament?

The words in which Christ made marriage a sacrament are

not recorded in Sacred Scripture. The institution of the sacrament may have taken place at the marriage feast of Cana—John 2:1-10, or on the occasion of Christ's remarks about marriage to the Pharisees—MARK 10:2-12. The Church teaches infallibly that Christ instituted the sacrament of Marriage, as he did all the others.

4. What does Christ accomplish through the sacrament of Marriage?

Through the sacrament of Marriage Christ confers:

a. an increase of the divine life;

b. all the actual graces needed throughout married life to bring about an ever deeper union of man and wife in soul and body to help them live up to what they promised in their marriage vows when they said: "I take you for my lawful wife (husband) to have and to hold, from this day forward, for better for worse, for richer, for poorer, in sickness and in health, until death do us part";

c. All the actual graces needed for the fulfillment of the vocation of parenthood.

5. What did our Lord teach about marriage?
Our Lord taught:

a. that marriage was instituted by God;

b. that husband and wife find their fulfillment in each other;

c. that marriage is to last for life;

d. that marriage must be between one man and one woman.

And there came to him some Pharisees, testing him, and saying, "Is it lawful for a man to put away his wife for any cause?" But he answered and said to them, "Have you not read that the Creator, from the beginning, made them male and female, and said, 'For this cause a man shall leave his father and mother, and cleave to his wife, and the two shall become one flesh'? Therefore now they are no longer two, but one flesh. What therefore God has joined together, let no man put asunder." They said to him, "Why then did Moses command to give a written notice of dismissal, and to put her away?" He said to them, "Because Moses, by reason of the hardness of your heart, permitted you to put

213

away your wives; but it was not so from the beginning. And I say to you, that whoever puts away his wife, except for immorality, and marries another, commits adultery; and he who marries a woman who has been put away commits adultery"—MATT. 19:3-9.

6. When did God institute marriage?

At the very beginning of the human race, when he created Adam and Eve, God instituted marriage.

Then God blessed them and said to them, "Be fruitful and multiply; fill the earth and subdue it. Have dominion over the fish of the sea, the birds of the air, the cattle and all the animals that crawl on the earth—GEN. 1:28.

Then the Lord God said, "It is not good that the man is alone; I will make him a helper like himself."

The Lord God cast the man into a deep sleep and, while he slept, took one of his ribs and closed up its place with flesh. And the rib which the Lord God took from the man, he made into a woman, and brought her to him. Then the man said, "She now is bone of my bone, and flesh of my flesh; she shall be called woman, for from man she has been taken." For this reason a man leaves his father and mother, and clings to his wife, and the two become one flesh

—GEN. 2:18, 21-24.

7. For what purpose did God institute marriage?

God instituted marriage for the procreation and education of children and for the mutual fulfillment of husband and wife.

Among the blessings of marriage offspring holds the first place. The Creator of the human race himself, who in his goodness has willed to use human beings as his ministers in the propagation of life, taught us this truth when in instituting matrimony in the Garden of Eden he bade our first parents, and through them all married persons who should come after them: "Increase and multiply and fill the earth." St. Augustine rightly draws the same conclusion from the words of the apostle St. Paul to Timothy: the apostle testifies that procreation is the purpose of matrimony when, having said, "I will that the younger women should marry," he adds immediately, as though he had been asked the reason, "so that they may bear children and become mothers of families"—Enc. on Christian Marriage 24, 25.

8. What did Christ teach about divorce?

Christ said, "What God has joined together, let no man put asunder." Therefore he taught that there can be no divorce. He said, "Whoever puts away his wife, except for immorality, and marries another commits adultery. . . ." Therefore he taught that an attempted marriage following a "divorce" would be invalid and adulterous.

In the Old Testament God had permitted divorce to the Jews because of the hardness of their hearts. The Old Law was imperfect in this as well as in other respects. Christ restored marriage to what God had intended in the beginning, a union of one man and one woman for life.

9. What did our Lord mean by the words "except for immorality"?

The word immorality refers to a union which was forbidden by Jewish law. In this case a man would have the duty of terminating an illicit and invalid union. The words do not mean that divorce is permissible in the case of infidelity.

10. What did Christ do for marriage by elevating it to the dignity of a sacrament?

In making it a sacrament Christ gave marriage a new meaning, a new beauty and a new power of sanctifying. Marriage is now not merely the lawful union of man and wife; it is a source of holiness, a means of a closer union of each with God as well as with each other. The union of husband and wife in Marriage is a type of the union of Christ and his Church.

11. In what way is the union of husband and wife a symbol of the union of Christ and his Church?

The union between Christ and his Church is a vital, life-giving union. The union of husband and wife is a life-giving union, imparting grace to their souls.

The union between Christ and his Church is an organic union, the union of head and body. The union of husband and wife is a union of two in one flesh and one spirit.

The union between Christ and his Church is a union of

infinite love, love which is constant and unwavering, love which is self-sacrificial. The union of husband and wife is also a union of love, love which is exclusively given to one's spouse, love which is unselfish, love which lasts as long as life.

12. What did St. Paul mean when he said that "the husband is the head of the wife"?

St. Paul said that the husband is the head of the wife just as Christ is Head of the Church. The husband has the final authority within the family; but he must use this authority as Christ does, who "also loved the Church and delivered himself up for her." The husband must nourish and cherish his wife "as Christ also does the Church." What is more, husbands are commanded to "love their wives as Christ also loved the Church."

13. Who administers the sacrament of Marriage?

The bride and groom administer this sacrament to each other. The first gift they give to each other as man and wife is the gift of the divine life.

14. What laws safeguard marriage?

a. Since marriage was instituted by God, there are divine laws, such as the indissolubility and unity of marriage.

b. Since marriage was made a sacrament by Christ, the head of the Church, there are laws made by the Church which protect it. For example, the Church demands that Catholics be married before a priest and two witnesses. It is Church law which fixes the age for marriage, forbids mixed marriages, etc.

c. Since marriage is the basis of human society, the state makes laws governing it. Such laws are those which require a marriage license, blood test, etc.

15. Has the state the power to grant a divorce?

The state has no power to dissolve a valid marriage. Consequently, the Church does not ordinarily recognize the subsequent marriages of divorced persons, even if the parties involved are non-Catholics. The state may, however, dissolve the civil

216

aspects of a valid marriage. This is called in civil law a divorce; but in the eyes of God the marriage still exists.

16. Has the Church the power to grant a divorce?

Not even the Church has the power of dissolving a valid, sacramental marriage which has been consummated. Therefore, when the Church declares that a marriage is null and void, she is merely declaring that something existed at the time of the marriage which rendered the marriage invalid from the very beginning; e.g., in the case where one of the parties to the marriage did not give true matrimonial consent.

There are cases in which the Church (not the state) has the power of dissolving the *natural* bond of marriage. One such instance is the well known "Pauline Privilege"—cf. 1 COR. 7:12-16.

Practical Points

1. Since Marriage is one of the sacraments of the living, it is necessary to be in the state of grace to receive it licitly. The first gift which a bride and groom give each other is the gift of the divine life. It would be a great misfortune to be unable to receive this gift because of the obstacle of unrepented mortal sin. Moreover, since Marriage is a sacrament which usually is received only once in a lifetime, the dispositions of soul with which one receives it are particularly important. The couple who are about to receive the sacrament should prepare themselves not only by confession but by a longer period of prayer and reflection. The best preparation for Marriage is a few days spent in prayer and recollection in a lay retreat house.

2. No one would accept a position from which he could never resign without a great deal of thought and investigation. No one would enter a profession without adequate preparation. Yet thousands enter into marriage with little or no preparation. To remedy this situation some dioceses provide Pre-Cana conferences or other types of marriage preparation. Engaged couples should avail themselves of these services.

3. Married couples can derive great benefit from a Cana Conference for husbands and wives. In some places these days are held regularly in various parishes throughout the diocese. They provide an excellent means of stirring up the graces which are in the married couple, in order that their union may become ever more perfect.

4. The graces of the sacrament of Marriage are given to be used in the daily life of a Christian husband and wife. They are meant to work in conjunction with, not independently of the graces of the other sacraments. Married people should use the sacraments of Penance and Holy Eucharist often, and they should use them with their state of life in mind, seeking by means of confession to rid themselves of the faults which prevent a more perfect marriage union and family life, and by means of Communion to grow in love for one another in Christ.

5. "Divorced" persons, we must remember, are still married in the eyes of God. To keep company with such a person would be a serious sin. Many a marriage outside the Church has resulted from such company-keeping.

6. Every Catholic must be married before a priest and two witnesses. Otherwise the marriage is not a valid one, and the two parties are not really husband and wife. The marriage of non-Catholics is valid, as long as they are not bound by any impediment.

7. The Church has set up certain impediments to marriage, conditions which render a marriage either unlawful or both unlawful and invalid. When there is a sufficient reason to do so, the bishop may grant a dispensation from certain impediments, provided the impediment does not affect the essence of marriage.

8. Couples planning marriage should consult the parish priest of the bride at least a month before the marriage. The publication of the banns in church is done usually on the three Sundays before the marriage date.

9. Catholics should be married at Mass. Only for a serious reason should a Catholic couple deprive themselves of the great privilege of being married at Mass.

The Sacramentals

Then were brought to him little children that he might lay his hands on them and pray; but the disciples rebuked them. But Jesus said to them, "Let the little children be, and do not hinder them from coming to me, for of such is the kingdom of heaven." And when he had laid his hands on them, he departed from that place—MATT. 19:13-15.

OUR LORD has given us seven sacraments, by which he sanctifies and strengthens us and fits us for our role in his Mystical Body. In imitation of Christ, her head, the Church has given us the sacramentals, by means of which she sanctifies the ordinary things of life, calls down God's blessings upon us and reminds us in a practical and vivid way of the truths by which we live. The Church blesses many of the objects which we use in daily life. We need never be out of reach of her blessing. We are never abandoned to our own weakness in any emergency. The Church is constantly at our side, asking God to bless us and the things we use.

1. What are sacramentals?

Sacramentals are special blessings or blessed objects which the Church gives us in order to inspire our devotion and to gain for us certain spiritual and temporal favors.

2. How do the sacramentals differ from the sacraments?

Christ instituted the sacraments; the Church the sacramentals. The sacraments were instituted to give grace; the sacramentals to impart a blessing or some special protection.

3. What are the effects of the sacramentals?

The effects of the sacramentals are:

a. the remission of venial sin and of the temporal punishments due to sin;

b. the repression of evil spirits;

c. the giving of actual grace through the prayer of the Church;

d. health of body and material blessings.

4. What are some of the principal sacramentals?

The ceremonies, actions and prayers which surround the essential act in the sacraments are sacramentals. The anointings in Baptism, the prayers used in the Last Anointing and the nuptial blessing given in Marriage are a few examples of such sacramentals.

The sign of the cross, holy water, the rosary, the way of the cross and benediction of the Blessed Sacrament are examples of sacramentals which are used frequently.

5. What are the sacramentals which are given on certain days during the year?

Candles are blessed and distributed on Candlemas Day, Feb. 2. The blessing of throats is given on St. Blaise Day, Feb. 3. Blessed ashes are placed on our forehead on Ash Wednesday, to remind us of our death and to urge us to do penance during Lent. Blessed palms are distributed on Second Passion Sunday, as a reminder of our Lord's triumphal entry into Jerusalem to begin his Passion. The blessing of fields takes place on August 15. Other sacramentals, such as the blessing of a home or of a mother after childbirth, can be given at any time.

6. How should we use the sacramentals?

We should use the sacramentals with faith and reverence, as the Church instructs us to do. We must avoid superstition in our use of medals and other blessed objects, remembering that they, as well as the other sacramentals, produce their effect not automatically, but as a result of the prayers of the Church and the devotion they inspire in us.

Devotion

Many laymen wish to associate themselves with various religious orders in order to participate in the prayers and good works of those orders. Originally these people were allowed to wear the religious habit of the order with which they were associated. Now they wear the scapular—two small pieces of cloth connected by strings and worn over the shoulders. There are sixteen scapulars in which Catholics may be invested. The oldest and most common of these is the scapular of our Lady of Mount Carmel, by which the wearer shares in the fruits of the good works and prayers of the Carmelite Order.

In place of the actual scapular one may wear the scapular medal, which has an image of the Sacred Heart on one side and of our Lady on the other. There are many spiritual privileges attached to wearing the scapular. Converts may be enrolled in any or all of the scapulars after they have made their First Communion.

Practice

▶ Pictures, statues and crucifixes can be an aid in prayer and in keeping us mindful of God and the things of God. Every Catholic home should have a crucifix or some religious picture or statue in a prominent place.

Care should be used in selecting these objects, however. They should be in good taste, not merely "religious," the kind which will inspire devotion, rather than mere sentiment. Nowadays good religious art is available. We need not be satisfied with anything less.

Encyclical of Pius XII on the Sacred Liturgy, Washington, D. C., N.C.W.C., 10¢.

> The official papal teaching on the worship of the Church. Beautiful and inspiring reading. Available paper bound in several editions.

Of Sacraments and Sacrifice, HOWELL. Collegeville, Minn., Liturgical Press, 183 pp., 90¢ (paper)

> Required reading for all who want to know the meaning of prayer, the Mass and the sacraments. Despite the profundity of its subject and its thought, this wonderful book is very easy to read.

Christ Acts Through the Sacraments, ROGUET. Liturgical Press, 162 pp., $1.25 (paper)

> One of the best short books on the nature and the effects of the sacraments.

My Mass, PUTZ. Westminster, Md., Newman Press, 151 pp., $1.50 (paper)

> An excellent treatment of sacrifice and of the Mass as a sacrifice. Not difficult reading.

Holy Mass, ROGUET. Collegeville, Minn., Liturgical Press, 120 pp., $1.75 (paper)

> A very fine work on the nature of the Mass. Should be read.

Study the Mass, PARSCH. Collegeville, Minn., Liturgical Press, 118 pp. $.35.

> A condensation of a longer book which outlines the origin, history and meaning of the parts of the Mass. Invaluable for all.

Fides Albums, Chicago, Ill., Fides, 24 or 32 pp., 25¢ per album.

> The sacraments and the Mass presented in an ingenious form which combines the best in photographic art with excellent written commentary. Albums on Baptism, Marriage, Confirmation, the Mass, the Priest, the Sacraments of the sick and the Passion are available.

Sacred Signs, GUARDINI. St. Louis, Pio Decimo Press, 106 pp., $1.75.

> A delightful book on the sacramentals and things connected with worship. Very easy to read.

The Church's Year of Grace, PIUS PARSCH. Collegeville, Minn., Liturgical Press, $2.25 a vol.

> Three volumes of this masterpiece are now translated into English. A fourth is on the way. Explains the meaning of each Mass of the year and of the liturgical seasons.

Christ the Life of the Soul, 373 pp. $5.00.
Christ in His Mysteries, 407 pp. MARMION. St. Louis, Herder, $5.00.

> Two wonderful books integrating the liturgy and the spiritual life. Difficult reading, but very rewarding.

PART V

THE COMMANDMENTS OF GOD

section **35** | **The Great Powers of a Christian**

Beloved, let us love one another, for love is from God. And everyone who loves is born of God, and knows God. He who does not love does not know God; for God is love. In this has the love of God been shown in our case, that God has sent his only-begotten Son into the world that we may live through him. In this is the love, not that we have loved God, but that he has first loved us, and sent his Son a propitiation for our sins. Beloved, if God has so loved us, we also ought to love one another—1 JOHN 4:7-11.

In this we have come to know his love, that he laid down his life for us; and we likewise ought to lay down our life for the brethren. He who has the goods of this world and sees his brother in need and closes his heart to him, how does the love of God abide in him? My dear children, let us not love in word, neither with the tongue, but in deed and in truth—1 JOHN 3:16-18.

WE HAVE been made children of God, having been "born again of water and the Holy Spirit." In Baptism we have received a new life from Christ. We must therefore live a new life, a life consistent with the dignity of a Christian.

The Christian life is a life of love. "Thou shalt love the Lord thy God with thy whole heart, and with thy whole soul, and with thy whole mind." This is the greatest and the first commandment. And the second is like it, "Thou shalt love thy neighbor as thyself"—MATT. 22:37-39.

"A new commandment I give you," Jesus said, "that you love one another. By this will all men know that you are my disciples, if you have love for one another"—JOHN 13:34-35. "This is my commandment, that you love one another as I have loved you. Greater love than this no one has, that one lay down his life for his friends. You are my friends if you do the things I command you"—JOHN 15:12-14.

We would not be able to love God or one another as children of God without a special gift from God, the gift of charity. This gift is one of the great powers which God gives us with the gift of the divine life, the power to believe God, the power to hope in him and the power to love him and to love our fellowmen as children of God, the virtues of faith, hope and charity. These gifts, together with the gifts of the Holy Spirit and the other helps which God gives us enable us to live according to the new life which is ours as members of the Mystical Body of Christ, to make a return to God for the gifts he has given us. The return gift we give to God must be no less than God's gift to us—Christ. We return Christ to God by allowing Christ to live in us, by living the Christ life ever more fully.

1. Why do we receive the divine life here on earth?

We receive the divine life here on earth because God wants us to be born again and begin to share his life here and constantly increase it. The greater the degree of the divine life we possess, the more like God we become, the greater glory we give God and the happier we shall be in heaven.

2. How do we receive the divine life?

The ordinary way of receiving the divine life is through Baptism, to which we are led by faith.

He who believes and is baptized shall be saved—MARK 16:16.

3. How does the divine life grow within us?

When God gives us the divine life he also gives us new powers which enable us to *act* and grow in that life. These new powers are the virtues of faith, hope and charity, the moral virtues of prudence, justice, temperance and fortitude and the gifts of the Holy Spirit.

4. What is faith?

Faith is a power given us by God which enables us to believe God in whatever he has told us. Our minds cannot fully

226

understand the mysteries which God has revealed to us. But faith makes us *certain* of the truth of everything God has said, more certain than we are about things we see or hear, because faith rests on the authority of God himself.

5. Can we earn the gift of faith?

No. We receive faith from God as a free gift. There is nothing we can do to earn it. But God, "Who wishes all men to be saved and to come to the knowledge of the truth"—I TIM. 2:4, offers the gift of faith to all men.

6. What is an act of faith?

An act of faith is an *expression* we give to the gift of faith. An act of faith is a great act of humility; it demands that we submit our minds to God and accept his word for something we cannot see for ourselves.

> *Amen I say to you, whoever does not accept the kingdom of God as a little child will not enter into it*—LUKE 18:17.

7. How do we live by faith?

We live by faith by acting according to what we believe rather than according to what the world tells us. To live by faith means also to strive ever for a deeper faith and to desire the will of God rather than our own.

> *What will it profit, my brethren, if a man says he has faith, but does not have works? Can the faith save him? And if a brother or a sister be naked and in want of daily food, and one of you say to them, "Go in peace, be warmed and filled," yet you do not give them what is necessary for the body, what does it profit? So faith too, unless it has works, is dead in itself. But someone will say, "Thou hast faith, and I have works." Show me thy faith without works, and I from my works will show thee my faith*—JAMES 2:14-18.
>
> *For just as the body without the spirit is dead, so faith also without works is dead*—JAMES 2:26.

8. What is hope?

Hope is a power given us by God which enables us to have confidence that God will grant us pardon for our sins, the divine life, and heaven itself. Hope also includes a desire for the rewards which God has promised those who love him, a desire to possess God, the source of everlasting happiness.

> You who fear the LORD, wait for his mercy,
>   turn not away lest you fall.
> You who fear the LORD, trust him,
>   and your reward will not be lost.
> You who fear the LORD, hope for good things,
>   for lasting joy and mercy.
> Study the generations long past and understand;
>   has anyone hoped in the LORD and been disappointed?
> Has anyone persevered in his fear and been forsaken?
>   has anyone called upon him and been rebuffed?
> Compassionate and merciful is the LORD;
>   he forgives sins, he saves in time of trouble
>   —SIR. 2:7-11.

9. What is an act of hope?

An act of hope is an *expression* we give to the gift of hope. Like the act of faith it is a great act of humility. Left to ourselves we have no right to hope for forgiveness or to aspire to heaven. But clinging to Christ, our Saviour, who has paid the price of our salvation, we rely on the goodness of God, who has promised to save us if we cooperate with the help he gives.

10. What is charity?

Charity is the gift given by God which enables us to love him above all things for his own sake and to love ourselves and all our brothers as children of God.

11. How are faith, hope and charity increased within us?

Faith, hope and charity are increased within us by use; the more we exercise faith the stronger becomes our faith; the more we exercise hope and love the stronger become our hope and love.

12. What are the moral virtues?

The moral virtues are:

a. prudence, the virtue which inclines us to form right judgments about what we should or should not do,

b. justice, the virtue which inclines us to give to all men whatever is due to them, *c. temperance,* the virtue which inclines us to govern our appetites according to what is right and pleasing to God,

d. fortitude, the virtue which inclines us to do what God desires, even when it is hard and disagreeable.

13. What are the gifts of the Holy Spirit?

The gifts of the Holy Spirit are:

a. counsel, the gift which moves us to act with prudence, especially in difficult cases,

b. piety, the gift which moves us to love God as our Father and to have affection for all persons and things consecrated to him,

c. fear of the Lord, the gift which moves us to fear offending God and being separated from him whom we love,

d. fortitude, the gift which moves us to do great things for God joyfully and without fear of difficulties and obstacles,

e. knowledge, the gift which moves us to see the things of this world in their true perspective, in their relation to God,

f. understanding, the gift which moves us to a deeper insight into the truths that God has revealed to us,

g. wisdom, the gift which moves us to judge all things, human and divine, as God sees them and to have a relish for the things of God.

All the gifts of the Holy Spirit make us docile and receptive to the guidance of God and the graces he sends us, and so enable us to act quickly and easily in the performance of his will.

14. How can we express our love for God?

As children of God we can express our love for our Father:

a. by offering him ourselves and everything we do;

We offer ourselves to God in the Morning Offering and throughout the day by doing all we do as well as we can out of love for God.

. . . whether you eat or drink, or do anything else, do all for the glory of God—1 Cor. 10:31.

We offer ourselves to God above all in the Mass. In the Mass

229

we offer ourselves in and with and through Christ. There is no better way of offering ourselves than by daily Mass.

b. by doing his will, by making our own the prayer of Christ,

Not as I will, but as thou willest—MATT. 26:39.

This means, first of all, that we keep the commandments and do not separate ourselves from God by serious sin. Secondly, we must strive to avoid all sin, even that which is not serious.

In this we know that we love the children of God, when we love God and do his commandments. For this is the love of God, that we keep his commandments—1 JOHN 5:2-3.

c. by imitating Christ, whom God has sent not only as our Saviour but also as our model.

Learn from me, for I am meek and humble of heart . . .
—MATT. 11:29.

d. by uniting ourselves to Christ by eating his flesh and drinking his blood in the Eucharist;

He who eats my flesh and drinks my blood abides in me and I in him—JOHN 6:57.

e. by recalling God's mercy to us; he has forgiven our sins; we can love him all the more by being grateful for his forgiveness;

Wherefore I say to thee, her sins, many as they are, shall be forgiven her, because she has loved much. But he to whom little is forgiven, loves little—LUKE 7:47-48.

f. by praying; our prayers should not be merely those in which we ask God for favors; we should also tell him we love him and ask him for an increase of the gift of love;

g. by loving others; we love God only if we love one another.

He who has the goods of this world and sees his brother in need and closes his heart to him how does the love of God abide in him?—1 JOHN 3:17.

15. *How do we express love for our fellow-men?*

We express love for our fellow-men by treating all men with the reverence which is due them as sons of God. This means much more than "not bothering" people or refraining from insulting or injuring them. We must treat every man as we would Christ himself. We must practice the works of mercy. Christ tells us that at the last judgment he will say to us:

*Come, blessed of my Father, take possession of the kingdom
prepared for you from the foundation of the world; for I
was hungry and you gave me to eat; I was thirsty and you
gave me to drink; I was a stranger and you took me in;
naked and you covered me; sick and you visited me; I
was in prison and you came to me. Then the just will answer
him, saying, "Lord when did we see thee hungry, and feed
thee; or thirsty and give thee drink? And when did we see
thee a stranger, and take thee in; or naked, and clothe thee?
Or when did we see thee sick, or in prison, and come to
thee?" And answering, the king will say to them, "Amen I
say to you, as long as you did it for one of these, the least
of my brethren, you did it for me*—MATT. 25:34-40.

16. What are the works of mercy?

The works of mercy are:

to feed the hungry,	to admonish the sinner,
to give drink to the thirsty,	to instruct the ignorant,
to clothe the naked,	to counsel the doubtful,
to visit those in prison,	to comfort the sorrowful,
to shelter the homeless,	to bear wrongs patiently,
to visit the sick,	to forgive all injuries,
to bury the dead,	to pray for the living and the dead.

Often we fail to see opportunities to practice the works of
mercy because we fail to understand them properly. "The naked"
are not only those who have no clothes at all, but those who do
not have enough clothes. "The homeless" are not only displaced
persons, but families who cannot find a decent place to live because landlords refuse to rent to couples with children or to people of certain races. The words of St. John, "He who has the
goods of this world and sees his brother in need and closes his
heart to him, how does the love of God abide in him?"—1 JOHN
3:17—apply to nations as well as to individuals. Yet today there
are countries which are too small in area to support their people,
while other countries with enormous space restrict immigration.
There are countries where abject poverty is so widespread as to
be the rule, countries which need financial and technical aid in
order to feed and clothe their people. A Christian, mindful of
these words of St. John, may not close his eyes to such conditions,

nor condone a policy of apathy or opposition to measures which would help his brothers in need in other countries.

17. *Why do we have to love all men?*

When Jesus was asked the question, "Who is my neighbor?" he replied by telling the story of the good Samaritan, which teaches us that our neighbor is *every man*, not only those who belong to *my* race, *my* country, *my* religion. Even those who hate us and injure us must be included in our love. Jesus tells us in the Sermon on the Mount:

> *But I say to you, love your enemies, do good to those who hate you, and pray for those who persecute and calumniate you, so that you may be children of your Father in heaven, who makes his sun to rise on the good and the evil, and sends rain on the just and the unjust*—MATT. 5:44-46.

Practice

Study the acts of faith, hope and love. If possible memorize them. At least become familiar enough with the content of these prayers to be able to express your faith, hope and love to God in your own words.

An Act of Faith

O my God! I firmly believe that thou art one God in three Divine Persons, Father, Son, and Holy Spirit. I believe that thy Divine Son became man and died for our sins, and that he will come to judge the living and the dead. I believe these and all the truths which the holy Catholic Church teaches because thou hast revealed them, who canst neither deceive nor be deceived.

An Act of Hope

O my God! relying on thy infinite goodness and promises, I hope to obtain pardon of my sins, the help of thy grace, and life everlasting, through the merits of Jesus Christ, my Lord and Redeemer.

232

An Act of Love

O my God! I love Thee above all things with my whole heart and soul because thou art all-good and worthy of all love. I love my neighbor as myself for the love of thee. I forgive all who have injured me, and ask pardon of all whom I have injured.

In your examination of conscience check as to whether you are actually sharing with others the knowledge you are acquiring about God and his Church.

Are there any sick friends or acquaintances whom you have not visited lately? Are there any newcomers in the neighborhood whom you might welcome by a visit?

✠   ✠

section **36** | ## Sin and Its Consequences

*This, therefore, I say and testify in the Lord, that henceforward you are not to walk as the Gentiles walk in the futility of their mind, having their understanding clouded in darkness, estranged from the life of God through the ignorance that is in them, because of the blindness of their heart. For they have given themselves up in despair to sensuality, greedily practising every kind of uncleanness. But you have not so learned Christ—for surely you have heard of him and have been taught in him (as truth is in Jesus) that as regards your former manner of life you are to put off the old man, which is being corrupted through its deceptive lusts. But be renewed in the spirit of your mind, and put on the new man, which has been created according to God in justice and holiness of truth—*EPH. 4:17-24.

GOD THE FATHER looking down upon his Son, Jesus Christ, said: "This is my beloved Son, in whom I am well pleased"—MATT. 3:17. Through Christ we have become adopted sons of God. As good and loving children of God, it should be our constant desire to live under the smile of our Father, to merit his approval, to hear in our hearts the Father saying, "These, too, are my beloved children, members of the Body of my Son, in them I am well pleased."

In order to be pleasing to our Father we must, like Christ, do always what is pleasing to him. We must at the very least refrain from acting ungratefully and rebelliously against him. We must avoid sin.

When we speak of sin and the evil of sin we usually mean serious, or mortal sin. Mortal sin is the greatest of all evils. It is a rejection of God, a breaking of our friendship with God.

Venial sin is not to be compared with mortal sin. It is not a rejection of God. It is an offense against him, but in a manner which does not destroy our friendship.

But it is only by comparison with mortal sin that venial sin seems slight. In itself venial sin is no trivial matter. It is an offense against God or our neighbor, and therefore a failure to love as a child of God should love.

As children of God we must, as St. Paul exhorts us, "put on the new man, which has been created according to God in justice and holiness of truth." We must avoid not only mortal sin, but deliberate venial sin as well.

1. What is sin?

Sin is willful disobedience to God. This disobedience may be an action, a thought, a desire or an intention.

2. How can an internal act be sinful?

Actually, the essence of sin lies in the thought, desire or intention. As soon as we deliberately desire or intend to perform a sinful act we have already offended God. We may lack the courage or the opportunity of putting our desire into action, but that does not change the fact that we have withdrawn our obedience from God. All actions for which we are responsible begin with a desire or intention; the action is merely the carrying out of that desire or intention. This fact explains the words of Christ,

234

> But I say to you that anyone who even looks with lust at a
> woman has already committed adultery with her in his heart
> —MATT. 5:28.

3. What are the different kinds of sins?

The different kinds of sins are:

a. original sin, the sin of our first parents. We suffer from
the *effects* of original sin, but we are not personally guilty of it;

b. personal sin, a sin which we ourselves commit. Personal
sin may be mortal or venial.

4. What is mortal sin?

Mortal sin is a *serious* offense against God. That a sin be
mortal three conditions must be fulfilled:

a. The offense in itself must be *serious,* i.e., something that
has been forbidden or commanded by God under pain of losing
his friendship; e.g., to tell a lie which would seriously injure
someone's reputation would be a mortal sin; to tell an ordinary
lie, which does no serious injury, would be a venial sin.

b. The person who commits the sin must *realize what he is
doing* and that what he is doing is a serious *offense against God;*
e.g., to kill a man deliberately and unjustly would be a mortal sin;
to kill a man accidentally would be no sin.

c. There must be *full consent of the will.* A person acting
under any circumstance which deprives him of free will would
not be guilty of mortal sin.

5. What are the effects of mortal sin?

a. Mortal sin destroys our divine life; hence the word mortal, meaning death dealing.

> For when you were the slaves of sin, you were free as re-
> gards justice. But what fruit had you then from those things
> of which you are now ashamed? For the end of these things
> is death. But now set free from sin and become slaves to God,
> you have your fruit unto sanctification, and as your end,
> life everlasting. For the wages of sin is death, but the gift
> of God is life everlasting in Christ Jesus our Lord
> —ROM. 6:21-23.

b. Mortal sin makes a man displeasing to God. Nothing one
does while in the state of mortal sin can be pleasing to God.

c. Since it is a rejection of God, mortal sin renders the sinner liable to eternal damnation.

6. What is venial sin?

Venial sin is a less serious offense against God. Venial sin is a sin which does not sever our relationship with God, but which does weaken our love for God.

For in many things we all offend—JAMES 3:2.

In venial sin, either the offense itself is not a serious matter (e.g., an ordinary lie of excuse, a small theft, a slight disrespect towards God) or else the sinner is not sufficiently aware of the seriousness of his action, or does not give full consent of his will.

7. Can a sin be fully deliberate and yet be only venial?

Yes. Such a sin is called a deliberate venial sin. Deliberate venial sin weakens the will and paves the way for mortal sin. Deliberate venial sin also lessens the intimacy between us and God. Habitual venial sin brings about a state of lukewarmness which is very dangerous.

8. How do we know whether an action is sinful?

Our conscience tells us whether an action is right or wrong, a mortal or a venial sin.

9. How does our conscience know what is right and wrong?

Our conscience is merely our mind judging on moral matters. Therefore, it must be instructed. We must learn from Christ, teaching through his Church.

10. Can mortal sin be forgiven?

Yes. God will forgive any mortal sins and any number of them if the sinner truly repents. When God forgives the sin he not only restores the divine life and the gift of charity, he even restores all the divine life previously possessed.

11. What happens to one who dies in the state of mortal sin?

One who dies in the state of mortal sin will continue to re-

236

ject God for all eternity. He will never repent, will never turn back to God. He must, therefore, spend eternity in hell.

12. What is hell?

Hell is the state of eternal damnation. When a man, whose destiny is God, has died rejecting God, he must spend eternity deprived of God, and therefore of all happiness.

> Then he will say to those on his left hand, "Depart from me, accursed ones, into the everlasting fire which was prepared for the devil and his angels"—MATT. 25:41.

13. In what does the pain of hell consist?

The principal pain of hell is the loss of God. In addition, there is another pain, the "pain of sense," which is so terrible that it is comparable to the pain caused by earthly fire.

> If thy hand is an occasion of sin to thee, cut it off! It is better for thee to enter into life maimed, than, having two hands, to go into hell, into the unquenchable fire. "Where their worm dies not, and the fire is not quenched." For everyone shall be salted with fire, and every victim shall be salted
> —MARK 9:42, 43, 48.

14. How can the all-merciful God send anyone to hell?

Actually, it is not God but the sinner who sends himself to hell. Mortal sin is a rejection of God. Hell is mortal sin carried to its logical and eternal conclusion.

15. What happens to one who dies with unforgiven venial sin?

One who dies with unforgiven venial sin or without having made sufficient reparation for his sins must undergo further purification in purgatory.

16. What is purgatory?

Purgatory is a state of purification after death. The souls in purgatory possess the divine life and know that they are saved; but they long to see God. They cannot help themselves, but can be helped by the prayers and sacrifices of the faithful on earth and the souls in heaven.

17. What is temptation?

Temptation is an inducement to sin. Deliberate sin, whether

mortal or venial, does not "just happen"; it is *preceded* by an inducement to sin, which is called temptation.

18. *What are the sources of temptation?*

The sources of temptation are three: the world about us, the devil, and our own inclinations to sin. These inclinations are: pride, covetousness, lust, anger, gluttony, envy and sloth.

Practice

▶ Since mortal sin is so common and is treated so lightly by the world, we must constantly strive to keep alive in ourselves a real horror of it. We can do this by reflecting frequently on two truths, the Passion and death of our Saviour and the fact of hell.

The awful sufferings and death which the Son of God endured were the price God himself paid for the mortal sins of men.

Mortal sin is a rejection of God. A man chooses something that God says he may not have if he wishes to remain a friend of God. If a man dies in such a state of soul God grants him his wish in eternity, namely to be separated from God.

In order to avoid mortal sin we must try to avoid deliberate venial sin. If we are faithful to God in smaller things we shall be faithful to him in serious matters.

We should pray for help from God when we are tempted to sin. If we pray, God will always give us strength to overcome temptation.

In order to avoid sin we must also avoid any person, place or thing which in all probability will lead us into sin. To place ourselves in such an occasion of mortal sin without sufficient reason would be itself a mortal sin.

By prayer and thought try to discover what particular fault in your character you ought to be striving especially to overcome. Work on that fault in your examination of conscience.

The First Three Commandments

And behold, a certain man came to him and said "Good Master, what good work shall I do to have eternal life?" He said to him, "Why dost thou ask me about what is good? One there is who is good, that is God. But if thou wilt enter into life, keep the commandments." He said to him, "Which?" And Jesus said,

> *"Thou shalt not kill,*
> *Thou shalt not commit adultery,*
> *Thou shalt not steal,*
> *Thou shalt not bear false witness,*
> *Honor thy father and mother, and,*
> *Thou shalt love thy neighbor as thyself"*
>
> —MATT. 19:16-19.

THE GREAT commandment of love requires of us that we act towards God as his children and that we act towards our fellow man as brothers, children of the same Father, members of the Body of Christ.

Our duties towards God and towards our neighbor are set forth in the ten commandments:

I am the Lord thy God. Thou shalt not have strange gods before me.

Thou shalt not take the name of the Lord thy God in vain.

Remember thou keep holy the Sabbath day.

Honor thy father and thy mother.

Thou shalt not kill.

Thou shalt not commit adultery.

Thou shalt not steal.

Thou shalt not bear false witness against thy neighbor.

Thou shalt not covet thy neighbor's wife.

Thou shalt not covet thy neighbor's goods.

If we love God we will keep the first three commandments; they tell us our duties towards God. If we love ourselves and our neighbor we will keep the other seven commandments; they tell us our duties towards ourself and our neighbor.

The ten commandments are not laws which were enacted to establish order or to test our obedience. They flow from our very nature as human beings. Because we were created by God and depend on him completely we must, as intelligent responsible beings, acknowledge that dependence. We must praise God, love him, believe him and show reverence for his name. Because each human being has certain rights which he receives from God, we must respect those rights.

In studying the ten commandments, therefore, we are studying the laws which tell us how a man must act because he is a man, how he must act towards God and towards his fellow man. But, more than that, in studying the ten commandments, we as children of God, are studying the laws which help us fulfill the great law of love.

Thou shalt love the Lord thy God with thy whole heart, and with thy whole soul, and with thy whole mind. . . . Thou shalt love thy neighbor as thyself—MATT. 22:37-39.

* * *

THE FIRST COMMANDMENT:

I am the Lord thy God. Thou shalt not have strange gods before me.

1. *To what are we bound by the first commandment?*

The first commandment binds us to believe in everything which God has revealed, to worship him, to trust him and to love him above all things. In other words, the first commandment commands us to practice faith, hope and charity.

2. *How do we practice faith, hope and charity?*

We practice faith by believing all the truths which the Church teaches as revealed to us by God, by professing our faith and never under any circumstances denying it.

240

We practice hope by relying on God's mercy and never doubting that he will forgive our sins if we are truly sorry for them, and that he will give us all the help we need to reach heaven.

We practice charity by keeping all the commandments and doing the works of mercy.

If you love me, keep my commandments—JOHN 14:15.

3. How serious are sins against faith?

Sins against faith are most serious, because they strike at the very foundation of our relationship to God.

4. What are the sins against faith?

The sins against faith are:

a. the denial of all or any of the truths which God teaches through the Church,

b. deliberate doubt about any truth of faith,

c. the complete rejection of the Catholic faith, with the result that one no longer considers oneself a Catholic,

d. failure to profess the faith when obliged to do so,

e. failure to obtain necessary religious instruction,

f. reading books forbidden by the Church as dangerous to our faith (as guardian of the faith, the Church has legislated that a Catholic should read only those bibles and books about religion which have her stamp of approval),

g. refusal to accept the authority of the pope as visible head of the Church,

h. the worship of some created thing instead of the true God,

i. worship of the true God in a manner not approved by the Church (e.g., active participation in a non-Catholic religious service),

j. superstition (this includes astrology, belief in good luck charms, dreams, fortune tellers, etc. Superstition may be a venial sin. But to guide one's life by superstition would certainly be a mortal sin),

k. attendance at spiritualistic seances or the consultation of mediums.

5. *What are the sins against hope?*

The sins against hope are presumption and despair.

6. *How does one sin by presumption?*

One sins by presumption by taking for granted that salvation can be obtained by one's own efforts without God's help, or by God's help without one's own cooperation.

7. *What is despair?*

Despair is a refusal to trust that God will forgive our sins and give us the means of salvation.

8. *What are the sins against charity?*

All sins are in some way sins against charity. Specific sins against charity are treated under the fifth commandment.

* * *

THE SECOND COMMANDMENT:

Thou shalt not take the name of the Lord thy God in vain.

9. *How do we keep the second commandment?*

We keep the second commandment by showing reverence to God, and especially to his holy name.

10. *What are the sins against the second commandment?*

The sins against the second commandment are:

a. blasphemy, i.e., mocking, ridiculing, despising God, his Church, the saints or holy objects (this is one of the most serious of sins);

b. irreverence in using the name of God, Jesus or the saints (this sin is usually venial);

c. cursing, i.e., calling down evil upon another (cursing would be a mortal sin if one were serious; ordinarily one is not);

d. swearing, i.e., calling upon God to witness the truth of what we are saying, when what we are saying is not true or when there is no sufficient reason to call upon God (perjury, i.e., lying while under oath, is a mortal sin);

242

e. breaking a vow, i.e., a deliberate promise made to God to do something which is particularly pleasing to him (to break a vow would be a mortal or venial sin depending on how one is bound by the vow).

* * *

THE THIRD COMMANDMENT:
Remember thou keep holy the Sabbath day.

11. How do we keep the third commandment?

We keep the third commandment by worshipping God in a special way and refraining from unnecessary work on Sunday.

12. Why did the Church change the Lord's Day from the Sabbath to Sunday?

The Church, using the power of binding and loosing which Christ gave to the pope, changed the Lord's Day to Sunday because it was on Sunday (the first day of the week) that Christ rose from the dead and that the Holy Spirit descended upon the apostles.

13. How are we obliged to worship God on Sundays and Holy Days.

The law of God does not specify the amount of worship required. But there is a Church law which binds us to assist at Mass on Sundays and Holy Days. By observing this law of the Church we are observing also the divine law of worship on the Lord's Day.

14. Is assistance at Mass all that is required on Sundays and Holy Days?

Assistance at Mass on these days is all that is required under pain of sin. But the spirit of the law requires further worship, a real sanctification of the whole day.

Let the public and private observance of the feasts of the Church, which are in a special way dedicated and consecrated to God, be kept inviolable: and especially the Lord's day which the apostles, under the guidance of the Holy Ghost, substituted for the Sabbath. Now, if the order was given to

243

*the Jews, "Six days shall you do work: on the seventh day is
the Sabbath, the rest holy to the Lord. Every one that shall
do any work on this day shall die:" how will these Christians
not fear spiritual death, who perform servile work on feast-
days, and whose rest on these days is not devoted to religion
and piety but given over to the allurements of the world?
Sundays and Holy Days, then, must be made holy by divine
worship, which gives homage to God and heavenly food to
the soul. Although the Church only commands the faithful
to abstain from servile work and attend Mass and does not
make it obligatory to attend evening devotions, still she desires this and recommends it repeatedly: moreover, the needs
of each one demand it, seeing that all are bound to win the
favor of God if they are to obtain his benefits—Enc. on the
Sacred Liturgy 150.*

15. What kind of work is forbidden on Sunday?

The kind of work that is forbidden on Sunday is heavy
work, manual work, work which is done more with the body than
the mind.

16. Is any such work permitted on Sunday?

Such work which is necessary is permitted on Sundays.
Some work is necessary for the common good. For example, it is
necessary for policemen, railroad men, drug store and delicatessen
workers, etc., to work on Sundays.

Some work is necessary for other reasons; e.g., cooking and
dishwashing in the home, etc. Some work becomes necessary
because of an emergency or in an unusual situation. In the latter
case, if there is any doubt, one should ask one's confessor. Con-
ducting business which is not necessary for the common good is
forbidden on Sunday.

17. What kind of sin is it to do forbidden work unneces-
sarily on Sundays?

The sin would be mortal or venial depending on the amount
of time spent in such work.

Practice

▶ 1. We cannot love someone we do not know. God has told us of himself in order that we might love him. Because we are God's children we know our Father far better than do those who have not the gift of faith. But we can never know God well enough. Our love for our Father should prompt us to seek more and more knowledge of him. We may not be content with the knowledge of our faith gained by reading and study. The better our education the deeper should be our knowledge of the faith. Far too many laymen think that only priests need be concerned with the study of religion. This is a very false idea. We are all God's children. We should all have a knowledge of our faith commensurate with our age, our intelligence and our education.

2. Difficulties about matters of faith are not the same as doubts. Difficulties are questions which occur because of an inquiring mind, the need of further knowledge or mistaken information. These difficulties should not be side-stepped. They should be met squarely by seeking information on the point.

3. Many stores and businesses which formerly had remained closed on Sundays are now open for business on that day. This is an abuse which Christians should oppose as an outright violation of Sunday observance. Many bishops have cried out against this abuse. Everyone should cooperate with the bishops' appeals by refusing to patronize on Sunday those places of business which traditionally have been closed on that day.

4. Heavy housework and repairs about the house on Sundays are sometimes excused on the grounds that there is no other time in which to do these things. This excuse does not apply if Saturday is spent in rest and leisure. Many people nowadays do not have to work on Saturday. In this case they should use that day, not Sunday, to catch up on work about the house.

*My son, take care of your father when he is old; grieve him not as long as he lives. Even if his mind fail, be considerate with him; revile him not in the fullness of your strength. For kindness to a father will not be forgotten, it will serve as a sin offering—it will take lasting root. In time of tribulation it will be recalled to your advantage, like warmth upon frost it will melt away your sins. A blasphemer is he who despises his father; accursed of his Creator, he who angers his mother—*Sir. 3:12-16.

WHEN GOD sent his Son into the world he sent him as a member of a family. Jesus chose to have a human mother and a human foster-father and to be subject to them. By so doing he taught us the importance which God places on the family. By his life at Nazareth as a member of the Holy Family Christ has sanctified family life and given us an example of what that life should be. He taught us the dignity of parenthood by the reverence he showed to Mary and Joseph; he saw them as the representatives of his Father.

In the fourth commandment God reminds us that as his children we must respect authority within the family by honoring and obeying our parents. He reminds us, too, that we must respect and obey his other representatives, those who exercise lawful authority over us in the larger family of man, which is the family of God.

* * *

Honor thy father and thy mother.

1. How do we keep the fourth commandment?

We keep the fourth commandment by obeying all lawful authority and exercising it conscientiously. Parents keep this commandment by providing for the needs of their children, their spiritual as well as their material needs, by giving them affection,

246

protection, discipline, education and good example, by preparing them to live as children of God in this world, and so to attain eternal union with God. Catholic parents are obliged under pain of mortal sin to send their children to Catholic schools whenever it is possible to do so.

Sons and daughters keep this commandment by obeying, honoring and respecting their parents, and by providing for them in their old age.

2. Whom must we obey?

a. Children who are under age and still dependent on their parents must obey them in everything which is not in opposition to the laws of God or the Church.

b. We must obey the Church. Christ the King acts through the pope and through the spiritual ruler of the diocese, the bishop.

> *And I say to thee, thou art Peter, and upon this rock I will build my Church, and the gates of hell shall not prevail against it. And I will give thee the keys of the kingdom of heaven; and whatever thou shalt bind on earth shall be bound in heaven, and whatever thou shalt loose on earth shall be loosed in heaven*—MATT. 16:18-19.

c. We must obey the civil government. Whether a law binds us under sin or merely compels our obedience under threat of a penalty depends on the mind of the law-maker.

3. Does the fourth commandment oblige us to love our country?

Yes. The fourth commandment obliges us to fulfill our duties as citizens of our country, to respect its laws and institutions, to cooperate for the common good and to defend our country when the cause and the means used are just.

4. Is it possible to commit mortal sin against the fourth commandment?

Yes. If the person exercising authority intends to bind under serious sin, and the matter is serious, a violation of his command would be a mortal sin. Usually, however, parents do not intend to bind their children under mortal sin except in something extremely serious.

Practice

▶ 1. The right and duty of educating their children belongs to the parents.

The family . . . holds directly from the Creator the mission and hence the right to educate the offspring, a right inalienable because inseparably joined to the strict obligation, a right anterior to any right whatever of civil society and of the State, and therefore inviolable on the part of any power on earth—Enc. on the Christian Education of Youth.

Parents, therefore, may not leave the education entirely to the school. The school is meant to assist the parents, not supplant them in this important duty.

2. Parents have a great responsibility towards their children in the matter of giving good example. It is idle to suppose that children will develop right attitudes in regard to respect for law, the use of money, respect for others, tolerance, etc., if their parents display the fact that they themselves have un-Christian attitudes towards these things.

3. The good or harm which a parent can do by way of example is most evident in the matter of prayer and the sacraments. Parents who are never seen to pray, who miss Mass, or who rarely receive Holy Communion can hardly expect their children to develop good habits in regard to prayer and the sacraments. On the other hand, parents who do pray and teach their children to pray and who receive Holy Communion every time they assist at Mass are giving their children excellent example, and are in a position to encourage their children to do likewise.

4. One of the duties we have as citizens of our country is that of voting and of doing so intelligently. Nowadays there are organizations which can give us information on candidates for office. A good Christian should take his privilege of voting seriously and exercise it wisely. Remembering that our Lord called us "the salt of the earth," "the light of the world," the good Christian should take an interest in and participate in civic

affairs. Only thus can he expect to carry the principles of Christ into civic affairs.

5. Parents should respect their children's choice of vocation. Those who stand in the way of their children's desire to study for the priesthood or the brotherhood or to enter a convent would be guilty of serious sin. Parents are frequently wrong in encouraging their children too strongly to follow pursuits which are merely lucrative rather than those which contribute to society, e.g., teaching or nursing.

✠   ✠

section 39 | **The Fifth Commandment**

You have heard that it was said to the ancients, "Thou shalt not kill"; and that whoever shall murder shall be liable to judgment. But I say to you that everyone who is angry with his brother shall be liable to judgment; and whoever says to his brother, "Raca," shall be liable to the Sanhedrin; and whoever says, "Thou fool!" shall be liable to the fire of Gehenna. Therefore, if thou art offering thy gift at the altar, and there rememberest that thy brother has anything against thee, leave thy gift before the altar and go first to be reconciled to thy brother, and then come and offer thy gift. Come to terms with thy opponent quickly while thou art with him on the way; lest thy opponent deliver thee to the judge, and the judge to the officer, and thou be cast into prison. Amen I say to thee, thou wilt not come out from it until thou hast paid the last penny—MATT. 5:21-26.

AS MEMBERS of the family of God we must treat all men as our brothers in Christ; we must assist all men in their journey through life back to the Father. We must, therefore, respect the rights of our fellow men, rights of soul and body. The fifth commandment reminds us that we must practice brotherly love within the family of God and that we must not injure the body or soul of our neighbor. The fifth commandment

249

reminds us, too, that we must acknowledge that our lives as well as those of our neighbor belong to God, and that we must therefore, preserve our own life and health and refrain from risking them rashly or needlessly.

* * *

Thou shalt not kill.

1. How do we keep the fifth commandment?

We keep the fifth commandment by preserving our own life and health and by respecting our neighbor's right to life and health of body and soul.

2. What are the sins against the fifth commandment?

The sins against the fifth commandment are:

a. murder,

b. abortion,

c. mercy killing,

d. suicide,

e. mutilation of one's body without a sufficient reason,

f. risking one's life without a sufficient reason,

g. excessive eating and drinking,

h. unjust anger, which leads to hatred, revenge, fighting and quarreling.

3. Is it ever permitted to take the life of another?

Yes. To kill in legitimate self-defense is not sinful. The state has the right to punish serious crime with the death penalty.

To take part in a just war (one in which the cause and the means are just and in which there is reasonable hope of success) is not against the fifth commandment.

4. Why are abortion and "mercy killing" against the fifth commandment?

Abortion and "mercy killing" are mortal sins against the fifth commandment because in both cases human life is taken unjustly. Abortion is so serious a crime that the Church punishes it by excommunication.

5. How are we obliged to preserve our own life and health?

We are obliged to use every ordinary means in preserving our own life and health. We may not, therefore, risk our life except for a sufficient reason, for example, to rescue another; nor may we allow our body to be mutilated or deprived of an important function unless it be necessary to save the body itself, e.g., an amputation or a hysterectomy in cancer cases.

6. How serious a sin is it to mutilate the body unnecessarily, to deprive it of an important function, or to shorten one's life?

Sterilization, except in the case of legitimate removal of a diseased organ, is a mortal sin because the function of sex is an important function. The use of narcotics, except in licit medical practice, is a mortal sin.

Deliberately to deprive oneself of consciousness or moral judgment by over-indulgence in alcohol is a mortal sin. To impair the faculties by the use of alcohol is a venial sin. To drink to the point where the mind and speech are affected, even though consciousness or moral judgment is not lost, would be a venial sin.

7. What is hatred?

Hatred is wishing evil to another. It is a matter of the will, not the feelings. We are not guilty of sin because we feel an aversion to certain people, as long as we do not encourage or manifest such a feeling. We are obliged to *love* our neighbor, not to like him. Liking is a matter of the feelings and is not always under the control of the will. Nor is it incompatible with supernatural love.

8. Are religious and racial prejudice against the fifth commandment?

Yes. Prejudice is unreasonable and always opposed to charity. To judge and condemn any person because he happens to belong to a certain religious group, nationality or race injures that person. To manifest prejudice in action hurts the feelings of our neighbor, and is therefore a sin against charity. To deny him his rights is a sin against justice as well as charity. This is particularly true in the case of joining an organization which promotes segregation or any other denial of human rights.

9. May we seek revenge or refuse to forgive injuries?

No, we may not. Jesus insisted that our sins will not be forgiven by God unless we forgive our brother's offenses against us.

For if you forgive men their offenses, your heavenly Father will also forgive you your offenses. But if you do not forgive men, neither will your Father forgive you your offenses
—MATT. 6:14-15.

10. What is scandal?

Scandal is any evil action or one which has the appearance of evil, which does spiritual harm to another. Bad example is frequently scandalous, since it may easily lead another into the same sin. Bad example given to the young is particularly serious.

And whoever causes one of these little ones who believe in me to sin, it were better for him if a great millstone were hung about his neck, and he were thrown into the sea
—MARK 9:41.

11. How serious are sins of hatred, scandal, cooperation in sin, and uncharitable words and actions?

The seriousness of such sins is determined by the seriousness of the harm done to our neighbor. Deliberately to wish serious evil to another, to cooperate with him in a serious sin, to give serious scandal or to talk or act against our neighbor in such a way as to injure him seriously is a mortal sin against the fifth commandment.

Practice

▶ In the field of race relations Christians have a great opportunity for giving the world an example of justice and charity. It would be a shocking thing if the behavior of Christians in regard to segregation and other injustices were no different from that of others. We must never forget that our Lord said, "By this will men know that you are my disciples, if you have love one for another."

Or do you not know that your members are the temple of the Holy Spirit, who is in you, whom you have from God, and that you are not your own? For you have been bought at a great price. Glorify God and bear him in your body
—1 COR. 6:19-20.

OUR FATHER has given us a world in which human skill and artistry can add to the order and beauty of his creation. But God was not content to allow men to share in his creation merely as workers and artists. He desired to give men and women a share in his fatherhood, a share in the creation of new human beings who are destined to share in the divine life, to be his adopted sons and daughters, to share his happiness for all eternity in heaven. Thus he gave to his children the wonderful power of sex.

The bringing of new life into the world is the first purpose of sex. But this wonderful power in human beings is also something else, something deeply mysterious. It is the means whereby a man and woman with God's blessing give themselves to one another in love, and thereby find their fulfillment in one another and a closer union with God through one another.

Among all the powers that we possess the power of sex is unique. It is the only gift we have which we may not use for our own sake. Our eyes, our ears we use in order to bring the outside world into our mind. Our power of nourishing ourself we use in order to build up our own body. But our power of sex we possess in order that we might give ourselves to another in a union of body and soul which is to last a lifetime.

Love always expresses itself by an attempt to give oneself to the loved one. We give gifts to those we love, the gift of attention, interest, time. We give presents to those we love; the deeper the love the more precious and personal the present. In all this we are seeking ways of giving ourselves to those we love. Our power of sex is in some mysterious way peculiarly, deeply, ourself. The very words, intimate, private, personal, applied to the sexual faculty give evidence of this fact. Thus it is the means whereby men and women can give themselves to one another in a love which is fruitful in new human beings, children who are both God's and theirs. The joy and fulfillment to be found in married love are our Father's rewards to his sons and daughters who enter into the vocation of marriage and parenthood.

Sex, therefore, is not merely a means of obtaining pleasure; it is far deeper than that. Still less is it something shameful or sordid. Rather it is something sacred. It is only the misuse of sex that is shameful, all the more shameful because it is the misuse of something sacred. Sex in human beings may never be divorced from love. The misuse of sex is a sin against love, not only against divine love, as is every sin, but against human love as well.

* * *

Thou shalt not commit adultery.
Thou shalt not covet thy neighbor's wife.

1. How do we keep the sixth and ninth commandments?

We keep the sixth and ninth commandments by using the power of sex lawfully, according to the plan of God. For married people this means that they use their marriage rights properly, that they freely give the use of those rights to one another, and that they remain faithful to one another.

For unmarried people this means that they do not use the power of sex at all, since its use is lawful only in marriage.

For all, keeping the sixth and ninth commandments means that we cultivate modesty and chastity by guarding our eyes, our ears and our thoughts and imaginations from anything that would lead us into sins against the sixth and ninth commandments.

2. What is the proper use of the sexual power?

The use of the sexual power is the sacred privilege of married couples. It is the means whereby they cooperate with God in procreation and achieve union with one another in body and soul. By its very nature, therefore, the sexual power may be used only in marriage.

3. What are the sins against the sixth and ninth commandments?

The sins against the sixth and ninth commandments are:
adultery,
unjust refusal of the marriage right to one's spouse,
fornication,
birth control,
self-abuse,
intimacies between unmarried persons,
reading obscene books, magazines, etc.,
looking at pictures, sights, etc. which are sexually arousing,
lewd conversations,
deliberate thoughts, desires or imaginations against modesty or chastity.

For an unmarried person any deliberate seeking of or consent to sexual pleasure, or any sexual act committed either alone or with another is a mortal sin. For married persons any sexual act with someone other than their spouse, birth control or unreasonable denial of marital rights is a mortal sin.

Let marriage be held in honor with all, and let the marriage bed be undefiled. For God will judge the immoral and adulterers—HEB. 13:4.

For know this and understand, that no fornicator, or unclean person . . . has any inheritance in the kingdom of Christ and God—EPH. 5:5.

Let the husband render to the wife her due, and likewise the wife to the husband. The wife has not authority over her body, but the husband; the husband likewise has not authority over his body, but the wife. Do not deprive each other, except perhaps by consent, for a time, that you may give yourselves to prayer—1 COR. 7:3-5.

4. Are demonstrations of affection between unmarried persons against the virtue of chastity?

Demonstrations of affection between unmarried persons are

255

right and good as long as they are true demonstrations of affection and are not the sort of actions which by nature arouse passion. Prolonged or passionate kissing and actions of a more intimate nature belong only to the married state, and would be mortally sinful for unmarried persons.

5. Why is birth control condemned by the Church?

Birth control in the sense of contraception, i.e., the performance of the marriage act in such a way as to prevent conception—is an abuse of the sacred faculty of sex. It is, therefore, against the natural law. The Church does not forbid birth control as she forbids meat on Friday; she merely declares that God has revealed such an abuse of nature to be a sin against nature which can never be justified. To practice contraception is, therefore, a serious sin for all people, not only for Catholics.

> *But no reason, however grave, may be put forward by which anything intrinsically against nature may become conformable to nature and morally good. Since, therefore, the conjugal act is destined primarily by nature for the begetting of children, those who in exercising it deliberately frustrate its natural power and purpose, sin against nature and commit a deed which is shameful and intrinsically vicious . . .*
> —Enc. on Christian Marriage 37.

6. Is birth control always a mortal sin?

Yes, because of the importance of the faculty misused, deliberate birth control is always a mortal sin.

> *Our mouth proclaims anew: any use whatsoever of matrimony exercised in such a way that the act is deliberately frustrated in its natural power to generate life is an offense against the law of God and of nature, and those who indulge in such are branded with the guilt of a grave sin . . .*
> —Enc. on Christian Marriage 38.

7. Why are thoughts and desires against chastity sinful?

Any deliberate desire to commit a sinful act is in itself sinful. If the act we desire to perform would be a mortal sin, the deliberate desire to commit it would be in itself a mortal sin. Our Lord said, "You have heard that it was said to the ancients, 'Thou shalt not commit adultery.' But I say to you that anyone who

256

even looks with lust at a woman has already committed adultery with her in his heart"—MATT. 5:27-28.

Thoughts or imaginations of a sexual nature can easily arouse sexual feelings, especially in the young. For an unmarried person, who has no right to the use of sex, to consent to such feelings would be a mortal sin.

8. What is the virtue of modesty?

The virtue of modesty is the virtue which protects chastity by inclining us to guard our senses, so as not to invite temptation and to be considerate in our dress and behavior, so as not to cause temptation to others.

9. Are immodest looks, etc., sinful?

Looks, reading and other such actions which are opposed to the virtue of modesty can be sinful according to the circumstances. If one who has no right to the use of sex were to indulge in such things merely out of curiosity, without consent to any sexual feelings, he would commit a venial sin. To do so with consent to such feelings would be a mortal sin for an unmarried person. In this matter there can be, too, an occasion of serious sin, sometimes even for a married person—the danger of consenting to an unlawful desire for another person. If one, married or unmarried, has a good reason for pursuing a good action which may produce sexual feeling to which he does not consent— e.g., the study of medicine, seeking necessary information—there would be no sin involved.

10. Why is the sixth commandment sometimes called "the difficult commandment"?

Because of the effects of original sin the desire to experience sexual pleasure outside of marriage and unlawfully is easily aroused in us. Our eyes, our ears, our sense of touch, even our imagination can bring us into contact with objects which stimulate the sexual faculty. Yet for unmarried persons, since they have not the right to the use of sex, there can be no deliberate acquiescence in such stimulation, much less a seeking of it, without serious sin.

257

11. *How do we preserve chastity?*

We preserve chastity:

by prayer—the habit of prayer, and prayer in time of temptation,

by cultivating devotion to our Blessed Mother,

by the frequent reception of the sacraments of Penance and the Holy Eucharist,

by avoiding occasions of sin, such as certain types of books, pictures, entertainments and companions.

Practice

▶ 1. The pagan society in which we live has little regard for the virtue of chastity. Parents and teachers should take special care to inculcate in the young an appreciation of this important virtue. Chastity should be presented not as a repression of the instincts but as a positive virtue which is essential to manliness and womanliness. Above all, they should stress the fact that sex is something good and holy, that there is nothing evil about any part of the body, that the body, good by nature, has been made the temple of the Blessed Trinity. If sex is presented as good and sacred and its importance in marriage explained, it can easily be pointed out why any misuse of sex is a tragic misfortune rather than a daring adventure.

2. Steady company-keeping between young boys and girls has become an accepted practice in many places. Boys and girls in their teens who are in no position to think of marriage for several years, or who have no thought of marriage at all, see the same person regularly, frequently and exclusively. Often there is an exchange of rings or pins to signify that they in some sense "belong to one another." Besides the obvious disadvantage of such exclusiveness in dating (it narrows the field from which young people can select a partner for marriage) there is another more immediate danger; such steady company-

keeping is usually a proximate occasion of mortal sins against chastity. Older couples experience this difficulty; but in their case it is a necessary occasion, and, using the ordinary precautions, they can expect the necessary help from God to keep from sin. Such is not the case with younger boys and girls. In the face of this widespread practice, therefore, even over the protests of their teen-age children, parents have a duty of taking a very determined and strict stand.

✝　　　✝

section 41 | The Seventh and Tenth Commandments

God said, "Let us make mankind in our image and likeness; and let them have dominion over the fish of the sea, the birds of the air, the cattle, over all the wild animals and every creature that crawls on the earth."

God created man in his image.
In the image of God he created him.
Male and female he created them.

Then God blessed them and said to them, "Be fruitful and multiply; fill the earth and subdue it. Have dominion over the fish of the sea, the birds of the air, the cattle and all the animals that crawl on the earth." God also said, "See, I give you every seed-bearing plant on the earth and every tree which has seed-bearing fruit to be your food. To every wild animal of the earth, to every bird of the air, and to every creature that crawls on the earth and has the breath of life, I give the green plants for food"—GEN. 1:26-30.

OUR LORD taught us to be poor in spirit, not to be attached to nor too desirous of material things. "What does it profit a man if he gain the whole world but suffer the loss of his own soul?"—MATT. 16:26. Material possessions can distract us in our efforts to reach heaven. On the other hand, the Church tells us that it is good for men to own things, indeed, that the ownership of some property can be a positive help on our way to heaven. So anxious is she that all should be able to own property that she calls for a better distribution of wealth in the world.

The seventh and tenth commandments regulate the possession and use of the things God has entrusted to us and to others.

There is much injustice in the world today on the part of individuals, groups and governments. Some people are avaricious and greedy. Communist governments deny the right of a person to own productive property. The man who steals, whether he is a pickpocket, an employer or a worker, the Communist state which unjustly deprives a man of what is his, the child who damages property, all these offend against the right order which God has established between his children and the things he has given them for their use.

* * *

Thou shalt not steal.
Thou shalt not covet thy neighbor's goods.

1. How do we keep the seventh and tenth commandments?

We keep the seventh and tenth commandments:
by respecting the property of others,
by paying our just debts,
by dealing honestly in business,
by paying a living wage to our employees,
by doing a full day's work for a full day's pay,
by living up to our agreements and contracts,
by returning things we have found.

2. What are the sins against the seventh and tenth commandments?

The sins against the seventh and tenth commandments are:
stealing,

260

cheating,
vandalism,
acceptance of bribes,
use of false weights and measures,
charging exorbitant prices,
wasting time,
careless work,
violation of contracts and agreements,
envy of another's possessions.

3. How is the seriousness of sins against the seventh commandment determined?

The seriousness of sins against the seventh commandment is determined by the seriousness of the harm done either to the individual or to the community. Ordinarily it is considered serious if the injustice is equivalent to one day's wages for the injured party. A considerable amount taken from even a wealthy person or a corporation would constitute a serious sin against justice.

4. When is there an obligation of making restitution?

Whenever there has been a violation of justice, one is bound to make full restitution. One guilty of injustice is bound in conscience to restore the object unjustly possessed, withheld or destroyed, according to the value it had at the time, together with any natural increase. The sincere intention to restore the value of the goods is necessary before a sin against justice can be forgiven. If one who is guilty of an injustice can no longer find the owner or his heirs, he is obliged to give the stolen goods or their value to the poor or to use them for some charitable cause.

5. What does the Church say about the right to private property?

The Church says that the right to private property is a natural right, one that may not be taken away. This does not mean, however, that a man may do with his property whatever he pleases. It is wrong for him to waste it, misuse it, or to use it in a way that will be harmful to others. Then, too, the good of society may dictate that a man give up the ownership of some particular property, but only when he is justly compensated for his loss.

> At the same time a man's superfluous income is not left entirely to his own discretion. We speak of that portion of his income which he does not need in order to live as becomes his station. On the contrary the grave obligations of charity, beneficence and liberality which rest upon the wealthy, are constantly insisted upon in telling words by Holy Scripture and the Fathers of the Church—Enc. on Reconstructing the Social Order 50.

The most serious error of Communism is its atheistic materialism. But it errs, too, and in a serious way, in its denial of the natural right of a man to own property.

6. What is social justice?

Social justice is that form of justice which requires from each individual all that is necessary for the common good.

Speaking of social justice, Pius XI declares:

> But social justice cannot be said to have been satisfied as long as workingmen are denied a salary that will enable them to secure proper sustenance for themselves and for their families; as long as they are denied the opportunity of acquiring a modest fortune and forestalling the plague of universal pauperism; as long as they cannot make suitable provision through public or private insurance for old age, for periods of illness and unemployment. In a word, to repeat what has been said in our Encyclical Quadragesimo Anno: "Then only will the economic and social order be soundly established and attain those goods which the wealth and resources of nature, technical science and the corporate organization of social affairs can give." These goods should be sufficient to supply all necessities and reasonable comforts, and to uplift men to that higher standard of life which, provided it be used with prudence, is not only not a hindrance but is of singular help to virtue—Enc. on Atheistic Communism 52.

7. What does the Church teach about a living family wage?

Pope Pius XI said, "In the first place, the worker must be

paid a wage sufficient to support him and his family. . . . It is an intolerable abuse, and to be abolished at all costs, for mothers on account of the father's low wages to be forced to engage in gainful occupations outside of the home to the neglect of their proper cares and duties, especially the training of children. Every effort must therefore be made that fathers of families receive a wage large enough to meet ordinary family needs adequately. But if this cannot always be done under existing circumstances, social justice demands that changes be induced as soon as possible whereby such a wage will be assured to every adult workingman. . . ."

"In determining the amount of the wage, the condition of a business and of the one carrying it on, must be taken into account. . . ."

"Lastly the amount of the pay must be adjusted to the public economic good. . . ."—Enc. on Reconstructing the Social Order 71-73.

Practice

▶ 1. The Church vindicates the right of workers to join trade unions and urges them to do so and to take an active part in them, not only for the workers' protection but also for the establishment of an economic order characterized by justice, tranquillity and order. To this end she encourages associations among employers also, envisioning an order in which these various associations will work together for the good of all.

2. The ideal wage is one paid with the family in mind. Pope Pius XI said: "The wage paid to the workingman must be sufficient for the support of himself and his family. . . ."

3. The prevalence of certain unjust practices does not alter the fact that they are sins against justice. Among such practices would be included business deals which are based on the slogan, "Let the buyer beware." To sell a defective article

the defects of which are carefully camouflaged is unjust, and therefore un-Christian.

4. To steal from the government or from a great many people is as sinful as to steal from an individual. The cynical excuse, "everyone does it," is unworthy of a Christian.

☩   ☩

section 42 | **The Eighth Commandment**

*For in many things we all offend. If anyone does not offend in word, he is a perfect man, able also to lead round by a bridle the whole body. For if we put bits into horses' mouths that they may obey us, we control their whole body also. Behold, even the ships, great as they are, and driven by boisterous winds, are steered by a small rudder wherever the touch of the steersman pleases. So the tongue also is a little member, but it boasts mightily. Behold, how small a fire—how great a forest it kindles! And the tongue is a fire, the very world of iniquity. The tongue is placed among our members, defiling the whole body, and setting on fire the course of our life, being itself set on fire by hell. For every kind of beast and bird, and of serpents and the rest, is tamed and has been tamed by mankind; but the tongue no man can tame—a restless evil, full of deadly poison. With it we bless God the Father; and with it we curse men, who have been made after the likeness of God. Out of the same mouth proceed blessing and cursing. These things, my brethren, ought not to be so. Does the fountain send forth sweet and bitter water from the same opening? Can a fig tree, my brethren, bear olives, or a vine figs? So neither can salt water yield fresh water—*JAMES 3:2-12.

JESUS CHRIST is the way, the truth and the life. Because he is Truth itself, he detests lying and hypocrisy. Our Lord always dealt gently with sinners; but the lying, hypocritical Pharisees he sternly denounced time and time again. Christ expects us to "worship the Father in sincerity and truth," to love the truth as he loves it.

The eighth commandment reminds us that, as members of Christ, we must love truth and refrain from lying, deceit and hypocrisy. Such things come from the devil, "a liar and the father of lies"—JOHN 8:45; they have no place in the family of God.

As members of Christ we must also be solicitous to protect the good name of others. We must imitate the example which Jesus gave us at the Last Supper, when, with the utmost delicacy, he let Judas know that he was aware of his betrayal, but nevertheless did not name him as the traitor before the other apostles.

* * *

Thou shalt not bear false witness against thy neighbor.

1. *How do we keep the eighth commandment?*

We keep the eighth commandment by speaking the truth, and by being careful not to injure the good name of others.

2. *What are the sins against the eighth commandment?*

The sins against the eighth commandment are:
lying,
calumny,
detraction,
revealing certain secrets.

3. *What is a lie?*

A lie is the expression of something which we know to be untrue, made with the intention to deceive.

4. *What kind of sin is it to tell a lie?*

To tell a lie is ordinarily a venial sin. If a lie injures someone seriously or is told while under oath (perjury), it is a mortal sin.

5. *Is it ever permissible to tell a lie?*

No, it is never permissible to tell a lie, even to avoid evil or to accomplish good. When there is sufficient reason, however, we may use a mental reservation.

6. What is mental reservation?

A mental reservation is an expression which may be taken two ways. In social and business life there are many commonly used mental reservations; e.g., "Mrs. Smith is not at home," may mean that the lady of the house is actually out, or it may be an accepted polite way of saying that she does not wish to see the caller.

7. What is calumny?

Calumny is lying about someone in such a way as to injure his good name.

8. What is detraction?

Detraction is the unnecessary revelation of something about a person which is true but which injures that person's good name.

9. How serious are the sins of calumny and detraction?

Both calumny and detraction are mortal sins if the thing said about another person is seriously damaging to his reputation. They are venial sins if what is said about the other person is not serious. Gossip when it constitutes calumny or detraction is sinful.

One who has committed either calumny or detraction must make whatever effort is required to restore the good name of the injured person. The resolution to make such restitution is necessary in order to obtain forgiveness of these sins.

10. How serious is the obligation of keeping a secret?

The seriousness of the obligation of keeping a secret is determined by the importance of the secret to the person who confided it.

The secrecy of the confessional may never be violated by the priest for any reason whatsoever, even at the cost of his life.

Practice

► 1. Gossip columnists enjoy such prestige today that we are apt to forget the fact that the unnecessary revelation of the sins and crimes of others is unjustifiable and can be seriously sinful. It is surely out of place for a Christian to read or support a certain type of defamatory magazine which specializes in innuendo, scandal and detraction.

2. An exaggeration can be a lie. This fact should be remembered not only in social life but in business as well. There is no justification for making exaggerated claims for a product in order to make a sale. A Christian should remember that honesty in speech ought to be one of his hallmarks both in social life and in business dealings.

3. It is very easy to criticize and complain about others, especially in their absence, to discuss their faults needlessly and pass judgment on their actions. We should, rather, bring out the good points of the person under discussion and defend him as we would ourselves when he is being criticized.

✠   ✠

section 43 | The Commandments of the Church

*Amen I say to you, whatever you bind on earth shall be bound also in heaven; and whatever you loose on earth shall be loosed also in heaven—*MATT. 18:18.

AFTER THE WORSHIP of God, which is her first concern, the Church is concerned with the salvation and sanctification of her members. She remembers, if we sometimes forget, that our Lord insisted on the necessity of penance and mortification. She realizes that penance and other practices which we must observe are necessary for our very salvation. As a wise and practical mother she also realizes that, left to ourselves, we would keep putting off doing these necessary things. Accordingly, she places on her children the obligation of fasting, of worshipping God, of doing at definite times and places that which we might otherwise neglect, to our peril.

The laws of the Church, unlike the laws of God, are subject to change by the Church. She has made them; she can change them; she can modify them; she can grant dispensations from them. The laws of the Church, moreover, are not meant to work an undue hardship on her children. When a Church law becomes a very great burden, much more difficult than intended, we are automatically excused from its observance. The Church is the same gentle Christ whose yoke is sweet and whose burden is light.

In obeying the commandments of the Church it is Christ we are obeying, Christ, who said, "He who heareth you, heareth me."

1. Where are the commandments of the Church to be found?

The commandments of the Church are to be found in her collection of laws, which is called the "Code of Canon Law."

2. What are the principal commandments of the Church?

The principal commandments of the Church are:

a. to assist at Mass on Sundays and holy days of obligation;

b. to fast and abstain on certain days;

c. to receive Holy Communion during the Easter season;

d. to confess our sins once a year;

e. to contribute what is necessary for divine worship, for the maintenance of the Church;

f. to observe the Church's regulations on marriage.

3. What are the holy days of obligation?

The holy days of obligation in the United States are the following feasts:

the Circumcision—January 1

the Ascension of our Lord—forty days after Easter

the Assumption of our Lady—August 15
All Saints—November 1
the Immaculate Conception—December 8
Christmas—December 25.

4. How serious is the obligation of assisting at Mass on Sundays and holy days of obligation?

We are obliged under pain of mortal sin to assist at Mass on these days.

A serious inconvenience excuses one from this obligation. For example, illness or indisposition which would normally keep one home from work or from a social obligation would constitute a sufficient reason for missing Mass.

5. Is it a sin to miss part of Mass on Sundays or holy days?

Yes. It is a sin to miss part of Mass on these days. Such a sin is mortal or venial depending on the importance of the part missed. We are obliged under pain of mortal sin to be present for at least the three principal parts of the Mass, i.e., the Offertory, the Consecration and the Communion.

6. What are the laws of fast and abstinence?

The laws of fast and abstinence are laws of the Church which oblige us to limit the quality and/or quantity of food we eat on certain days. Fasting limits the quantity of food. Abstinence forbids the eating of meat.

FASTING

Everyone over 21 and under 59 years of age is bound to fast on all the weekdays of Lent, on the Wednesdays, Fridays and Saturdays of the Ember weeks, the vigils of All Saints, of the Immaculate Conception, Christmas and Pentecost. Sometimes the bishop grants a dispensation for some of these days.

On days of fast, only one full meal is allowed. Meat may be taken at this meal, except on Fridays, Ash Wednesday, the vigil of the Immaculate Conception and the vigil of Christmas. Two other meatless meals, sufficient to maintain strength, may be taken according to one's needs; but together they should not equal another full meal.

Eating between meals is not permitted; but liquids, including milk and fruit juices, are allowed.

When health or ability to work would be seriously affected, the law does not oblige. In doubt, a parish priest or confessor should be consulted.

ABSTINENCE

Everyone over seven years of age is bound to observe the law of abstinence. Complete abstinence is to be observed on Fridays, Ash Wednesday, the vigils of the Immaculate Conception and Christmas. On days of complete abstinence meat and soup or gravy made from meat may not be used at all.

Partial abstinence is to be observed on the Wednesdays and Saturdays of the Ember weeks, on the vigil of Pentecost and on the vigil of All Saints (unless a dispensation has been granted). On days of partial abstinence meat soup or gravy from meat may be taken only at the principal meal.

Practical Points

1. In some instances one is automatically excused from a law of the Church, e.g., one who has diabetes is excused from fasting. In other cases, where keeping the law would be unusually difficult, there is reason to ask for a dispensation. In such cases it is not lawful to assume that one does not have to keep the law; one must first obtain a dispensation from a priest.

2. It should be remembered that a pastor in making appeals for funds is not asking for money for himself. He is acting as a steward who administers the property of the Church. It is his unpleasant duty to have to ask for money which is needed to keep buildings in repair, etc. If all parishioners (instead of a little better than half of them) contributed according to their means such appeals would not be necessary.

3. The Church has, of necessity, made many laws and regulations concerning marriage. In individual cases when there is need to know the law on some aspect of marriage one should consult a priest.

section **44** | # The Final Glory of the Church

And I saw a new heaven and a new earth . . . And I saw the holy city, New Jerusalem, coming down out of heaven from God, made ready as a bride adorned for her husband. And I heard a loud voice from the throne saying, "Behold the dwelling of God with men, and he will dwell with them. And they will be his people and God himself will be with them as their God. And God will wipe away every tear from their eyes. And death shall be no more; neither shall there be mourning, nor crying, nor pain any more, for the former things have passed away"—APOC. 21:1-4.

WHEN THE SON of God came into this world he came as a helpless infant. He lived a life of extreme poverty. He was rejected by the people he came to save. His death on the cross, although actually a triumph, had all the appearances of failure. And yet Christ, even as he stood in humiliation before the court which condemned him to death, proclaimed that he was king. He prophesied that he would return to earth one day, no longer in poverty and humiliation, but in triumph to judge the living and the dead.

Belief in the second coming of Christ sustained the early Church even in the darkest hours, when persecution raged about her and threatened to overwhelm her. However dark the picture, the early Christians never forgot that the final victory would be Christ's.

Today the forces of evil are powerful and well organized. Men and governments refuse to acknowledge Christ as their king, openly defy him and persecute and kill his followers. This is to be expected. Our Lord warned us that such things would happen. While we spare neither effort nor prayer in extending the kingdom of Christ on this earth, therefore, we, too, should remember that, however powerful the enemy, the final victory will be

Christ's. He will return in glory and triumph. His enemies will be forever vanquished; and those who are united to him and share his life will share in his eternal victory.

1. Will the work of the Church ever end?

The Church's work of distributing grace will cease when the world comes to an end; but its work of praising and glorifying God will continue forever in heaven.

2. What will the happiness of heaven be like?

In heaven we shall be happy in a way far greater than any man has ever been happy, even in his happiest moments on earth.

a. There will be no sorrow, no pain, no hardship, no want.

*And God will wipe away every tear from their eyes. And death shall be no more: neither shall there be mourning, nor crying, nor pain any more, for the former things have passed away—*Apoc. 21:4.

*And the redeemed of the Lord shall return, and shall come into Sion with praise: and everlasting joy shall be upon their heads. They shall obtain joy and gladness: and sorrow and mourning shall flee away—*Is. 35:10.

b. There will be no struggle, no temptation, no possibility of sin or disorder. All will be perfect peace and joy.

But the souls of the just are in the hand of God,
and no torment shall touch them.
They seemed, in the view of the foolish, to be dead;
and their passing away was judged an affliction and
their going forth from us, utter destruction.
*But they are in peace—*Wis. 3:1-3.

c. There will be perfect rest, not the rest of inactivity, but the rest which is the perfect satisfaction of all longing, the rest which the heart finds in the contentment of perfect love.

*May the angels take you into paradise: may the martyrs come to welcome you on your way, and lead you into the holy city, Jerusalem. May the choir of angels welcome you, and with Lazarus, who once was poor, may you have everlasting rest—*Ritual.

d. There will be final and complete union with God, the source of all joy and happiness. In this world we can know God only by faith. In heaven we shall see God as he is, face to face, and we shall be overwhelmed by his beauty and goodness.

We see now through a mirror in an obscure manner, but then face to face. Now I know in part, but then I shall know even as I have been known—1 COR. 13:12.

e. There will be complete ease and familiarity in our conversation with God. Prayer, which is frequently difficult here on earth, requiring great application and effort, will be a supreme joy in heaven. Our conversation with God will be infinitely more delightful than any we have had, even with those whose company we have enjoyed most on earth.

f. There will be companionship with all the members of our Father's great family, the angels and the saints and all those we have known and loved in this world. There will be no farewells, no separation, no end of the love, peace and joy which will prevail among the children of God.

Whatever we find pleasant, beautiful or desirable in this world attracts us because it is a faint reflection of God. We have moments of exaltation, periods of joy and contentment here on earth; but they never last. They cannot last long nor satisfy us for long, because in them we have only the merest reflection of God. If such hints of the beauty and lovableness of God can delight us here, we can only begin to imagine what happiness will be ours when we behold the reality, God himself, the inexhaustible source of all happiness.

3. Will the world ever end?

The world as we now know it will end some day. However, there will be "new heavens and a new earth"—2 PET. 3:13, the details of which are still veiled in mystery.

4. When will the world end?

Only God knows the day and the hour. Our Lord spoke of the end of the world several times; but because his words are prophecies they are mysterious and are capable now of being interpreted in various ways.

And as he was sitting on the Mount of Olives, the disciples came to him privately, saying, "Tell us, when are these things to happen, and what will be the sign of thy coming and of the end of the world?" And in answer Jesus said to them, "Take care that no one leads you astray. For many will come in my name, saying 'I am the Christ,' and they will lead many astray. For you shall hear of wars and rumors of wars. Take care that you do not be alarmed, for these things must come to pass, but the end is not yet. For nation will rise against nation, and kingdom against kingdom; and there will be pestilences and famines and earthquakes in various places. But all these things are the beginnings of sorrows. Then they will deliver you up to tribulation, and will put you to death; and you will be hated by all nations for my name's sake. And then many will fall away, and will betray one another, and will hate one another. And many false prophets will arise, and will lead many astray. And because iniquity will abound, the charity of the many will grow cold. But whoever perseveres to the end, he shall be saved. And this gospel of the kingdom shall be preached in the whole world, for a witness to all nations; and then will come the end"

MATT. 24:3-14.

Then if anyone say to you, "Behold, here is the Christ," or, "There he is," do not believe it. For false christs and false prophets will arise, and will show great signs and wonders, so as to lead astray, if possible, even the elect. Behold, I have told it to you beforehand. If therefore, they say to you, "Behold, he is in the desert," do not go forth; "Behold, he is in the inner chambers," do not believe it. For as the lightning comes forth from the east and shines even to the west, so also will the coming of the Son of Man be. Wherever the body is, there will the eagles be gathered together. But immediately after the tribulation of those days, the sun will be darkened, and the moon will not give her light, and the stars will fall from heaven, and the powers of heaven will be shaken. And then will appear the sign of the Son of Man in heaven; and then will all tribes of the earth mourn, and they will see the Son of Man coming upon the clouds of heaven with great power and majesty. And he will send forth his angels with a trumpet and a great sound, and they will gather his elect from the four winds, from end to end of the heavens—MATT. 24:23-31.

Watch therefore, for you do not know at what hour your Lord is to come—MATT. 24:42.

274

5. How did the early Christians interpret these prophecies?

Some undoubtedly expected the end of the world in their own lifetime, even though they had been warned by St. Peter,

> This first you must know, that in the last days there will come deceitful scoffers, men walking according to their own lusts, saying, "Where is the promise of his coming? For since the fathers fell asleep, all things continue as they were from the beginning of creation. . . ."
>
> But, beloved, do not be ignorant of this one thing, that one day with the Lord is as a thousand years, and a thousand years as one day. The Lord does not delay in his promises, but for your sake is long-suffering, not wishing that any should perish but that all should turn to repentance. But the day of the Lord will come as a thief; . . . But we look for new heavens and a new earth, according to his promises, wherein dwells justice. Therefore, beloved, while you look for these things, endeavor to be found by him without spot and blameless, in peace. . . . You therefore, brethren, since you know this beforehand, be on your guard lest, carried away by the error of the foolish, you fall away from your own steadfastness—2 PET. 3:3-17.

However, even those who did not expect the second coming of Christ before they died lived in such a way as to be prepared for it. They looked forward with eagerness to the second coming of Christ as the final and glorious fulfillment of all that a Christian should hope for.

6. What will be the great event at the end of the world?

The great event will be the return of Christ to this world. Christ's work on earth will not be finished until he returns in glory to reveal his triumph to all mankind. He himself describes this scene:

> But when the Son of Man shall come in his majesty, and all the angels with him, then he will sit on the throne of his glory; and before him will be gathered all the nations, and he will separate them one from another, as the shepherd separates the sheep from the goats; and he will set the sheep on his right hand, but the goats on the left. Then the king will say to those on his right hand; "Come, blessed of my Father, take possession of the kingdom prepared for you

275

from the foundation of the world; for I was hungry and you gave me to eat; I was thirsty and you gave me to drink, I was a stranger and you took me in, naked and you covered me; sick and you visited me; I was in prison and you came to me." Then the just will answer him saying, "Lord, when did we see thee hungry, and feed thee; or thirsty, and give thee drink? And when did we see thee a stranger, and take thee in; or naked, and clothe thee? Or when did we see thee sick, or in prison, and come to thee?" And answering the king will say to them, "Amen I say to you, as long as you did it for one of these, the least of my brethren, you did it for me." Then he will say to those on his left hand, "Depart from me, accursed ones, into the everlasting fire which was prepared for the devil and his angels. For I was hungry, and you did not give me to eat; I was thirsty and you gave me no drink; I was a stranger and you did not take me in; naked, and you did not clothe me, sick, and in prison, and you did not visit me." Then they also will answer and say, "Lord, when did we see thee hungry, or thirsty, or a stranger, or naked, or sick, or in prison, and did not minister to thee?" Then he will answer them, saying, "Amen I say to you, as long as you did not do it for one of these least ones, you did not do it for me." And these will go into everlasting punishment, but the just into everlasting life—MATT. 25:31-46.

7. Will the judgment which Christ makes at the end of the world be a real judgment?

It will not be a real judgment in the sense that Christ will be rendering a decision. At his death each man gives an accounting of his life. Nothing decided at this final accounting will be changed in the last judgment. The damned will still be in hell and the saved in heaven. Christ will announce who has been saved and who has been damned.

8. What happens at our death?

At death we will not go before a judgment seat to hear the Lord pronounce sentence upon us. Rather, by a special illumination, God will let us know whether we are ready for eternal happiness in heaven, whether we must undergo further purification in purgatory, or whether we must spend eternity in hell.

9. What do we mean by the resurrection of the dead?

At the end of the world the bodies of the dead will arise.

St. Paul, speaking of the bodies of the just after the resurrection says:

> For this corruptible body must put on incorruption, and this mortal body must put on immortality . . .—1 COR. 15:53.

The body will be spiritualized, immune to sickness and death. It will be able to move from place to place with the speed of thought. The beauty of the soul will shine forth. The glorified body will be able to pass through solid objects. In a word, it will be beautiful, as Christ's was at the Transfiguration, and will possess all the qualities of Christ's body after the Resurrection.

10. How should we prepare for the second coming of Christ?

Our preparation for the end of the world and the second coming of Christ should be positive rather than negative. Instead of dreading the end of the world and anxiously looking for signs and portents, we should prepare ourselves to meet our Saviour by endeavoring to lead a holy life and doing our part in spreading the kingdom of God.

> He who testifies to these things says, "It is true, I come quickly!" Amen! Come, Lord Jesus! The grace of our Lord Jesus Christ be with all. Amen.

With these words of expectation, St. John ended the Apocalypse, the last book of the Scriptures.

Conclusion

It is heartening to remember that the final victory will be Christ's and that we shall share in that victory if we remain in union with our Saviour. But before the final victory there is much to be done. The Church Militant must constantly strive to conquer the world for Christ. The final victory is assured; but there are other victories possible here and now for the achievement of which God requires our cooperation. There are others, our relatives, friends and acquaintances, who may come to love Christ more, perhaps, even become members of his Mystical Body, provided our example and our efforts are what they should be. Others should be able to see that our lives have been enormously enriched because we have been joined to the Mystical Body of Christ. They should be able to see in our lives evidence of that deeper union with God which comes from prayer. They should be able to see that we live by faith, that we are sustained by hope, that we practice love of God and our neighbor in our daily life.

All the means which will enable us to live up to the great challenge of living the Christian life are at our disposal. God will sustain us in our efforts. No prayer will go unanswered. Aid from our brothers in the great family of God will be forthcoming if we call on the saints in heaven and the souls in purgatory.

The life-giving sacraments are there to give us holiness and strength. We should receive them often. Above all, the great source of grace and love, the Eucharist, is there for our daily use. If we wish to be more deeply united to Christ and our neighbor we should make *daily* Mass and Communion our aim.

Help and encouragement will come to us from association with our fellow-members in the Mystical Body. The more deeply we enter into the life of the parish, the more effective we shall be as Catholics. Above all, we should enter wholeheartedly into the great act of the family of God, the Mass. We should take our part, too, in the parish organizations, and if possible in whatever movement of the lay apostolate is open to us.

Finally, we should remember always the words of Pope Pius XII:

> *For nothing more glorious, nothing nobler, nothing surely more honorable can be imagined than to belong to the holy, Catholic, apostolic and Roman church, in which we become members of one Body as venerable as it is unique; are guided by one supreme Head; are filled with one divine Spirit; are nourished during our earthly exile by one doctrine and one heavenly Bread, until at last we enter into the one, unending blessedness of heaven*—Enc. on the Mystical Body 91.

* * *

RECOMMENDED READING—PART V

Five Great Encyclicals, New York, Paulist Press, 215 pp., $1.25.
The monumental Encyclicals on the social order: The Condition of Labor, by Leo XIII and Reconstructing the Social Order and Atheistic Communism, by Pius XI together with the latter's great Encyclicals on The Christian Education of Youth and Christian Marriage. No mature Catholic should be unacquainted with these great papal teachings.

Moral Guidance, 351 pp., *Christian Guidance*, 245 pp., *Marriage Guidance*, 411 pp. HEALY. Chicago, Loyola University Press, $3.00 per vol.
Three easy to read volumes on Christian morality. Solid and authoritative, but popularly written.

Christian Design for Sex, BUCKLEY. Chicago, Fides, 216 pp., $3.50.
A thorough treatment of this important subject. Not easy reading.

The Catholic Viewpoint on Race Relations, LA FARGE. N. Y. Hanover House, 190 pp., $2.95.
An excellent treatment of the difficult and vital question of race relations, by one who has labored long in the field.

The Pope Talks about Labor Relations, SMITH. St. Paul, Catechetical Guild, 63 pp., 15¢.
A pamphlet which gives a summary of the papal doctrine on labor.

The Gospel in Action, DAY. St. Paul, Catechetical Guild, 64 pp., 15¢.
An application of the teachings of the Gospel to the modern social scene.

GENERAL BOOKS

A Handbook of the Catholic Faith, VAN DOORNIK. New York, Image Books, 514 pp., $1.35.

> A wonderfully clear, concise and positive presentation of the Catholic Faith. Highly recommended to all readers.

A Catholic Catechism, New York, Herder and Herder, 439 pp., $4.95.
> This new German Catechism is a fine presentation of Catholic doctrine. Although it is intended for children, it can be read by anyone.

The Teachings of the Catholic Church, SMITH. New York, Macmillan, 2 volumes, 1282 pp., $12.50 per set.

> A complete exposition of most of Catholic dogma for the person who wishes to make a further investigation into the faith.

Theology for Beginners, SHEED. New York, Sheed & Ward, 241 pp., $3.00.
> A short explanation of the dogmas of the Church. Very readable and sound.

A Map of Life, SHEED. New York, Sheed & Ward, 144 pp., $2.00.
> A concise treatment of the basic doctrines of the faith. Easy to read.

My Way of Life, FARRELL & HEALY. Brooklyn, Confraternity of the Precious Blood, 604 pp., $1.35.

> A popularized presentation of St. Thomas' Summa Theologica. Delightful to read.

MARY

The Reed of God, HOUSELANDER. New York, Sheed and Ward, $2.25.
> A beautiful book on our Lady. One which will give all a deeper love for Mary and a better appreciation of her role in our lives.

The Mary Book, SHEED. New York, Sheed & Ward, 409 pp., $4.00.
> A collection of poems, essays, etc., on the Blessed Mother which are well worth reading.

True Devotion to the Blessed Virgin, DE MONTFORT. Bay Shore, N. Y., Montfort Publications, 245 pp., $1.50.

> The classic book on devotion to Mary, written by St. Louis DeMontfort.

PRAYER

Hours of the Day, TOURNAE, Belgium, Desclee & Co., $8.00.
> All the hours of the divine office except Matins, for all the seasons of the liturgical year are presented in this book, English in one column,

Latin the other. Excellent for those who would like to make their own the official hymns and prayers of the Church.

A Short Breviary. Edited by WILLIAM G. HEIDT, O.S.B. Collegeville, Minn., Liturgical Press, abridged 764 pp., $3.90; unabridged 1200 pp., $6.00.

> For religious and laity. Psalms, hymns and scriptural readings for each day of the week, taken from the divine office. Excellent for those who are not bound to say the complete office but wish to pray according to its spirit.

Prayer in Practice, GUARDINI. New York, Pantheon, 228 pp., $3.50.
The Lord's Prayer, GUARDINI. New York, Pantheon, 125 pp., $2.75.

> Two excellent books in the Guardini tradition. Deep and beautiful ideas presented in a form which is easy to read.

Progress Through Mental Prayer, LEEN. New York, Sheed & Ward, 276 pp., $3.50.

> A guide to the practice of mental prayer. Not too difficult.

MARRIAGE

Life Together, HOPE. New York, Sheed & Ward, 199 pp., $2.75.

> A fine little book on the Christian ideal of marriage.

Marriage, The Great Mystery, KOTHEN. Westminster, Md., Newman 115 pp., $2.50. A more difficult book, but a rewarding one. It develops the theme of St. Paul.

What They Ask about Marriage, CONWAY. Chicago, Fides, 317 pp., $3.75.

> A book of questions and answers about the usual problems that people have about marriage. It is easy to read and very informative.

PENANCE

Pardon and Peace, WILSON. New York, Sheed & Ward, 257 pp., $3.00.

> An excellent book on the sacrament of Penance. Ideal for those who would like to derive more benefit from the sacrament. Easy to read.

CHURCH HISTORY

Outline History of the Church by Centuries, McSORLEY. St. Louis, Herder, $12.00.

> A bird's-eye view of the history of the Church. Easy to read.

A Short History of the Reformation, HUGHES. New York, Doubleday, $4.00.

> A brief, but informative history of the Protestant Reformation. Basic reading on this important subject.

A Popular History of the Catholic Church, HUGHES. N. Y., Image Books, 85¢.

> An amazing amount of information, usually found only in works of many volumes, is here presented in an interesting way by the outstanding Catholic Church historian writing in English today.

The Greatest Faith Ever Known, OURSLER. New York, Permabooks, 35¢. A book about the early days of Christianity. Very easy to read.

THE BIBLE

Foreword to the Old Testament Books, MORIARTY. Weston, Mass., Weston College Press, 113 pp., $1.00.

> An excellent little book introducing each book of the Old Testament. There is a selection of suggested readings which will give one a comprehensive view of the Old Testament.

The Two-Edged Sword, McKENZIE. Milwaukee, Bruce, 312 pp., $4.50.

> A wonderful book, which gives the purpose and nature of the Old Testament. It outlines the religious ideals and values found in the Old Testament.

They Saw His Glory, WARD. New York, Sheed & Ward, 278 pp., $4.50.

> An introduction to the Gospels and Acts. It gives the main themes and main lines of thought of each of the books.

A Catholic Commentary on Holy Scripture, ORCHARD. New York, Nelson and Sons, 1296 pp., $15.00.

> The only line by line commentary of the Scriptures in English. An outstanding book, packed with information; for the person who truly wants to understand the Bible.

LAY APOSTOLATE

Lend Me Your Hands, MEYER. Chicago, Fides, 241 pp., $1.50 (paper)

> An easy to read book about the lay apostolate and the various forms it can take. Well worth reading.

Forward the Layman, PERRIN. Westminster, Md. 176 pp., $3.25.

> A book which treats of the theology of the lay apostolate. The author explains the task of the layman in the Church and the world.

Index

Prayers—

First printing July 1958—32,000
Second printing Sept. 1958—100,000
Third printing Feb. 1959—100,000
Fourth printing Jan. 1960—100,000
Fifth printing Sept. 1961—200,000
Sixth printing June 1963—200,000
Eighth printing Jan. 1968—150,000
Ninth printing Jan. 1972—50,000

Printed in England in 1959 by Sheed and Ward, under the title,
CHRIST IN US

Also printed in India, Mexico, Formosa.

Printed sets of questions to accompany this text are available.
Set A, 300 questions; Set B, 500 questions—40¢.

TYPOGRAPHIC DESIGN BY EDWARD FITZGERALD

 5